THE 101 HABITS OF
HIGHLY SUCCESSFUL
SCREENWRITERS

Insider Secrets from
Hollywood's Top Writers

BY
KARL IGLESIAS

Adams Media Corporation
Avon, Massachusetts

Dedication

To all aspiring screenwriters who sacrifice so much to share their soul through the screenplay. May these 101 habits be the seeds that inspire your next masterpiece.

• • •

Published by
Adams Media, an F+W Publications Company
57 Littlefield Street, Avon, MA 02322, USA
www.adamsmedia.com

ISBN: 1-58062-550-9

Printed in Canada.

J I H G F E

Library of Congress Cataloging-in-Publication Data
Iglesias, Karl.
The 101 habits of highly successful screenwriters : insider secrets
from Hollywood's top writers / by Karl Iglesias
p.   cm.
Includes index.
ISBN 1-58062-550-9
1. Motion picture authorship. 2. Screenwriters--United States--Interviews.
I. Title: One hundred one habits of highly successful screenwriters. II. Title: One hundred
and one habits of highly successful screenwriters. III. Title.

This publication is designed to provide accurate and authoritative information with regard to the subject matter covered. It is sold with the understanding that the publisher is not engaged in rendering legal, accounting, or other professional advice. If legal advice or other expert assistance is required, the services of a competent professional person should be sought.
—From a *Declaration of Principles* jointly adopted by a
Committee of the American Bar Association
and a Committee of Publishers and Associations

This book is available at quantity discounts for bulk purchases.
For information, call 1-800-872-5627.

Acknowledgments

When most of the words in this book belong to the 14 screenwriters interviewed for this project, it is clear where my appreciation lies. First and foremost, a heartfelt thank-you and deep appreciation must go to those 14 screenwriters for granting me their time and energy despite their hectic Hollywood schedules and for their willingness to share their knowledge and experience with the reader. They are, in alphabetical order: Ron Bass, Steven DeSouza, Gerald DiPego, Leslie Dixon, Akiva Goldsman, Amy Holden Jones, Nicholas Kazan, Jim Kouf, Scott Rosenberg, Eric Roth, Michael Schiffer, Tom Schulman, Ed Solomon, and Robin Swicord. Your insightful comments are the soul of this book.

Extra special thanks to:

Claire Gerus and Dawn Thompson for their helpful comments, editorial support, and commitment to nurture this book to completion.

Patsy Hilbert for her thorough review and proofing of the manuscript.

Paula Munier Lee for believing in this project as much as I did.

Richard Krevolin for introducing me to Paula and for the intense 11-point tennis games.

Kathryn Makris and Meera and Steve Lester for inviting me to the Selling to Hollywood Conference.

Pat Cummings and Hilary Cline at the Writers Guild Foundation for generously helping with the mailings.

Edward James Olmos for opening the doors.

Sandy Martin for allowing me to prove myself.

All past and present Team #5 members (they know who they are) for their enthusiastic moral support, inspiration, and humor.

And most of all, to my friends and family, for their caring and support.

HABIT *n.* 1. a. A recurrent, often unconscious pattern of behavior that is acquired through frequent repetition. b. An established disposition of the mind or character. 2. Customary manner or practice: *a person of ascetic habits.* 3. An addiction.

—THE AMERICAN HERITAGE DICTIONARY
OF THE ENGLISH LANGUAGE, THIRD EDITION

The secret to success in any field is to find what successful people do, think about and act on, and do the same.

—ANTHONY ROBBINS

CONTENTS

FOREWORD
by Lew Hunter

· Karl Iglesias asked me to write about the importance of habits for screen-writers. I barely waited for him to finish the sentence before I shouted "Yes!"

Wonderful screenwriting is 90 percent perspiration, 10 percent inspiration. The originator of this edict has yet to be authenticated, but the only truer words in screenwriting advice come from Jack Sowards (*Star Trek II: The Wrath of Khan*): "FINISH!" he cries.

Stephen King suggests that many people consider the muse to be shaped like a woodland fairy who wafts from the forest and whispers in the writer's ear sweet inspiration to encourage him or her to the next line of prose, poetry, or screenwriting. King, however, envisions his muse to have a flattop crewcut à la Jack Webb in *The D.I.* yelling "GET YOUR ASS BEHIND THAT KEYBOARD, KING!" I'm with Stephen King. I'm a "seat writer."—"Seat of the pants to the seat of the chair."

I'm also with Noel Coward, who quipped: "I adore professionalism. I loathe writers who can only write when it's raining."

When I began professing at UCLA in 1979, the crown jewel screen-writing class, 434, required an outline for a feature-length motion picture and a minimum of seventy pages of script. I implored my colleagues to insist that the script be finished in each quarter's ten-week time frame.

You see, from holding a screenwriter's feet to the fire via a deadline, comes habit. From habit comes discipline, a career, money, angst, joy, and countless cups of coffee.

Before habits (good ones, of course) come mentors. I'm also on the faculty at the Sorbonne in Paris. When I first spoke at a gathering in the Richelieu Room, the oldest lecture hall in the world, I reported that someone once said, "You can't teach screenwriting." Not so. To say that screenwriting cannot be taught is to say that Aristotle did not need Plato, that Monet did not need Manet. I ticked off the mentors of Maria Callas, Rudolph Nureyev, and the teachers of those whose huge portraits surrounded us in that assembly of learning—Racine, Maupassant, Hugo, Molière. Why would screenwriting be the only writing received by divine inspiration?

You need mentoring even after you become a professional writer. In this book are 14 mentors who violate that George Bernard Shaw quip, "Those who can't do, teach." You have 14 members here who can do and teach.

I must also say that Mr. Iglesias has put together a unique "interview" book that defies traditional structure for screenwriting or any other writing book I have studied. Within these pages is "everything you've always wanted to know about screenwriting but were afraid to ask the masters of the craft." Karl has asked the questions and received the richest variety of responses about desire, commitment, the creative process, creating a writing environment, writing habits, time management, writer's block, rewriting, storytelling basics, the audience, the Hollywood System, networking, getting an agent, pitching, and the four Ps: Patience, Perseverance, Passion, and Practice. Put this special book on the "must read and reread" shelf of your screenwriting library.

You can't be Ron Bass, Leslie Dixon, Nicholas Kazan, my ex-student Scott Rosenberg, UCLA-trained Eric Roth, Ed Solomon, or any of these marvelous screenwriters on these pages. However, you can reach the heights that come with perseverance, "seat writing," and mentoring. So here you are, on the threshold of greater knowledge.

And from this knowledge will come habits that can help you be a "highly successful screenwriter." Read, then write. It's not so difficult. It's "seat writing," remember? "Seat writing" four hours a day, the rest of your life. You can do it!

Write on!

Lew Hunter
Superior, Nebraska
June, 2001

INTRODUCTION
Fade In

We are what we repeatedly do.
Excellence then is not an act, but a habit.
—ARISTOTLE

Meet Joe Executive. He's a successful studio producer with a long list of box-office hits and award-winning films. Despite the old adage attributed to William Goldman, "Nobody knows anything," there's one thing Joe knows for sure: It all starts with a great script. And in a town where only one in a thousand screenplays can be considered great, he knows one when he reads one.

And that's his problem, you see. Most of the scripts that cross his desk are terrible, mediocre, by the numbers, or "almost-good," which means that in order to feed the industry's ravenous appetite for good stories, executives are *desperately* looking for great material. Every day, upon grabbing the next script from the top of the pile, Joe prays that it's the one.

If you want something you've never had,
you have to do something you've never done!
—KIMNESHA BENNS

So he wonders, "How could it be that, with so many people writing scripts, their quality is substandard?" After all, although it used to be that most American writers yearned to write the Great American Novel, since the early 1990s, they've been trying to write the Million-Dollar Spec Script. Who can blame them? With readily available spec sales news in trade publications (and more recently on the Internet) captivating aspiring writers with dreams of a quick fortune like a nightly dose of *Who Wants to Be a Millionaire,* screenwriting has become the newest American lottery. Good or bad, it's still a strong incentive.

But Joe has a theory. Maybe the problem is not craft. Maybe it's the temperament of the so-called "writers"—their traits, skills, talents, and habits—that are not allowing them to write a great screenplay. It may sound harsh, but the sad truth is that more than half the scripts currently making the rounds in Hollywood were written by writers who have no business being screenwriters. Sure, everyone goes to the movies and knows when they're good or bad, and everyone has access to a computer on which to write their screenplay. But think about this: Everyone can recognize a funny joke, but can everyone create one that's as funny, and has never been told before?

Joe Executive is aware of the multimillion-dollar business devoted entirely to giving outdated prescriptions, rules, and formulas to aspiring screenwriters in an industry that frowns on formulas. He's browsed the bookstores and seen entire shelves devoted to screenwriting. He's seen flyers and newspaper ads and Web sites for script doctors, consultants, seminar gurus, pitching conferences, and contests, so he knows just how many aspiring screenwriters are willing to pay anything to get that magic key that will open the door to a spec sale that will instantly change their lives.

Problem is he's still looking for great scripts, and they ain't coming. Sure, he's inundated with material at a mind-boggling rate, but he's tired of reading bad scripts and seeing the waste of paper, money, readers' time, messenger costs, and overworked Beverly Hills postal carriers.

One hasn't become a writer until one has distilled writing
into a habit, and that habit has been forced into an obsession.
Writing has to be an obsession. It has to be something as organic,
physiological and psychological as speaking or sleeping or eating.
—NIYI OSUNDARE

But Joe Executive is an idealist and a dream maker; that's what he does for a living. He turns dreams into reality. And his dream is to raise that standard of scripts from terrible to great. He's tired of all the books that teach formulas, that don't really give any information about how to be a screenwriter and how to develop habits that will lead to more joy in the process and better material for the industry. Don't get him wrong, it's still an entirely selfish motive: better material for him and less manure to sift through in order to find it.

While cooking dinner one evening, an idea jolts him. In order to write a great script, you have to be a real screenwriter, because, like an aged wine, it takes time and hard work to develop the necessary craft to write great scripts. You can't just be a fly-by-night, dreaming of the big score.

> *Winners have simply formed the habit of doing*
> *things losers don't like to do.*
> —ALBERT GRAY

"I know!" he says, "I'll invite one lucky aspiring screenwriter (the apprentice) to my mansion for an in-depth, no-holds-barred question and answer session with a group of the top screenwriters in the business (the masters) who would share their thoughts on what it's like to be a real screenwriter." After all, that's how Joe became a successful executive. He started out as an assistant to an executive, who mentored him and showed him the ropes.

He's always believed in the "work smarter, not harder" philosophy. The difference between successful screenwriters and unsuccessful screenwriters is that successful screenwriters do all the things that unsuccessful ones want to do but can't do or don't know how to do. Modeling what works is the philosophy at the heart of every master–apprentice craft. Why not screenwriting? Someone is doing it right—many, in fact. Why not ask them how they do it? "Hey, successful-screenwriter-dude, what are your habits? What works for you? Enlighten me."

> *If I wanted to become a tramp, I would seek information and advice*
> *from the most successful tramp I could find. If I wanted to become a*
> *failure, I would seek advice from people who have never succeeded.*
> *If I wanted to succeed in all things, I would look around me for those*
> *who are succeeding, and do as they have done.*
> —JOSEPH MARSHALL WADE

Has he ever seen this done before? Not really. During his days as an aspiring screenwriter, he'd read a couple of great interview books, and he sometimes found them useful when a professional discussed his process.

The problem was that he would have to read the whole book just to get the particular tidbits he was hunting for. For instance, when he was having trouble with discipline, he'd have to read a whole interview, hoping the writer would discuss discipline. Not the most efficient way to learn, and often a waste of time. But since he was procrastinating anyway, he never saw it as a waste of time. Sound familiar?

"This is going to be different," he thinks. "This focus will not be on how to write a formulaic script but on what it takes to become the writer who creates a unique one. In other words, what the habits and traits are that would increase the odds of not only writing your version of a great script but also developing a successful career as a screenwriter."

Well, guess what? You, the reader of this book, are the lucky apprentice about to discover what it means to be a screenwriter from real, successful screenwriters, in their own words.

What This Book Is About

This book is not intended to replace any of the books on craftsmanship. As Robert McKee says, "No one needs another recipe book to reheat Hollywood leftovers." Whereas the more than one hundred books on the craft attempt to teach the reader *what* to do, this book outlines, by asking those who are already doing it successfully, *how* to do it. It focuses on the necessary habits, so that the "how" becomes second nature to you. In other words, it explains how to *be* a screenwriter.

This book departs from the established interview books in that its structure is organized by topic rather than by individual interview, following a much more efficient model of reverse engineering. In other words, it focuses on a particular habit, trait, or indispensable skill, and then has a group of highly successful screenwriters share their thoughts on the subject, much like a panel of experts discussing a specific topic.

Presented here are simple habits of action and thought. Many will seem obvious, but they bear repeating because they're often ignored by aspiring screenwriters. Others are surprising and sometimes even shocking. By themselves, they may not make you a successful writer. But developing new habits and combining them with your talent will definitely make you a *better* writer. All this book can accomplish is to share with you what highly successful screenwriters believe and do on a regular basis in the hope that you will be intrigued and inspired enough to emulate them.

How This Book Is Organized

What sets this book apart is its structure and its focus on the specific habits that have made some screenwriters highly successful. It is based on the simple philosophy of modeling excellence and the commonsense approach of the apprentice-master relationship.

Because each screenwriter is unique and has habits that work for him or her, you'll notice that several habits listed seem to contradict each other. For example, the habit of rewriting after finishing the first draft conflicts with the habit of rewriting as you go along. These habits are not gospel but simply what works for each of the screenwriters featured here. It's up to you to try them out and see if they work for you.

Part 1, *Passion*, discusses what makes screenwriters different from other people, their common traits and skills, their reasons for becoming a screenwriter despite all the drawbacks. Included in this part are thoughts on believing in your talent; being committed to a career, not just one spec script; how to overcome various fears associated with the writing vocation; and learning the craft.

Part 2, *Creativity*, focuses on the creative process, how working screenwriters summon their muse to come up with fresh ideas and how they flesh out a story. It also explores their writing environments and favorite times to write.

Part 3, *Discipline*, the heart of this book, guides you through the basic components critical to success, including the writing habit and time management, and offers tips on overcoming procrastination, dealing with writer's block, and the rewriting process.

Part 4, *Storycraft*, shares insider secrets and specific tips to make each of the basic elements of a great script easier to manage, from conflict and characters to dialogue and evoking emotion on the page. It also explores what makes a great story and what differentiates good from bad writing.

Part 5, *Marketing*, focuses on the business side of screenwriting and how to market yourself as a writer, offering tips on the importance of establishing a network of supporters, mentors, and contacts in an industry that runs on relationships, from getting your first agent to pitching with enthusiasm and overcoming nervousness.

Part 6, *The Four Ps*, examines the need for patience, dealing with the Hollywood System, and keeping the dream alive, from perseverance and belief in your material to handling rejection like a pro.

Finally, a closing chapter, "Fade Out," leaves readers with final words of inspiration as they return to their favorite task, writing their next project—coming soon to a theater near you.

What This Book Will Do for You

This book is for any writer, novice to professional, who is aware of the basic elements of the screenwriting craft, but is missing the mechanics or daily habits that will make the process much easier.

It is also aimed at the intermediate to professional writer who has developed a set of habits that sometimes impede rather than help him in his writing output, and who is looking for better habits to develop. (In the interest of brevity/simplicity, without any sexism implied, masculine pronouns will be used hereon to refer to writers.) Maybe he's curious about what he may be doing wrong and, seeing what his peers are doing successfully, he may want to try some new ones. Or maybe reading about similar habits will validate his own and boost his self-confidence.

Look at this book as an effective way to have all the interviewed screenwriters be your personal mentors. Study their habits, learn from them, and maybe their wisdom will rub off on you and arm you with enough knowledge and self-confidence to accomplish your goals.

It is my hope that you'll discover what it really takes to be a successful screenwriter in Hollywood, and realize that maybe there's a great deal more to it than seeing a mediocre movie and thinking you could write one better, or reading one of the more than one hundred screenwriting books.

It is also my hope that in reading and discovering the particular habits of highly successful screenwriters, you will either begin to see similarities in your attitudes and ways of thinking or be inspired to adopt new ones.

There's an old industry adage that in Hollywood, it's not who you know but who knows you. I will add that it's also not what you know but what you do. It's all about action.

But we can't act until we discover the 101 habits that have made our 14 screenwriters successful. Let's find out who they are and how they made the leap from aspiring to professional screenwriters.

Screenwriters Panel

Ron Bass (*Passion of Mind, Snow Falling on Cedars, Entrapment, Stepmom, What Dreams May Come, How Stella Got Her Groove Back, My Best Friend's Wedding, Waiting to Exhale, Dangerous Minds, When a Man Loves a Woman, The Joy Luck Club, Sleeping with the Enemy, Rain Man, Black Widow*)

In 1982, I made an investment that went wrong and I needed to make more money. My previous two novels had been published, and I had an idea for a third novel. My literary agent said he had a contact at Reader's Digest Condensed Books, and he had this idea for a World War II spy novel. If I could write up a proposal that would get his contact excited enough to make a Reader's Digest commitment to my publisher, he could get me a $20,000 advance. The thing was that I hated World War II stories. They're kind of corny, Nazi stories. So I decided to write the "Anti-World War II" story, the kind of story that could have happened anywhere, anytime, that showed that people, even Nazis, and beautiful resistance people, and American counterspies were still people, with fears and loves, dreams and hopes. So I got excited about it. For about three months, I started getting up at three A.M., and I wrote this 115-page treatment, and it sold, and I got an advance that was even bigger than expected. It was a dream come true that I could get paid for this thing. The novel was published and when the film rights were bought, I insisted on writing the screenplay.

So I did the same thing as I did with my novels. I got up at three, wrote until six, the kids got up, I spent time with them until seven, and then got to work by eight and was a good lawyer until six, had dinner with my wife, and played with the kids. All weekend long I'm writing, and on vacations I'm writing like crazy. I wrote four scripts in a year and a half while I was practicing law.

And then a good friend who happened to be the head of Fox at the time said to me, "How many blind deals would you need from me to be able to quit law entirely and just write?" I thought about it, did the calculations, and it came down to two scripts. He said, "You got it." I thought about it, talked with my wife and with my partner at the firm, who was also my mentor. He said, "That's great, you're a great writer, you're making the right decision. If you ever fail or if you want to return to your old job and be a lawyer again, there'll always be a place for you here." He made it really easy to follow my calling of love.

Steven DeSouza *(Street Fighter, Knock Off, Judge Dredd, Beverly Hills Cop III, The Flintstones, Ricochet, Hudson Hawk, Die Hard 2, Die Hard, The Running Man, 48 Hours)*

My reason to write came out of a sort of laziness. By that I mean my original ambition, ever since I was 8 years old, was to be a cartoonist for Walt Disney. I remember spending hours trying to do my best at what they call in the comic business "swipes," i.e. knock-offs. I made animated cartoons with an 8-mm camera, I did Claymation and cartoons for the junior high school newspaper. Then someone asked me to write a piece, and I discovered it was much more efficient to tell a story by writing than to spend hours with my India ink and scratch board. That's when I switched to prose. I started reading *Writers Digest*, where I gleaned the basic knowledge that, in order to be hired as a screenwriter, playwright, or television writer, you needed to have script samples. So I wrote two spec scripts in the genres I was familiar with, science-fiction and detective. At that time, there was nothing in any of these magazines about "screenwriting." I was just committed to being a writer.

Then I got a short piece published in a magazine. I went to college, still trying to get things published. A great year would be when I made $150 here, $350 there. But in college, there was a film teacher who took me aside one day and told me to leave school and go to Hollywood right away. I'd like to think I took his advice immediately, but I didn't have any friends or relatives in the industry, so I waited. I did a stint in the Army Reserve, got married, and then stumbled into my first show-biz job in Philadelphia, working at a local television station as a writer-producer. Eventually I got laid off, but through networking I managed to get from one TV station to another, did talk shows, local commercials, cooking shows, evangelist shows on Sundays. It got to a point where I couldn't take this anymore. I had all these writing samples, so I decided to go to Hollywood. I had an emotional talk with my wife because we had just had a little baby at the time, and I took a bargain basement flight to Los Angeles where I had an uncle and aunt.

My aunt said, "I can help you. I play bridge with my best friend and she's Merv Griffin's secretary." So I go see her and she says, "Gee, we only do *Wheel of Fortune* and *Jeopardy* here and all we hire are question writers, but there's not a lot of turnover, so maybe we'll call you next year if there's an opening." She also said I definitely needed an agent, and she happened to know a lawyer who had quit to become an agent. So I called him up, sent him my samples, he liked them, asked me if I would deign to do television.

I said sure, I want to work. So he gave my samples to one of his clients who was desperate for writers, and who happened to be the producer of these bionic shows at Universal. As soon as he read them, he hired me. Six days after I arrived in town, I signed a contract with Universal Studios. I was even written up in *Variety* as one of these stories that never happen: Instant success! Of course, 13 weeks later, I got laid off when the show got canceled. But since Universal was a television factory making most of the shows for all three networks, I got swapped around between shows like a baseball player. Someone hires you for a detective show across the hall or a little work on a lawyer show. It's a tremendous exposure to all kinds of genres and to a certain discipline because you only have seven days to make these suckers. I sweated my first hiatus, and then got a lot of offers because I was the new guy in town or the new blood in television. Paramount quickly lured me away from Universal to write pilots for them, which sold, and I had the dumb luck of being asked to write dramatic pilots. One of them was called *The Renegades*, which was Patrick Swayze's first gig, and the producer on that was Larry Gordon. One day, he calls me into a meeting, and there is Joel Silver, who was his protégé, and Michael Eisner and Jeffrey Katzenberg. At that time, there was no firewall between the television and film departments as it is now at most studios. They'd seen my work on these pilots under tough situations, and I had a reputation for doing action adventure with a sense of humor. So they offered me this movie they'd been developing for about six years. They said, "We need to make it funny without sabotaging the action, and we think you're the guy." And that was *48 Hours*.

So a lot of this is about being at the right place at the right time, a lot of dumb luck, working for people to whom you can prove yourself and show them what you can do so that when opportunities present themselves they think of you. It's not like I had some conscious plan: "*Bowling for Dollars* will lead to the *Bionic Woman* and then it's a short hop to Eddie Murphy." It just happened without me thinking about it.

Gerald DiPego (*Angel Eyes, Instinct, Message in a Bottle, Phenomenon, Sharky's Machine*)

I was always doing some kind of writing. I was a prose writer and a reporter through college, and I took courses in film in graduate school. Ultimately they led me to making my living as an educational and industrial film writer, which are still markets most people are unaware of. I was living in Chicago doing these industrials, already freelancing for a couple of years, and I had time to develop my own spec script and, like a lot of other people, bring it with me to Hollywood, thinking I could support myself writing industrials until I got my break. My dream was not necessarily to sell it, but use it as a sample, and that's what happened eventually. I showed it to enough people that it landed, ultimately, on the right desk at the right time.

Leslie Dixon *(The Thomas Crown Affair, That Old Feeling, Look Who's Talking Now, Mrs. Doubtfire, Loverboy, Overboard, Outrageous Fortune)*

I had no formal education whatsoever, completely on my own from the age of 18, financially and every other way, working crappy jobs, playing in a bluegrass band for a while, always having some guitar boyfriend or other. And then one day, I had an epiphany. I think I was 23, I said to myself, "if I'm still here living this life with these people and doing this 10 years from now, I'll kill myself." So in a calculated move, I decided to go to L.A. to become a screenwriter. I didn't have one extra dollar, worked crummy jobs to support myself, didn't have health insurance, drove around without car insurance, and most of the time my car didn't run so I didn't drive at all. I couldn't afford any screenwriting classes, but I was able to get a library card at AFI, which was great because I got to read great scripts that way. I probably learned more from that than a small stint at a Z-grade production company, reading all the scripts that came in. Those were so awful that it puffed up my ego and made me think I could do better than this, that I shouldn't be so intimidated. I was in L.A. for almost a year before I found an idea that was commercial enough. I actually wrote it with a friend because we were both broke, miserable, and desperate. He was very funny and I was very funny, and we thought we could make each other funnier. And we sold it. It wasn't a huge deal, people weren't making million-dollar deals then. But we were off and running. And of course, as these things go in Hollywood, we became insufferable to each other, professionally broke up, and I went my own way. One deal later, I wrote *Outrageous Fortune.*

Akiva Goldsman *(The Sum of All Fears, Memoirs of a Geisha, A Beautiful Mind, Lost in Space, Batman & Robin, A Time to Kill, Batman Forever, Silent Fall, The Client)*

Before screenplays, I wrote fiction and short fiction, but mainly *unsold* fiction. I've been writing since I was in seventh grade and always had the dream of becoming a writer. I don't know why I was so enamored of the idea. I think it was because my parents used to scream at each other, and I discovered that when I went by myself into a single room and I wrote, the shouts seemed to disappear. I wasn't particularly good, but I was very persistent. I went to college and got a graduate degree in creative writing, got a job working with severely emotionally disturbed children, and wrote at night. During my NYU days, I was invited to take a private writing course taught by an extraordinary writing teacher, Gordon Lish. He believed there were too many loud voices out there, and unless you had a clear voice, no one could hear you, so you had to be very authentic. The class was six hours straight, with no pee breaks. Gordon believed that if you didn't have the will to control your bladder for six hours, you didn't have the will to write, which sounds fabulous in theory, but it was unbelievably agonizing. You'd get there and start reading your story aloud to the class and often you'd get no further than a sentence or two before Gordon would tear you apart in front of everyone. He'd say, "Let me tell you why this sucks," and would say it in a very articulate way, which was really painful, but the process was as much psychological as it was literary. It was shearing off all pretense so you were forced to dig deeper and deeper and find your own voice, because it wasn't like next week you could come back with the same story. You had to write a new story every week. By the time I got to read a whole page aloud, it was a profoundly gratifying experience. So I'd put these stories in envelopes and send them out everywhere, and I'd get these really charming rejection notes. By the time I was 28 or 29, I realized I wasn't going to make it as a fiction writer and I thought, "My God, there's gotta be some way of doing this." I've always loved the movies, so I took Robert McKee's Structure class, which I highly recommend, and then I wrote a script, and I'm a bad example because it sold.

Amy Holden Jones *(The Relic, The Rich Man's Wife, The Getaway ('94), Indecent Proposal, Beethoven, Mystic Pizza, Maid to Order, Love Letters)*
My first aspiration was to be a documentary filmmaker but I quickly found that in order to do that you had to be independently wealthy, which I wasn't. So I became a film editor until Roger Corman gave me my first chance to direct. Then I had to rewrite the script. I had to keep writing things for myself to direct. Now, I much prefer writing to directing.

Nicholas Kazan *(Enough, Bicentennial Man, Fallen, Matilda, Dream Lover, Reversal of Fortune, Patty Hearst, At Close Range, Frances)*
I started by writing plays in college, and wrote them primarily for about seven years. The last two years of that, I began writing screenplays because I was always obsessed with movies, and I did that for about five

years full-time with very little success. And then one day, I wrote a screen-play in a completely different way. It was almost all images, and I used the images rather than the dialogue for dramatic effect. For me, that was the real transition from play writing to screenwriting.

Jim Kouf (*Rush Hour, Gang Related, Operation Dumbo Drop, Another Stakeout, Disorganized Crime, Stakeout, Miracles, The Hidden, Secret Admirer, American Dreamer, Class, Up the Creek*)

I took a date to see an exclusive engagement of *The Wild Bunch*. I walked out stunned by what I'd just seen on screen. From that moment on I wanted to make films. And the first thing you have to do when you want to make a film is . . . get someone to write it. So I started writing films for the fun of it, making them with 8- and 16-mm cameras and a bunch of friends. I used to charge them money to be in my films to finance the pic-tures. I wish I could use that concept now. I came out of college with a degree in English and History, and moved back to L.A. with only one career in mind, writing movies. My background up to that point really con-sisted of trying to grow up, graduate, and not get anyone pregnant. I had a job like everyone else. I sold paint, was a truck driver and insurance claims adjuster. I started making a living at writing three years later.

Scott Rosenberg (*Gone in 60 Seconds, High Fidelity, Disturbing Behavior, Con Air, Beautiful Girls, Things to Do in Denver When You're Dead*)

I grew up in Boston and always wrote, even from a young age. I was the kid in fifth grade who'd write the poem and read it to the assembly when a teacher was leaving. I wrote pretty much through high school. My favorite classes were always creative writing; I really sucked at science and math. And then I went to Boston University's School of Communications with a creative writing minor where I managed to get into the Graduate Creative Writing program. Upon graduation, I had no idea what I was going to do with my life, but the girl I was going out with moved to California, so I followed her. And when you're a writer in Los Angeles, you eventually discover this thing called a screenplay. Everyone I met was writing one, and I always loved the movies, so I started writing them. And everyone tells you to read *Chinatown* and *Lethal Weapon*, so I read the classic scripts and I just wrote. I was always writing, probably four or five scripts a year in my lean years while doing every crappy job, like driving a truck, selling stuff door to door, working as a production assistant for Dick Clark, which was one of those 18-hours-a-day things, so I decided to apply

to film school. I first went to USC at a time they didn't have a writing program. I was just making films and wasn't interested in that, so I transferred
to UCLA, which had a very intense writing program. Then, another girl I
liked moved to New York, so I transferred to NYU for a semester. But
while I was at UCLA, I placed third in the Samuel Goldwyn Award, and
that's how I got my first agent.

Eric Roth (*Ali, The Insider, The Horse Whisperer, The Postman, Forrest
Gump, Mr. Jones, Memories of Me, Suspect*)
    I grew up in New York, attended Columbia University's film program,
and did some graduate work at UCLA. I had some ideas of maybe becoming
a director, but I was uncomfortable with that. I always loved movies, but I
don't know what specifically made me want to become a screenwriter. I was
well versed in film, a certifiable film nut, my dad was a publicist and a producer, my mom was a story editor, so I grew up in film. I just found myself
writing a screenplay and I won the Samuel Goldwyn award at UCLA. So
that's how it happened: I wrote a script, it won an award, it got produced,
which led me to another job, and it all went up from there.

Michael Schiffer (*The Four Feathers, The Peacemaker, Crimson Tide,
Lean on Me, Colors*)
    I started writing prose when I was 25. I went overseas to get out of the
culture enough to be able to write about it, and traveled through Asia,
hitchhiked, had no money, spent seven months on the road and then, when
I came back from that experience about two years later, I really began to
write full time, writing all kinds of things. I wanted to be a writer and
started writing novels. I also wrote plays, but I couldn't get any support
from the playwriting world. I felt I got more respect out of the publishing
world because it took me more seriously as a fledgling writer and gave me
more creative support. So I put all my energy into doing that, but it wasn't
an accident that after hitting my limit as a novelist, I drove to Hollywood
when I was 35 to become screenwriter. Directing theater in college made
me want to write the stories myself. I gave myself five years and worked
really hard, writing 14 specs before I got hired for Colors.

Tom Schulman (*Holy Man, 8 Heads in a Duffel Bag, Medicine Man, What
About Bob?, Dead Poets Society, Honey I Shrunk The Kids, Second Sight*)
    Before writing, I was in production. I guess I began as a grunt,
working odd jobs. I started working for a company in Nashville that

made commercials and industrials, and my first job was carrying lights and doing pretty much everything. Then I came to Los Angeles and went to USC Film School, with aspirations be a filmmaker.

Ed Solomon *(Men in Black, Super Mario Bros., Leaving Normal, Bill and Ted's Bogus Journey, Bill and Ted's Excellent Adventure)*
I came into screenwriting because it seemed like the next step. I was writing on *Laverne and Shirley* when I was 21 and a senior in college, then went on to *It's Garry Shandling's Show,* and when I was 23, I wrote *Bill and Ted's Excellent Adventure.* I didn't get into it with much thought. In retrospect, I wish instead that I had an idea for a novel, and truly worked hard at it and sold it. I'd much prefer earning a living as a novelist because the process is the same. You sit in a room all by yourself and try to make up the most interesting, original and true thing that you can, except with screenwriting, the product gets chopped up and changed so much that the creative satisfaction is minimal.

Robin Swicord *(Practical Magic, Matilda, The Perez Family, Little Women, The Red Coat, Shag the Movie)*
I've always wanted to be a writer from the time I first started to read. Though I did all kinds of writing, I didn't think about screenwriting because I didn't completely understand that movies were written. I began writing plays first, but by the time I was 21, all I wanted to do was make films. I had worked as a photographer in college and had an understanding about the framing and images, which didn't translate to the stage. Someone had seen a play of mine in New York and got in touch with me. She asked me if I was interested in writing for film, so I sent her part of a screenplay. She read it, liked it, told me to finish it and that she would sell it. And she did. After that, people were talking about me as a screenwriter, not a playwright.

● ● ●

These 14 highly successful screenwriters have agreed to be your mentors in the context of this book, and generously share their thoughts on the traits, skills, and habits necessary for success as a screenwriter in today's film industry. Let's explore them, shall we?

PART I

Passion

The Urge to Screenwrite

Cats gotta scratch. Dogs gotta bite.
I gotta write.

—JAMES ELLROY

CHAPTER 1
Portrait of a Screenwriter

Before we can explore the habits of highly successful screenwriters, we have to know what they're like. Do you have what it takes to be a professional screenwriter? Since all writers are unique, you'll notice that the common traits that follow are unrelated to intelligence, education, environment, sex, age, or race. You'll also notice few screenwriter comments included with most of the first "obvious" traits, since it's somewhat embarrassing to comment on being creative, having talent, or being a natural storyteller. So what makes a successful screenwriter different from other people?

1. Being Creative and Original

*Imagination is being able to think of things
that haven't appeared on TV yet.*
—HENRY BEARD

It may seem unnecessary to include this trait, because most people know creativity is an essential part of the writer's makeup, especially in screenwriting. I've included it, however, because many beginning writers don't understand how important it is to be original. Reading hundreds of scripts and listening to thousands of pitches showed me how most of them were derivative of other movies, with familiar characters, uninteresting ideas, and clichéd plot twists. Beginning writers tend to develop the easiest idea that comes to mind, rather than working hard to generate original ones.

Our mentors are highly imaginative and can make creative connections between seemingly unrelated events. They're able to daydream about situations, characters, bits of dialogue, and get immediate answers to "what if" situations. As Pearl Buck eloquently puts it:

> The truly creative mind in any field is no more than this: a human creature born abnormally, inhumanly sensitive. To him a touch is a blow, a sound is a noise, a misfortune is a tragedy, a joy is an ecstasy, a friend is a lover, a lover is a god, and failure is death. Add to this cruelly delicate organism the overpowering necessity to create, create, create—so that without the creating of music or poetry or books or buildings or something of meaning, his very breath is cut off from him. He must create, just pour out creating. By some strange, inward urgency, he is not really alive unless he is creating.

No one can tell you what this mysterious creative energy really is. It's not a formula. You cannot control it, but you can certainly develop a relationship to it so that it will open itself to you more often than not.

Tom Schulman: Screenwriters need a determination to be original and an unwillingness to accept clichés. Most writers I know don't hesitate to change, or at least add something special as soon as they sense what they wrote has been done before.

2. Being a Natural Storyteller

We're only interested in one thing: Can you tell a story, Bart?
Can you make us laugh, can you make us cry, can you
make us wanna break out in joyous song?
—BARTON FINK, BY ETHAN AND JOEL COHEN

Usually, a desire to write movies or fiction not only implies an ability to tell stories—whether partly natural or gained through experience, reading, and watching movies—but also a deep love for all stories. But once again, this is a critical trait that is too often missing in today's aspiring writers. Working screenwriters have an insatiable addiction to all stories, good and bad. They are pushed to captivate an audience, and their work shows it.

Robin Swicord: Writers have the sort of mind that puts together narrative in a way that has a beginning, middle, and end. They notice cause and effect, that because this thing happened, that other thing is happening. These are the kinds of traits that come together into a mind that makes drama. People who don't have that natural bend for it have a very hard time really understanding what it is writers do. There's nothing more humbling for people who say, "I've always wanted to be a writer" than to actually try to create an alternate reality, only to find out it's really hard to play God.

3. Being Comfortable with Solitude

Writing is a lonely life, but the only life worth living.
—GUSTAVE FLAUBERT

Writing is a lonely business. As a writer once said, "It's like volunteering for solitary confinement without knowing the length of your stay." Writers must spend a lot of time alone, but because they tend to be introverted by nature, they usually find more psychological comfort in a book or in writing than in social interactions. This is not to say that if you're not comfortable with your solitude, you won't be able to write. One of the many surprises in chatting with our mentors is that many of them are actually extroverts who force solitude on themselves in order to do their jobs.

Ron Bass: I really prefer to write alone. Generally, when I have staff meetings, we talk about story and criticism, but I don't like to write with somebody else sitting there, because I'll talk out loud and I'll pace around. I can be physically active when I write. I usually sit but I also have standing desks wherever I go so I can write standing up, which enables me to pace around and charge back and forth, move my arms. It's a physical process, not just an intellectual one. I cross things out and I write bigger or darker depending on the emotion. If I'm in the park, I'll pace around. I must look really peculiar to people, so I try to find a place where I'm relatively alone, and certainly where I won't hear another human voice.

Leslie Dixon: In order to do the job really well, *you must spend prolonged periods of time in total isolation.* You must. I loved it for the first few years where I had total control of my time without anybody telling me what to do. But I still haven't figured out how to strike a balance between spending enough time by myself to produce a better grade of work versus not becoming a hermit.

Amy Holden Jones: The temperament that made me enjoy editing makes me enjoy writing, that solitary work where you get to refine over and over until you get it the way you want it. As a screenwriter, you need to be comfortable with that solitude for long periods of time, unless you work in television where it's a more social environment.

Tom Schulman: You need to create solitude so that you can hear the voices, and you need a willingness to live in the world of the story for long periods of time, forcing yourself into the world of the characters so that you can believe they exist. Many spouses of writers understandably complain that we're not living in the present.

Robin Swicord: A friend once gave me and fellow writers a personality test, and we all turned out to be introverts, which I don't think is a coincidence. Something like 20 percent of the general population is introverted, but I think most writers probably fall into that category. They feel very comfortable with solitude. They are probably better in one-on-one situations rather than dealing with lots of people. I know that when I'm in a room full of people, I tend to fall back as an observer.

4. Being a Natural Observer

Everything has beauty but not everyone sees it.
—CONFUCIUS

In order to describe, you need to observe. Most of us go through life only half seeing what goes on around us. We have too much going on to bother with observing details in life and in human nature. As a result, most beginning writers tend to reference what they've just seen on television and at the movies, rather than drawing from what they've observed in the real world. Successful screenwriters naturally develop the habit of observing others, which gives them an ear for the way people talk and an eye for the way they behave. They're aware of the most minute details of the world around them, silently making notes on everything, and seeing things vividly and selectively. Whether in coffee shops, airports, or restaurants, they cannot resist people-watching or eavesdropping on a conversation. In short, they pay attention.

Gerald DiPego: Many beginning writers don't do enough observing or enough listening when they're out and about in the world, on buses or in restaurants. Often, when I read a beginner's script, I find that the writer is not referencing life but rather what I see in movies and television.

Jim Kouf: I don't think the writer can leave it at the office. It's your life. You're constantly thinking, constantly listening to the conversation in the next booth, staring at the character with the eye patch, wondering what kind of character he is. It never leaves you.

Robin Swicord: Writers have the particular makeup of a person who looks at the world, observes human behavior, and finds themselves amused, intrigued, or emotionally moved by watching people.

Eric Roth: Everything is writing-related, you live with it 24 hours a day, so when you're out in the world, you're an observer of what people do and details of what's around you. Unconsciously, you try to save them and hopefully use them in a work at a later time.

5. Being Collaborative

Our mind is like a parachute. It only works when it is open.
—ANONYMOUS

In no other form of writing—novels, plays, poems, or journalism—is the habit of collaboration as important as in screenwriting. It is so engrained in the way scripts become movies that without this attitude, no screenwriter, unless he's a genius, can become successful. But as you'll also see later on, collaboration can be a downside.

Ron Bass: By being a screenwriter, you are choosing to be in a medium that is genuinely collaborative, but one in which you do not have the final vote. The collaborative process is wonderful when it's going well and terrible when it doesn't. You may feel passionately about something, and you get overruled by producers and directors. Anytime you get fired, it kills you. Anytime you get a set of notes and you think you got it, you made it work for you and them, and it works great and you love it, and they hate it, you can be angry at them and feel insecure about yourself. Writing screenplays is such a collaborative medium that not caring if anyone else likes it makes no sense to me. If you cannot handle this and the additional bad feelings that come with those moments when you're fired and another writer comes on and makes a total mess out of what you thought was wonderful, you should seriously consider another medium.

Gerald DiPego: It's a whole skill you have to develop apart from writing. Call it compromise, negotiation, or debate. You spend a lot of time in development, trying to do your best to explain and defend the material against harmful ideas, but at the same time, you have to stay open to the good ideas. Some people shut down and say, "The hell with them! They're all stupid." That's not going to work. Then again, you can't sit there like a stenographer and accommodate them because that will kill the material.

Michael Schiffer: You have to collaborate and listen, but you can't sell out your own work either. You try to navigate between their good and bad ideas and find a way to let them have what they feel they need without damaging what you feel is the emotional core and spirit of your piece. It's like being on a boat trip, somebody wants to go to the left bank and somebody wants to go to the right bank. There's no right or wrong. You have to allow people to go on the journey they want to go on if they are your partners. You try to respect the problems they are bringing up instead of thinking they're all a bunch of idiots. If you have that attitude, you're in big trouble because you're the idiot who will be fired first.

CHAPTER 2
Desire

6. Having a Driving Reason to Write

*Don't write with sales or money in mind—it poisons the
well at its source. If writing isn't a joy, don't do it.
Life is short. Death is long.*

—WILLIAM WHARTON

All the writers interviewed here have been writing for many years. They
didn't last or get to where they are today without having a driving and passionate desire to write. Every writer has a variety of reasons why he writes,
some more or less admirable than others. They are not like many aspiring
writers I meet sometimes whose only wish is to write a screenplay that will
sell for a million dollars so they can have the freedom to do what they
really love to do, whatever it may be. Whether it's their primary way of
expressing themselves, an outlet for their fantasies, or a desire to entertain
people, real writers don't get satisfaction out of doing anything else. They
love writing for its own sake.

But before you throw out your screenwriting software because your
motives are less than pure, remember that there are no good or bad reasons. You just need a *driving* reason. Most writers will tell you to do it
only if you love it, if you're so passionate about it that you cannot live
without doing it. But there may be some successful writers who hate
writing but are passionate about something else. It still drives them to
do good work. The most important ingredient is the passion and drive
to achieve your goals.

In his book, *A Mencken Chrestomathy*, H. L. Mencken calls the writer

one in whom the normal vanity of all men is so vastly exaggerated that he finds it a sheer impossibility to hold it in. His overpowering impulse is to gyrate before his fellow men, flapping his wings and emitting defiant yells. This being forbidden by the police of all civilized countries, he takes it out by putting his yells on paper.

We all want attention, recognition, immortality. And whether any writer admits it or not, egotism is a strong motivating factor in writing. But let's hear from our panel, in their own words:

Ron Bass: There's only one reason to become a screenwriter, or a writer of anything, and that is you can't avoid it. It's what you love to do. It's who you are. I write because there's no way I couldn't write. I was writing stories when I was six years old because I loved to do it and tell stories in my own way. I wrote a novel when I was teenager, then I became a lawyer to support my family and was away from writing prose for 16 years. And I really missed it. So I went back to it and didn't tell anyone that I was doing it. The second I started again, I just said to myself, "Why on earth did I take so long to come back to this?" There's absolutely nothing else in life that makes me feel the way that writing does.

Steven DeSouza: A good reason to become a screenwriter: It seems like a natural outlet for your creative energy. A bad reason: You just went to a screenwriting seminar at the Holiday Inn.

Gerald DiPego: For me, writing borders on an obsession. It's almost like I don't have a choice, like breathing. While you can certainly rack yourself with doubt, there is a persistence about it where it isn't a sense of "should I do this or not?" but more "I can't help this, I love it, I need to do it."

Leslie Dixon: I was one of those little girls whose English teacher always told her she should be a writer. My father was also a writer and my grandparents were artistic, so I guess it was genetically implanted and shoved into my head. I had a dreamy identity that I was going be a writer since I was eight years old. I wanted to find some form of writing where I didn't have to work a crummy job and write at night and since I was obsessed with movies, it seemed like the logical marriage of passion and commerce.

Akiva Goldsman: I couldn't think of a more perfect job for me. I've been lucky enough to work closely with directors and actors, hear how my words sound and change them in collaboration with the artists, and experience this kind of traveling summer camp that is a movie. This is important for me because the act of writing is itself wildly solitary, but the act of making a movie is very social, so for me, this is the perfect alternation: the solitude of writing and the community of building and making movies.

Nicholas Kazan: I started to write because I heard a line of dialogue and wrote it down, then I heard another one, and eventually I wrote a play. Without knowing anything about the play when I sat down, I wrote this 40-minute play simply by transcribing these lines of dialogue. And the experience of having this entire dramatic work delivered to me by my unconscious was such a riveting and narcotic effect that I was hooked.

Jim Kouf: I write because I enjoy writing and I love movies. But the most important reason I write is because someone else likes what I write and is willing to pay me for it. Otherwise, I'd rather go fishing.

Tom Schulman: I've been doing it for so long now that it has become a habit. It's like when I haven't walked in the morning, I'm not in a very good mood. I just can't get away from it. I tried writing a novel, but unfortunately, every scene was two and a half pages long. After a few chapters I thought, "Who am I kidding?" It requires the kind of patience that I just don't have. I don't even know if there are any bad reasons to become a screenwriter. Reasons and motivations are usually a cover for something else. Paddy Chayefsky once said that becoming a great lover was a good reason for writing screenplays, but you'd better have something else on you mind when you sit down at the typewriter.

Ed Solomon: I love a good movie just as I love a good book, but I don't love movies in general. I write because I enjoy sitting in the room making stuff up. I like thinking about dialogue and images and characters, which is fun and interesting, but putting it all together so that it becomes an interesting story is really hard for me.

Robin Swicord: I can't criticize anyone's dreams for wanting to become a screenwriter. Any reason is valid as long as it motivates you and you love to write. It's very difficult to make a living just writing, so every aspiring writer works two jobs. You have your day job, which helps you have a place to live and food to eat, and then you have your writing job, which takes place away from the rest of the world with very little support. Anyone who can do this for any length of time and is able to sell their work as a writer, no matter what it is, needs to be congratulated. So whether they want to be a screenwriter to be part of a microscopic minority of writers who actually make a living at it or whether they wake up in the morning with movies in their head and just have to write them down, whatever their reasons, they're perfectly valid.

CHAPTER 3
Belief

7. Believing You're Talented Enough

Having talent is like having blue eyes. You don't admire a man for the color of his eyes. I admire a man for what he does with his talent.
—ANTHONY QUINN

To do anything successfully, after the initial desire, we must believe it can be done. Strong belief is the driving force behind all art that was once visualized before becoming a reality. In Hollywood, it's not enough to have an "I think I can do it" attitude. It has to be "I *know* I can do it!" I'm a firm believer that, as human beings, we are all blessed with talent. Talent is simply what you have to say and your unique way of saying it by showing your soul through your writing. It's just a matter of noticing it and, more importantly, developing it.

But having some self-doubts can actually benefit writers by pushing them to become better at their craft. The problem, however—Hollywood being full of self-deluded dreamers—is that too many aspiring writers naively believe in something that isn't developed yet. Then again, delusion can be good. Look at Spud Webb, who at five feet tall wanted to become an NBA player more than anything in the world and did, despite many warnings against this silly dream. He even won a Slam Dunk contest one year, showing the rest of us that anything is possible if you believe it. As Henry Ford once said, "Whether you think you can or whether you think you can't, you're right."

Jim Kouf: You never know if you have talent. You're testing yourself with every script, so I never assume I've solved any riddles. I just keep trying to write something well. I never called myself a writer until somebody else called me a writer, and paid me for it. I wrote a script that got some attention and people started hiring me to rewrite other scripts. But it wasn't until I kept getting hired and I started making a living at it that I believed I was doing something right.

Eric Roth: Winning a contest helped validate me. It got me an agent. But I've always had a real sense that I had a good visual imagination. I've always had the arrogance or confidence that I could write good characters. That's about it. I went through a learning process just like anyone else.

Michael Schiffer: The first thing any writer has to ask himself is, "How do I know I have talent?" The answer is you don't know. When I first started out, I would cook dinner for my friends and then make them listen to what I had written that day. If I wasn't a good cook, there's no way anyone would have stayed. I could see them sitting there with such pity in their eyes, probably thinking this was just terrible and that I was just nuts.

Ed Solomon: Once in a while, you have an inkling that you may have a bit of talent when you make a little private connection by yourself in a room, a little scene that works or a great idea that surprises you. But the majority of the time, you're just slugging it out, confused, unable to see the forest from the trees, and doubting yourself, wondering if what you're saying has any value, or if you have the ability to make it work. Then when you finish something, and you think it's the greatest thing that's ever been written— three days later you feel it's an utter waste of ink and paper, and you wonder how you'll ever write anything again. I don't know how you overcome that. I just keep doing it because no one has offered me a better job yet.

Robin Swicord: I was lucky not to have a lot of extremely talented people around me where I grew up in a small town in the South. I was probably the only person there who wanted to be a writer. So I didn't find myself in a very competitive place, where I'd be comparing myself to other people's abilities. I guess it gave me a sort of delusion that I could do it because I was the only person doing it. Ironically, the first time I had doubts whether I would make it as a writer was after I had actually sold screenplays. I walked into someone's office when I first came to Los Angeles and saw shelves full of screenplays, thousands of them, covering an entire wall, and I thought, "My God, there are a lot of people doing this!" I was lucky not to be exposed to the real world until after I already had some validation.

CHAPTER 4
Enthusiasm

8. Being a Voracious Reader

Reading makes me want to write, and writing makes me
want to read. And both reading and writing make me joy to
be part of the great human adventure we call life.
—KATHERINE PATERSON

It is a rare writer who didn't grow up reading compulsively, feeding their minds with great stories and planting the seed for future inspiration to write their own. Reading teaches the writer about good storytelling the way watching an operation teaches a medical student about surgery. I absolutely love books. Bookstores and libraries are my second homes, and I wasn't surprised to hear that when our mentors are not writing or out socially they spend most of their free time reading. They have a passion for the printed word, whether it is fiction, nonfiction, or screenplays.

Ron Bass: I used to read a lot as a child. Now, I don't get to really read anything that I'm not assigned to write. I wish I had the time to read more. It's the biggest single sense of loss that I have about what I do and the choices I've made. When I think about retirement, the first thought in my mind is the beach in Maui and suitcases full of every book I've resented not having read over the years. The writing replaced the books, that window to a wider world and a way of looking at things, and when I started to write, I went to that place myself and created that other world rather than experiencing it.

Michael Schiffer: Though I'm usually burnt out on words by the end of most days, I try to read a little bit before going to bed, and I read voraciously on vacation. I love to put my writing down and devour books.

Tom Schulman: Essentially, if nothing goes in, nothing comes out. What we do as writers, even though we deal in images, is use words. And the way we become literate is through reading.

9. Being Passionate about the Craft

> *If you don't love it without the money,*
> *you won't love it with the money.*
> —TODD SILER

Passion is the most overused word in Hollywood, and for good reason. It is the critical quality that separates those who achieve the goal they set their minds to from those who simply dream about it. Every successful person I know has a passion for life, for their work, and for excellence, and our mentors are no exception. They have this all-consuming sense of purpose, which is, not surprisingly, far from a common trait among many aspiring writers. I'm alarmed when would-be writers come up to me and say, "I just can't find the time to write," because this is a clear clue they're not serious about becoming screenwriters. When you're passionate about something, you're dying to do it as often as you can. Passion is the drive that makes you want to write no matter what, when, or how.

Since this is a prominent trait among our mentors, I asked them what they loved most about being a screenwriter.

Gerald DiPego: You've got to love storytelling and be a really good audience for film. I loved film long before I started writing it. I love its magic and how it takes me away. That's what made me want to be a writer. I wanted to be a part of that magic. When you're writing the screenplay, first you take a journey and make the magic for yourself. It should be a journey of great joy and love in the work. It doesn't mean you won't struggle or sweat at the challenge, but if it's not based on a love for stories and film you're in trouble because you've got goals in mind instead of the process. I also like the thrill of seeing my work come alive on the screen. No matter how many years you're in the business, it's always a thrill to see all that's been assembled around this fragile little thing called a story. Suddenly, people are hammering nails, building sets, and actors are walking around saying your lines.

Leslie Dixon: I like being a part of the movie business; that's always a fantasy fulfillment. Your lifestyle, in patches, can be quite glamorous. You really do get to meet interesting and truly talented people you've always wanted to meet. Occasionally, you can dig deep into yourself and come up with surprising things you never knew you had in you and that's quite a challenge to yourself. And I'd be lying if I didn't say the money is great. There comes a point where, if you're not an idiot and don't get divorced multiple times, you're safe forever.

Amy Holden Jones: I like purging my demons and fulfilling my fantasies. I like working out themes that matter to me. It is enormously satisfying to be able to work them out through characters I create and ultimately have a work that entertains a lot of people, especially kids. I also like the writing process, especially the refining stage after I'm done with the first draft.

Nicholas Kazan: I like working my own hours. I like creating an alternative universe and the feeling of being possessed by the story. And I like the feeling of excitement—not knowing what is going to happen next.

Jim Kouf: You get to work alone . . . most of the time. You get paid well . . . some of the time. You get to be creative . . . until somebody buys the script. And, well, it's actually kind of fun . . . a lot of the time. I don't know what else I'd do.

Scott Rosenberg: I like that no day is the same. I basically do whatever I want, when I want. I get to learn about completely different subcultures. When I did a movie about car thieves, I immersed myself in the world of car thieves. When I did a movie about convicts, I got to go to prisons. You can work a lot of the demons in your life into your screenplays. Someone said to me that they felt sorry that I spent most of my days alone. They may think this, but the people I work with every day are a lot more interesting than the people in their office. The people I work with die when I tell them to die, make love when I tell them to make love, and cry when I tell them to cry.

Eric Roth: It's a wonderful adventure. It's a good way to explore yourself and other parts of the world and express yourself. The obvious thing is if you can be successful at it, you can make a great living at it.

Michael Schiffer: Oddly enough, I like screenplays as a form. People say that they're just blueprints, but I disagree. There's a lot more to it. I love their compression, their visuals, and their canvas. This sort of tight, internal reflectivity is really exciting and fun and very exacting. It's also a great thrill to see one's movie get made. The first time I sat alone in a dark screening room in New York and *Colors* went up on the screen it was a powerful, mind-blowing experience. Another plus is the actual process of writing the screenplay. I've written many scripts that didn't get made, but I was still deeply involved with them. I've shed tears when my characters wept and laughed when they did.

Ed Solomon: I don't particularly love movies. Don't get me wrong, I enjoy a good movie once in awhile but I'm not as passionate about them as most screenwriters. It's like asking a car designer if he likes traffic. He might like a good car but not most cars. I like a few movies but if you put a whole bunch of movies together, that's traffic. You don't have to love movies to love what you do. I write because I love to write. I like the idealized notion of a movie, what it can be, a beautifully realized visual and literal storytelling experience. What we do in the privacy of our little rooms is try to create idealized movies that exist in theory. What a movie usually ends up being is just two hours of junky celluloid. The more experience you have, the more you're able to create a movie that will approximate its final form.

Robin Swicord: I always loved creating a world, making up people and naming them, finding out who they are, what their great flaws are and what they do and what they think is funny. And I also like that I can wear my pajamas to work.

10. Being Passionate about Movies

Let the beauty we love be what we do.
—RUMI

Just as a fiction writer learns to write by reading books, a screenwriter learns by watching movies. It is this passion for movies, first and foremost, that makes writers want to tell stories for this most popular medium that affects mass audiences in meaningful ways.

Nicholas Kazan: What distinguishes the people off the streets who want to be screenwriters from those who are successful at it is that successful screenwriters love movies, breathe movies, and have an overwhelming, almost narcotic desire to be part of the process.

Jim Kouf: When I was in elementary school, I used to rush home to watch movies. When I was in high school, I convinced a chemistry professor to let me make a film instead of writing a term paper. When I was in college, I thought I'd write plays because I fell in love with the theater. But when I moved back home I didn't have enough money to move to New York. It just so happened I lived in Burbank and the guy next door was a camera operator and the guy down the street was a makeup man and a friend of my parents worked at Universal, so I was able to get my hands on some screenplays to see what they looked like. Once I figured out the form, I was off and writing.

CHAPTER 5
Commitment

11. Understanding the Downside of Being a Screenwriter in Hollywood

You pour your heart out into this, you take all this abuse, you take all this crap in grief, all for what? For a measly fortune.
—S. J. PERELMAN

Warning: this is an insightful look at the flip side to all the "first time writer goes from waiter to hot writer" success stories you've read about in the trades. Consider this a public service announcement on the realities of the business and the reason why everyone says you need a thick skin to survive as a Hollywood screenwriter.

Put every screenwriter on a bus out of town and see how quickly the industry comes to a halt. Producers have no movies to make, directors have no script to shoot, actors have no lines to speak, agents make no commissions, and so on with every job from production assistant to director of photography. No one has a job without a script, and yet screenwriting is the most disrespected element in the movie-making process. Why? Like it or not, it's still a medium driven by stars and directors. When a writer commits to a project, he goes home and writes it. When a star or director commits to a script, that project gets a green light for production.

Pay close attention. This is what awaits you as soon as you become a professional screenwriter:

Ron Bass: It's a very hard business. First, you're not the final decision maker of what the final text will look like. This isn't true anywhere else. If you're a novelist, like I was, you can reject all your editor's notes and they'll still publish the book. If you're a playwright, no one is allowed to change a word without your approval. When you're a screenwriter, and I mean features, because if you're in television, you have some final decision power at the executive producer level, you won't have the final word, unless you're the director, and you'll go through losing things that are very precious to you and losing arguments that you think are essential to the integrity of the story. Second, you're failing all the time as a screenwriter. The odds of anything getting liked are so small, and to get it made, they're even smaller. Even a wonderful script that everyone loves won't get made for all kinds of reasons. Even if it gets made, they may screw it up in making it or marketing it, and it may flop. Third, you're always being criticized and rejected. And yet, if you don't remain vulnerable to that, you're hurting yourself. Those who can harden their hearts to it and say, "To hell with them, I don't care what they say, I know I'm right" can become arrogant and lack the openness that maybe they don't have all the answers, maybe they're not doing such a great job and the criticism is correct.

Steven DeSouza: For me, the problem is not the rejection, but the random factors of the industry. You can have a picture that's ready to go and the star pulls out. Suddenly, there's no movie. They weren't going to make the movie because they loved the script but because the *star* committed to it. You could have a movie ready to go and the management changes. The good news is that they don't want to make the movie. The bad news is that they want to *reinvent* the movie. You have a team, everything is in place, and one factor changes and suddenly the whole thing spins off in another direction. So half the time it's a horrible experience because the movie gets canceled and the other half it's a horrible experience because the movie gets made anyway, completely reinvented.

Gerald DiPego: Film necessarily comes out of a clash of opinions, unlike writing a novel, which is a solitary journey. That in itself can be tough, especially in our film business, because the writer's opinion does not carry equal weight with the other players. I love the writing but after the writing comes the development. I don't know how many writers say they love development. That's where you're barraged by notes, and people give you changes. Some of them you respect as creative people, but others you wonder what are their qualifications, what makes them think they know how to make this scene better?

Akiva Goldsman: There are certainly downsides to all things but these are the choices we make. It's of course remarkably painful, without question, to get your ass kicked in reviews. I've gotten wonderful reviews and horrible ones and the truth is I've been the same writer from one picture to the next. Sometimes when a movie doesn't work, things get hung unfairly on one single individual when there's never a single individual who's responsible for a movie's success or failure. Sometimes I find that when writers get picked on in reviews, they get hit harder because they're hit by other writers. Ideally, if reviewers wanted to review a screenplay, they should read it and if they think it sucks, then they should say that.

Amy Holden Jones: Screenwriting is a terrible way to make a living and I always try to talk anyone out of it. Until you sit in a story meeting with the studio executives with no particular ability or actors who haven't even graduated from high school telling you exactly how to change your script, you haven't experienced what it's really like to be a screenwriter in Hollywood. Also, unlike novelists and playwrights, you don't own the copyright on your original material. It hurts when you sell a project you love and have management change it, or they have no intention of making it and suddenly the project you really cared about will never see the light of day.

Nicholas Kazan: In the theater, playwrights are revered and nothing can be changed without their permission. In film, directors rewrite you and actors change your lines without even realizing they're doing it. In that sense, it's a very frustrating profession. There are a million things that can go wrong with a movie. It can be miscast, a director can have the wrong tone, or a cinematographer can make the movie too beautiful or too ugly. And don't forget you can get fired. Even if you're successful, it still is incredibly painful. You write something you know would be a truly great film and it just gets destroyed. It may end up good or terrible, but it rarely is what it should have been, and you're the only one who knows this.

Jim Kouf: It's hard not to take it personally because here you are, the hero who slaved over these words, and as soon as you turn it in and everyone is happy with it, they couldn't care less what your thoughts are. It's a matter of giving up your child every time and letting somebody else raise it from that point.

Scott Rosenberg: Screenwriting is so intensely collaborative that it's not as pure as writing a play or a novel. There are too many cooks in the kitchen. Even when you get to the point where the producer and the studio finally see eye to eye, the director comes in and tinkers with it, then the actors come in and tinker with it, and even after the movie is done, a test audience causes changes. The final product is never as pure as when you first sat down to write it.

Tom Schulman: Writing can be excruciatingly painful. It can be emotionally grueling if you write something that's very close to you. Writing is constantly about chipping away at your ability, pushing yourself, always challenging yourself to come up with something better. Being a good writer requires a strong inner critic so when you do something you try to enjoy it while you do it. But as soon as you're done, you have to turn around and read it and really lay it to waste and start over. That is often a tough, demoralizing process full of highs and lows.

Ed Solomon: What I dislike is everything that happens once you're done with a script.

Robin Swicord: I don't like that it is so cut off from the actual film-making process and that it is all about who has the money and who shouts the loudest.

•   •   •

Still here? Good. You're tough enough to realize the realities of the business. Now we need to work on . . .

12. Being Committed to a Career, Not Just One Screenplay

Concerning all acts of initiative and creation, there is one elementary truth, the ignorance of which kills countless ideas and splendid plans: That the moment one definitely commits oneself, then Providence moves too. Whatever you can do or dream you can, begin it. Boldness has genius, power and magic in it. Begin it now.
—GOETHE

Do you dream of a screenwriting career? Sure, you still want to sell what you write, but are you committed to toughing it out for as long as it takes? Are you passionate about the craft? Do you feel it's your life and can't see yourself doing anything else? Or do you dream of just selling one screenplay for a million dollars, so you can then pursue another dream? Do you hope for fame, glory, and cash? If you're driven by the one-in-a-million chance of going from rags to riches overnight, nothing is stopping you from writing one spec script for money. But as you may already know, the odds are against you.

Nicholas Kazan: People who do anything for ulterior reasons are much less likely to get to the goal they anticipate. The one clear lesson of human behavior is that results are inadvertent. You have to get your pleasure intrinsically. Those who are successful at it love to write screenplays first and then are well rewarded for it. But even if they were paid a tenth of what they made, they'd still do it because they love to do it.

Scott Rosenberg: People doing it for the wrong reasons have a lottery mentality, but I remember my reason was actually the opposite. When I'd go home to visit, I'd be at a family gathering and my uncle would come up and hand me some article about screenwriting that said you had a better chance of hitting the lottery than becoming a paid screenwriter. It was an incredibly daunting statistic, so I always firmly believed that you make your own luck. Initially, you do it because you have to do it and you can't think of anything else to do. I write because I actually enjoy it. I have writer friends who'll do everything to avoid sitting at the computer. I'm always very comfortable sitting there. It's never the agony that it is for a lot of other people. I've always believed that we are paid more for our God-given talents than for anything else. Mark McGwire can hit a home run out of the ball park without effort every sixth time the same way that Jimmy Page can play the guitar or Jim Carrey can make you laugh. It's just natural talent. The idea of getting into the screenwriting business to make money is silly because the odds are stacked against you. The money is just the icing on the cake.

13. Having Precise Goals, Not Just Wishes

All people dream; but not equally. Those who dream by night
in the dusty recess of their minds wake in the day to find that it was
vanity. But the dreamers of the day are the dangerous people,
for they may act their dream with open eyes to make it possible.
—T. E. LAWRENCE

Look at all the habits so far. If they seem like too much work, you need to question whether your desire to write is a passion, a need, or simply just a wish. If you keep trying and failing to make the time to write, if your desire to write is not enough to keep you from doing more entertaining activities, then this may not be for you.

But if you've committed to a writing career, and want to write for the sake of writing, you need to realize that wanting and doing are two different things. With distractions and obstacles everywhere, singleness of purpose and a compelling sense of mission are essential. A writing career is created. When you commit to it, you need a plan of action and you need to act on that plan.

Ron Bass works an average of 14 hours a day, seven days a week. Eric Roth likes to wake up in the middle of the night, write for a few hours, take a nap and start again in the morning. He takes a break in the afternoon and writes again in the evening. Akiva Goldsman goes straight from bed to his computer and writes nonstop for 10 to 12 hours. The rest of our panel, with a couple of exceptions, are disciplined enough to keep regular hours, eight hours a day, five days a week, like any other job.

14. Not Letting Self-Doubts Get in the Way

Courage is not the absence of fear, but rather the judgment
that something else is more important than fear.
—AMBROSE REDMOON

Ask any aspiring writer why he has yet to write his first script or why he hasn't finished the one he's been working on for years, and without hesitation, he'll offer an endless string of excuses, "I don't have enough time . . ." "I'm not good enough . . ." "I have kids . . ." "I can't afford the latest screenwriting software . . ." "I don't have an agent . . ." These are often a front for fear and self-doubt. In fact, this whole industry runs on fear. Fear of saying "yes" to a potential box-office flop, fear of missing out on a hot script, fear of being found out and never working again, and so on. So you are not alone. Embrace the fears and do it anyway. Once again, this may be obvious, but it's an important habit to develop, because success in any field can only come after you overcome your fears and build self-confidence. The good news is that confidence is developed. No one is born with confidence. And in Hollywood, even a little bit goes a long way.

Ron Bass: Even today when I have a meeting at a studio, and somebody says, "Ron, we don't think the quality of this piece is up to your standard, it's just not what we expected," it still devastates me. I just go home and feel really, really bad. Even when my team says, "Oh, you're a great writer, you're brilliant, etc.," you still question your talent. Dustin Hoffman once said to me, "Every role is going to be my last; this is the one when they'll realize I can't act; I never could act. I will be found out, and this time I will fall off the tightrope, and they will tear me to pieces and I will never be allowed to act again." What he was saying is that this fear you're not that good is always there. You always have those fears because there's no objective standard. Even when your movie comes out, you realize it wasn't all you, it was Julia Roberts or a hundred other factors. Or your movie doesn't get made and the next one is a failure. It's hard to be in an industry where people alternately tell you you're brilliant and they didn't like something. Who's right and who's wrong? But you don't really want to give up your insecurity, because it's tied to the requisite humility. If you're not humble about the quality of your work and embrace the fear that it's not good enough, and everything that comes out of your mouth isn't just golden because you said it and you're famous, you're dead.

Leslie Dixon: All writers have doubts. But generally, as a person, I've always been comfortable and unafraid in most areas. I don't have this kind of desperation that most beginning writers have. It's just self-confidence without being arrogant. I think you need *more* self-confidence to say occasionally, "I don't think I can pull this off," and turn down the job if you know you're not the right writer for the project. It's just being honest that you don't always bat a thousand every time.

Akiva Goldsman: There's this wonderful notion, I think it's in *Three Kings*, where someone says, "Bravery is what happens afterwards." I've always believed that when you run across the battlefield with a flag in your hand, you're just trying to do desperately what the moment tells you to do. In the moment, you're just doing what's required. Afterwards, you have the time to feel scared and proud and courageous. I'm constantly afraid of failing, of being found out and revealed to be a fraud, of writing badly and not being allowed to write again. Quite frankly, any creative person who doesn't feel some of that runs the risk of becoming complacent and then your writing suffers. You need a bit of self-doubt to propel you.

Scott Rosenberg: In the beginning, I absolutely had doubts (and still do) but I wasn't crippled by them. I don't know why. I must have had this sort of misplaced arrogance about it. If I knew then what I know now, it may have been different.

15. Educating Yourself

Learning by reading is like making love by mail.
—LUCIANO PAVAROTTI

Can screenwriting be taught? The amazing proliferation of businesses and books catering to aspiring screenwriters shows that many believe it can. Despite some great writing workshops that help the writer find his unique voice, the result is thousands of formulaic spec scripts flooding an industry that abhors formulas (at least when it comes to buying spec scripts).

I'm not saying you should never attend a seminar or read a screenwriting book. They can be valuable in teaching you the basics. No one, however, can teach you the art of screenwriting because that's the unique magic only you can bring to a story. Seminars can be valuable for interacting with fellow writers, making you feel like you belong, and the fact that you've spent hundreds of dollars to attend may inspire you to take action and write your script. I have found that specific classes, such as at UCLA Extension, can also be instrumental in completing a script or a certain number of pages by an imposed date. It's the old deadline factor that most paid screenwriters benefit from, unless you impose them on yourself (see Habit 49). In essence, you're paying someone what amounts to a month's rent to force you to complete a project. Whatever works, right?

As you will hear from our mentors, the bottom line is that writing is self-taught. In addition to watching movies and reading screenplays and books about screenwriting, a screenwriter needs to learn about life, people, the human mind, emotions. Just as a musician learns by practice, working with and observing other musicians, or a painter by going to museums and studying the masters, you can learn by writing, observing other writers (what this book is about), reading other writers' works, and most importantly, watching a lot of movies.

Ron Bass: When I was a freshman at Stanford, I took a literature course on the American novel taught by a famous novelist, a real writer, big guy, hard drinking, who'd talk about his days with Hemingway and Scott in Paris. I came up to him after class one day and said, "I really want to write fiction. What writing courses should I take?" He said, "Never, ever, ever take a writing course, never read a book about writing, never let anybody tell you how to write. Take literature courses, read, steal, turn everything to your interpretation. As soon as you take a writing course, it's the beginning of the end, because you establish somebody else as the authority for how you can write, and it can't be. Writing is an art, it comes individually out of you. Only you can express your art your way, it's an expression of who you are. I couldn't tell you how to write, Fitzgerald couldn't tell you, Faulkner couldn't tell you. They may tell you how *they* write and you may listen to them and some of that may help you." My advice is to read screenplays, good ones and bad ones, so you can learn what you don't want to do, but more importantly, write a lot of stuff. You only learn to write by writing. Write every day. It shouldn't be a burden. If it is, you shouldn't be doing it.

Steven DeSouza: I scrounged up whatever books I could get, as there were precious few at that time. Since Amazon.com hadn't been invented yet, I would take the train from Philly to New York and go to Cinemabilia, a specialty film bookstore where I got a couple of books that I still read to this day and highly recommend. One is Eugene Vale's *Technique of Screenwriting*, which is still the best book on the craft I've ever read. The other is *The Art of Dramatic Writing* by Lajos Egri. The two complement each other because Egri's book is mainly about character while Vale's is more about structure and plot. Most of all, you need to see classic movies. The problem with most movies made today is that they're an imitation of last year's movies, which are imitations of the previous year's. Sometimes I mention a classic movie at a conference and no one in the room has ever heard of it. That's scary. It's like writing plays and never having read Shakespeare. You need to see all kinds of movies. Look at the silent ones, especially, because they had movies before they had dialogue. See how much they get across without dialogue. If you're depending only on dialogue to make your screenplays work, you're only working with half the ammunition that makes you a good writer. See a movie, then read its screenplay to see what was brought to the table by the actors and the director. Even a blockbuster can be a better learning tool than spending a weekend at a seminar.

Leslie Dixon: My favorite comedy of all time, the one that made me want to become a comedy writer, was *The Producers.* I've always had a sick sense of humor, so I thought singing, dancing Nazis was the funniest thing I'd ever seen in my life, and I never got over that. My mother was always dragging me to revival houses so I was familiar with Lubitch and Billy Wilder's work, for example. I guess you learn watching movies that you really like and trying to analyze why you really like them at the script level. Watch the movie and read the script for it. You can learn more from that than any class. I tried reading a copy of Robert McKee's *Story* that someone lent me, and to me, it felt like trying to understand human beings by analyzing their DNA. It was so full of little charts and graphs and rules, it was mind-boggling. So much of what you have to do here is by instinct, and I think the best way to learn is by watching the movies *you* like and find out why you like them. Of course, all this is completely useless if you don't have some ability to begin with. That's a prerequisite.

Amy Holden Jones: I was lucky to be given a script to rewrite and direct which was quite a learning experience. From that point on, I'd read the very best examples of the genres I was going to write. For instance, when I was writing *Love Letters,* I read *Kramer vs. Kramer, Ordinary People,* and other great dramas. If you read, analyze, and study them you begin to see patterns and techniques that work. Many beginning writers make the mistake of writing a particularly popular genre without even reading the classics in that genre. They also forget that the most important commercial factor in a movie is its visceral entertainment and that a script has to make you feel. I also took acting lessons because Corman makes everyone working for him take acting classes. You learn the process an actor takes to create a character, how dialogue works or what makes a scene work, all valuable things to learn as a writer.

Nicholas Kazan: I learned the craft by writing. I think most seminars are social activities where aspiring writers can gain comfort from meeting other aspiring writers. What they teach is so far from the outside that it gives very little information to real writers. If you write five screenplays, the fifth one will be better than the first. You'll refine your talent even without anyone reading them, even though it's better if others do read them, because you gain from what they don't understand or don't like. People's time would be much better spent trying to write screenplays than going to seminars. Make some labors of love. Write others quickly. Have the idea. Be inspired. Write it. Learn as you go. Watch movies. Read screenplays and write some more.

Scott Rosenberg: It's very difficult to teach someone how to write characters and dialogue. I believe that with the best screenwriters, it's a God-given talent. What you can learn, however, is structure. And you don't even have to go to film school to learn. You can pretty much get that out of a couple of books. The best course I ever took was taught by Frank Daniel, who used to be a dean at USC. He would show you a film, then the next class, he'd show it again but with the volume on low and he'd talk over the movie, basically explaining how the whole thing worked structurally, what was planted here and how it was paying off there. He would do this on all kinds of movies. It was the most fascinating experience and it taught you everything you need to know about structure. Once you have structure and if you can write character and dialogue, it's only a matter of coming up with good ideas. Another good thing about film school is that you have this shared experience with other writers and you don't feel so alone. You're also constantly getting feedback from other writers. Every week you have to turn in 10 pages for your classmates to read and comment on. What was also great about UCLA is that you have to write six screenplays before they let you graduate. That's amazing. When you leave school, you're already armed with a lot of material.

Eric Roth: I learned by just being a film buff. I loved movies and knew the language. The rest you learn by writing. I think people also have to learn literature and plays. Dramatic rules will always apply. And a classical education is as important as anything because a well-rounded kind of knowledge is the best for any kind of writer.

Michael Schiffer: One thing I found helpful was taking some UCLA Extension classes in acting and directing. It was great because it gave you a sense of what a good scene is, what dialogue is all about, by seeing what actors do. It showed you how you're writing for people to say these words, and it gave you some experience in drama making. I highly recommend that beginning writers take an acting class. Be active in it, direct a scene with actors and see what animates the scene and what you can leave off the page. You can build muscles for writing good dialogue. I've never taken a screenwriting course so I can't really say anything about them. If you take the occasional seminar and come away with one great tip you didn't know before, that's a good thing. But I've come to believe you only learn on your own by doing it, by trying to tell stories that work. When you write 14 to 20 screenplays, you begin to internalize a sense of timing and movement of the story, structure, and dialogue. It's not somebody else's rules that matter, it's your own. If you do it by trial and error from the inside out, your work will find its own unique storytelling voice.

Tom Schulman: Aristotle's *Poetics* and Lajos Egri's *Art of Dramatic Writing* are the two books that helped me a lot. Other valuable learning experiences included going to the actor's and director's lab, watching a lot of movies and having a circle of friends who were all movie and theater addicts and argued all the time about everything from performances to style.

Ed Solomon: The most helpful any of the screenwriting books and seminars have been to me is once I've had 18 years experience writing. I think they're helpful at the very beginning . . . if you don't take them as holy writ. And they're interesting to look at after you've been writing awhile and have had a chance to develop your own voice. But in most cases they can be dangerous. The book I'd recommend which is about writing in general is *Bird by Bird* by Annie Lamott. Mostly, I learned by asking friends, but I'm still learning. The only difference is that now I'm learning more. The leaps I take are bigger. One of my biggest surprises was that every script needs to be written differently. What worked for the last one doesn't necessarily work for this one. Every time I start a new script, I really feel I'm relearning how to write. You just learn by writing. You discover new ways of doing it by actually doing it. I know most writers learn by watching movies but I don't have the time. I have a wife and a child. I don't want my life to be all about movies. My most important creative source is living life. I try to understand this world and be a part of it. I try to have a point of view and not be too self-critical but at the same time not overly in love with everything I do. I just try to live and read books and be a part of the culture. I spend a lot of time with my son and wife, trying to be a good dad and a good husband and trying to make the most of this ridiculously short span of life.

Robin Swicord: I wasn't lucky enough to have a mentor, but finding someone who has the time and patience to sit with you can take years off the process. When I started to write seriously, I'd simply ask the help of people I'd meet whom I could see were smart, especially those who worked at the studios. It's very important to have someone from the outside who can read your work and be kind because you're risking everything when you are showing early baby work. At the same time, I'm not sure anyone can teach you how to write. All writing is self-taught. What you look for when you search outside yourself is only another pair of eyes to help you see what you are not able to see because you're too close to the work. For me, it was watching movies, often seeing them a second time, because I'm a sucker for narrative. When I see a movie I get sucked into the story so I have to see it again and really pay attention. Sometimes, I tell people to watch movies on video with the sound off and watch what the editor has done, where the cuts happen, how information is conveyed visually, why a scene begins here and not earlier or later. The ways humans learn is to absorb all that stuff and that understanding of other work goes into the understanding that makes our own work.

16. Being Willing to Work Hard and Make Sacrifices

> You can achieve anything you want in life if you have the
> courage to dream it, the intelligence to make a realistic plan,
> and the will to see that plan through to the end.
> —SIDNEY A. FRIEDMAN

Writing is hard, despite what you may think after reading a screenplay. It takes a lot of time, concentration, and discipline to sit down at a keyboard and write. Writers write. It's what they do. But with a burning desire to succeed, often bordering on obsession, committing to a screenwriting career also means sacrificing most of the things we take for granted, at least in the beginning stages of it, like a steady income, health benefits, or relationships. You watch your college friends become doctors, partners at law firms, and corporate vice presidents with six-figure salaries, or you hear your parents, who rarely understand your artistic struggles, ask "When are you going to get a real job?" Sound familiar? Successful writers get through this by focusing on one thing, and that's their passion for the craft they have committed to pursue with all their might.

Akiva Goldsman: I was lucky early on, but the downside was that my career became my life. Now I'm divorced and I might not be had my career not been as wonderful but as consuming as it was. This business is so hard to get into that once you do, you never want to let it go, and the ability to regulate your participation doesn't come easily. I still don't have it. I'm still wildly engaged with the idea of making movies and being part of them and it's as tantalizing and delicious as any experience, but with the good comes trading off. Sometimes, like with anything in life, other good things fall by the wayside.

Jim Kouf: I was committed to making it in show business. I refused to date or do anything else but write. I was writing nights and weekends and I wasn't happy until I did it. I ate, slept, and thought of nothing but writing. The only thing that would have forced me to quit is if I couldn't make it after 10 years; I would have said enough of this stuff. Luckily, I started making a living at it after three years and I haven't been unemployed since then, except for a couple of writers' strikes. I didn't have a family when I started out and I don't recommend having one when first starting out because at the very beginning, show business will steal your life. You have to be totally committed to getting in, you have to live, eat, breathe it, meet people in it and become friends with them.

Michael Schiffer: I wanted to be a writer and I was desperate. I was living on $3,000 a year. It was make it or die. That's a great motivation, not having any other way to live. I came to Hollywood with very little money and found odd jobs to support myself. I was willing to say I gave it my best shot. If it didn't work out, I was going to walk away from it at age 40. But the first part of that is to actually give it your best shot. None of us knows about our talent but we can address the hard work and the craft part.

17. Setting a High Standard of Excellence

I've learned early on, that no one discriminates against excellence.
—OPRAH WINFREY

Put simply, highly successful screenwriters are successful because they do the job better than anyone else. When starting out, our mentors took the necessary time to develop their craft. They knew what it took to make it and that they had to write more than one script to achieve the requisite craftsmanship to gain attention. Now, they're ruthless in their desire to do their best. They have to be. Their livelihood and reputation depend on it. A few slip-ups into substandard levels and they know they will be replaced by the latest hot-shot young writer. As a beginner, you need to know what this standard is and raise your work to it. What is this standard of excellence? It's easy to find out. Read great scripts and compare them to yours. You'll see the difference on the page and it hopefully will inspire you to raise the quality of your own work.

Leslie Dixon: As a screenwriter, I went through a horrific learning curve. My first script was basically sold on the idea. I continue constantly to feel my work is not good enough and try to improve it every day. To this day, I've never felt that my work pops out of the gate fully formed. So much of it is diligent and grinding application. It doesn't come easily to me.

Akiva Goldsman: Joel (Schumacher) taught me that if you just do your job well, you're doing better than 90 percent of the people doing it because so few people actually really do their job. He also taught me that there's room for error but no room for sloppiness, and this is really important to know because in the movie business, there are a lot of people relying on everything you do. If you take your work seriously from the get go, you have a better chance of fitting into the business once you're in it.

•   •   •

You've got passion, you've got desire, but have you mastered the habits that boost your creativity? Our mentors have. Let's find out how you can too.

PART II

Creativity

Summoning the Muse

O light supreme, raised so far above mortal thoughts,
lend again to my mind a little of your epiphany and
give my tongue such power that it may leave a single
sparkle of thy glory to future men . . .

—DANTE, THE DIVINE COMEDY

CHAPTER 6
The Creative Process

Books and theories abound when it comes to the study of creativity, from what it is to how you can get more of it. But no matter what theory you adopt, it all comes down to the same stages. Traditionally, the creative process has been divided into four distinct stages: First there's *Preparation,* which, for the purposes of this chapter, I divide into three substages I call "Feeding the Muse," "Nurturing the Idea," and "Playing with the Idea." This is where you develop the idea and gather the raw materials to grow it into a story. Next comes the *Incubation* period, which I call "Simmering the Idea," where you just get away from it and let your subconscious take over. This is followed by *Illumination,* or "Welcoming the Muse," which is the "Aha!" light bulb experience most are familiar with when an idea seems to come out of nowhere. Finally comes the *Evaluation* stage, which I label "Raising the Idea to Maturity," where your analytical self takes over to evaluate whether the idea is worth pursuing, and if it is, expanding it into an outline, then a screenplay.

It's important to keep in mind that the creative thinking process is not always linear and may jump around out of the order. Although the creative process is divided into clear phases, creation doesn't necessarily follow this order. Clearly, as writers, we've all had flashes of inspiration—an image, a character, an arena, or a line of dialogue— usually in the illumination stage, which we then followed with research, the preparation phase. Also, there are always ideas incubating in your subconscious throughout the creative process. Remember, this is just a demarcation and analysis, not rules to live by. When it comes to creativity, any order is valid as long your mind is free enough to attract ideas.

Feeding the Muse

In order to generate creative energy, first you must fuel the brain . . .

18. Getting Input As Often As Possible

> *In the midst of our daily lives, we must find*
> *the juice to nourish our creative souls.*
>
> —Sark

Many successful screenwriters are information junkies. The more information from as many diverse sources as possible, the more intellectual stimulation their minds receive. They abound with natural curiosity. There's a wonderful scene in the movie *Short Circuit* where the robot, Number Five, starving for knowledge, has gone through all the encyclopedias, magazines, newspapers, and television channels, but it's not enough. He pleads, "Input, input, need more input!"

Just like Number Five, and all artists, writers are sponges for information, and you need to immerse yourself in the outside world and soak up enough of it not only to know what's been done so you can be different, but also to fill your life with enough raw material that will eventually spill out with your unique signature, much like using your mind as a compost of fertile ground out of which great ideas will grow. I can't tell you how many pitches I've heard from beginners who prefaced it with, "This is a really original concept, it's never been done," only to realize, within seconds, that I could name at least three movies or published novels with that exact story. Then, it would sadden me when I'd hear the writer spent a year writing a script without bothering to research if a similar idea had been done. It's the old saying, "You need to know the rules before you can break them." And for that, you need a tremendous amount of input in order to output an ounce of originality.

Steven DeSouza: I'm a mad newspaper clipper. I have a wall completely devoted to filing cabinets, half of which are clippings, anything that gets my attention, like outrageous or clever crimes, incredibly stupid criminals, robberies, the latest technology, police techniques, military weapons. Technically, I research all the time, even though I don't know if it'll pay off some day. I also love the Internet because of the amazing access you have to things. I spend about 30 minutes a day zipping through news Web sites, and I also have an assistant who finds me obscure things.

Amy Holden Jones: Reading the newspaper is a big source for me. True stories of things people have done and the way they actually behaved often surprises me.

Scott Rosenberg: You definitely try to watch a lot of movies. I prefer not to read scripts because I don't want to know what's out there. When I'm not socializing, most of my free time is spent reading. But more importantly, it's about getting out there and living a life that's not related to the movie business, which is very hard to do in Los Angeles. If you spend enough time here, you come to realize that all the people you surround yourself with are in the movie business, used to be in the movie business, or want to be in the movie business. Sure, it can be very seductive when you find yourself at a party and there's Brad Pitt and Tom Cruise, but at a certain point, you have to say to yourself, "Wait a minute, I'm supposed to tell stories that are universally recognized and that's tough to do when I'm drinking a beer with Tom Cruise." It's not reality.

Tom Schulman: More than watching movies, I read a lot of fiction, nonfiction, newspapers, magazines, or I browse the Internet. But fiction is the most important. For some reason, if I don't read fiction, I have difficulty writing.

Robin Swicord: As writers, we need a lot of cultural input just for the sake of keeping our own mind alive. We also need to make ourselves get out of our pajamas and go out into the world and do something that's just human contact with other lives. As a human being, all you really have to write from are your own experiences, your own mind, and your own perception of the things that inspire you. You have to be interested in a lot of things. Do some volunteer work. Be involved with the world. The writing is just one aspect of who you are as a person, but who you are as a person is what feeds that writing.

19. Not Worrying about Finding Ideas

All the words you need are to be found in the dictionary.
All you have to do is put them in the right order.
—EMMA DARCY

Because a question often asked by beginners is "Where do you get your ideas?" I was surprised to hear that finding ideas is the least worry of our mentors. For them, it's more like, "so many ideas, so little time." You may think that they don't have to worry because they are successful, and there's a little bit of truth to that. At their level, ideas come to them from all sources, mainly through other people as offers for work. But even as beginners in their aspiring stage, our writers had developed the attitude of not being obsessed about finding ideas. The consensus was that ideas are everywhere around you. You just have to be open to them. It's like true love; it comes to you when you're not looking. What you should worry about is *executing* the idea masterfully once you commit to it. In Hollywood, the reality is that good ideas are a dime a dozen, but it's for their execution that successful screenwriters are highly paid. It's the reason why a studio sometimes hires up to 15 writers on a single project, usually a summer blockbuster, where a lot is at stake. Same idea, different renderings.

Ron Bass: Finding ideas has never meant that much to me. I've never felt very proud of that. I'm a storyteller. I'm not necessarily the person that gets the initial idea. They could come from anywhere, personal experience, people who work with me. Very often, it comes from the buyers. They tell me their idea and then I'll write the story around it, like spinning the pearl around the grain of sand.

Akiva Goldsman: I don't spend any time hunting for ideas. I find that the world is full of ideas and you just have to be open. They come to you and the really good ideas are the ones that possess you and you ultimately end up using.

Scott Rosenberg: For me, it's the opposite. I have too many ideas and it's very frustrating because there's no way I could get to them all. I aspire to get to a place where I can hire young writers to write a first draft under my supervision.

Ed Solomon: I find that when you're open to ideas, they come and when you search for them, they don't. The more you're open to the world around you and are thinking in that way, the more ideas come. It is absolutely true for me that writing breeds more writing and the more you are active in thinking and writing, the more ideas you get. A big part of it is pushing, nurturing, and fertilizing the ideas that come.

THE CREATIVE PROCESS   43

Robin Swicord: My problem is what am I going to do with all of them? I don't have enough time to write all the stories that come into my head. My mind is like Velcro. I don't look for them, they look for me.

Nurturing the Idea

Once you're blessed with the germ of an idea, you prepare by searching for raw materials that will become characters, plot, bits of dialogue, or situations, as you look at the big picture, ask questions, and let your mind wander.

20. Asking the Right Questions

> *The answer to any problem pre-exists.*
> *We need to ask the right question to reveal the answer.*
> —JONAS SALK

You immerse yourself in the idea, searching for any information that may be relevant. In journalism school, they teach budding reporters to ask the six universal questions for every story: Who, what, where, when, how, and why. When it comes to storytelling, the most popular story starter is "What if?" Asking the right questions often brings the right answers, like nails to a magnet. Most screenwriting books are filled with them: What is my story about? Who are my main characters? What do they want and what prevents them from getting it? Why do they want it? How far will they go to achieve it, and how far will someone go to stop them? Where and when is the story taking place? For me, the two most important questions I ask myself at any stage are "Is this unique and compelling enough to interest an audience?" and "Am I moved by this in any way?" Because if it doesn't move me, it definitely won't move an audience.

Asking questions can also be a valuable step before you go into the incubation phase of the creativity process, especially when you're stuck. Asking a question and then forgetting about it usually leads to fruitful illumination moments where the problems seem to work themselves out in the subconscious, and the answers pop out when you least expect them.

Ron Bass: Once I get the germ of the idea, there's a process I call "matrixing," which is everything that happens before I outline, a sort of gathering of ideas. I think about things in a deliberately disorganized way because I want to be free and open to anything. I gather everything in whatever way it strikes me. I go to the park and pace around and write out every idea that comes to me, whether it's about plot, structure, character, dialogue, theme, or tone. I'm writing everything like crazy for days or weeks.

Nicholas Kazan: Often an idea starts with a feeling, or you see a character in the street and he does something interesting, and you start wondering why, and you just follow that wherever it goes. Frequently, it goes nowhere, but what happens is that by writing it down an idea leads you to other ideas, and sometimes the ideas will fall together with other ideas and make a whole. I don't use cards or any structural paradigms. I just write notes and outlines, thoughts about characters, dialogue, and scenes, and I just try to play for as long as I possibly can. It's sort of an exploration of the world of the screenplay.

Eric Roth: I let the idea germinate for a little bit. I'm usually interested in the people and the theme associated with the germ of the idea. So I first need to know what it's about, the theme, because usually the story and characters should reflect that theme. Then I try to get very secure with what my opening will be and I know what the ending will be. The opening and the ending never change, and the middle is a big blur.

Tom Schulman: Usually an idea will come from a character that springs to mind for some reason. Something will always catch my eye while I take a walk. Once I realize it's got potential as a story, I usually follow it and push it along wondering where it will go. I write it down and forget about it. Then for reasons unknown, I might find that a few days later I'll be thinking about this story again. So I follow it some more and if it seems to open up, if I find that there is a character worth rooting for or some interesting theme starts to emerge, sometimes I'll find it's connected to something else I've been thinking about. Slowly, as I obsess on the growing story, I ask myself whether I'm interested in it. Is it compelling and exciting enough to warrant spending the next three months of my life on? If it is, I'll keep making notes on the story and then one day, the whole thing will just crystallize. An ending will occur or I'll realize what it's all about.

Robin Swicord: This is one of my favorite parts of the creative process. It's like writing the genetic code of the seed that will grow up to become a screenplay. I spend a lot of time thinking and making notes and playing out little scenarios in my mind to figure out the central theme of the story and things about the characters. I imagine ways to make it as visual as possible, how scenes will push other scenes or whose voice will be heard above the crowd. It's a very long process.

21. Researching

The mind is not a vessel to be filled but a fire to be kindled.
—WILLIAM BUTLER YEATS

Unless you have first-hand knowledge about what you're writing, research can stimulate your thinking and give your characters and events life and credibility. The method doesn't matter. It can be a visit to the library or bookstore and getting 50 books to read on the subject. It can be traveling to the particular world of your story, if it's contemporary, and observing, listening to, and interviewing real people. Or it can be left until after finishing the first draft to avoid any interruption of your creative flow. A note of warning: Researching can easily become a form of procrastination that can take more time than necessary and trap you from actually writing anything.

Steven DeSouza: I do whatever research I need as late as possible because I don't like to interfere with the creative flow. So if I'm writing about a city I haven't been in, I'll look at a map or read an article about it, just enough to get through, and I'll check on the details later. I don't want to stop in the middle of an emotional scene and have go to the library to get a travel guide to that city.

Leslie Dixon: Writers can get lost in research and use it as an excuse not to get on with the writing. Up until recently, I never did any research and faked absolutely everything. In the arena of comedy, it's more about giving the audience a good time. You really don't need to be factual and have the body of knowledge you would need if you were writing *The Insider,* for example. I know one writer who did six months of research and a lot of the momentum in her career was killed by staying out of the marketplace so long.

Michael Schiffer: I do some book research, but most often I go out with a tape recorder and spend as much time with people as they'll possibly give me. I like to talk to people who do the job I'm writing about. I spent six weeks in a bulletproof vest with cops and sheriffs for *Colors*. I've been on a nuclear submarine for *Crimson Tide*. It's the most fun part of my job. I get to go out into the world and meet the people who've been doing their job for many years, who love to talk about their work. I tell them the story I have in mind and ask them if it makes any sense. If they say, "Yes it does, but it would never happen like that," then I'll ask them how it would happen. I confess my ignorance up front and ask them to problem-solve issues within my story, and even my story logic itself. Because they're living in the field, they would know if something is bogus and would never happen. I always tell them I want to get it right and that I'm willing to throw away any preconceptions I have. If you just tell me what the truth is, I would rather work through the truth and find a way to make it exciting than to tell these gigantic lies that most bad movies are guilty of. So I use these personal interviews for research not just as a technical backup, but as a story resource.

Playing with the Idea

You transform and manipulate the resources you find by putting on your child's cap and letting your imagination roam free . . .

22. Becoming a Child

> *Genius is childhood recovered at will.*
> —CHARLES BAUDELAIRE

Remember when you were a child? Filled with wonder, free to play, spontaneous, living in the moment—life was a creative adventure. Everything around you seemed interesting, magical, and exciting. You loved to experiment, take risks, explore without boundaries, and touch. Think about the power of your imagination when you first discovered drawing, colored pencils, paper, or when you experimented with your first piece of Playdough. Or you were playing with Barbie dolls or G.I. Joes—make-believe, cops and robbers, imagining scenes and dramatic situations. Losing yourself in play brought you joy and excitement.

This is exactly what writers become when they're creating scenes and getting lost in them. Like a child, they have a fondness for play-acting and make-believe. At this stage of the creative process, they loosen up and get in touch with this same sense of wonder, curiosity, and risk. This is where they get to play and experience that joy of discovery, of being in the moment, and of taking chances and seeing where they lead.

Robin Swicord: In one corner of my office, I have dolls and childhood things because I feel the beginning of what we love and what we become happened when we were children. What I did as a child is the same as what I'm doing now so having things from my childhood are like talismans that remind me of what I'm really doing, which is sitting on the floor with my legs out, and on the floor between my legs, I have dolls and paper and glue and scissors and I'm making costumes and naming characters and whispering dialogue and planning great stories and having adventures in my mind. The only difference is that now I'm doing it for the pleasure of an audience. People sometimes forget to get in touch with that feeling. They don't give themselves permission to think of themselves as children playing. The most wonderful feeling is that of being at play as a child and it's our job as writers to let the child out and be creative. What is so amazing is that when we grow up we never have to stop playing. We have to be adults and be responsible, professional people. We have to turn our work in on time and be good collaborators, but at the most basic level, we get to go away from the rest of the world, shut the door, and play.

23. Becoming Possessed by the Story

> *Creation is a drug I can't do without.*
> —CECIL B. DE MILLE

Whereas the habit of becoming a child is more concentrated in specific moments and scenes within the story, there's a point in the creative process where you become obsessed with the story as a whole.

Amy Holden Jones: Sometimes I'll start with a scene or a mood, and elaborate on it, let it take me where it takes me. But often what happens is that I'll write 30 pages and there's nowhere to go after that. But from these 30 pages, I usually stumble on an interesting character, a scene, or a thought, and I go back to the other more secure process.

Nicholas Kazan: I like the feeling of being possessed by the story. Good screenwriters hear dialogue and see pictures. And while they have to devote enormous amounts of time to construction, they become possessed by their stories. By that I mean that they don't make up their stories. They don't say, "Gee, I wonder what's selling?" The good writers have an idea of what will happen, they see it, and then write down the pictures they see. They have an idea of what will happen in the scene and the characters speak to them. So rather than asking what the characters might say at a certain juncture, the writer watches the characters speak.

Scott Rosenberg: Once the idea occurs to me, I immediately people it and ask myself who are my characters. Then for about a month, I live with it for a while. I drive with it, I take it to dinner, it's the last thing I think about before I go to sleep and the first when I get up in the morning. I sort of let it percolate.

Simmering the Idea

At a certain point, you need to let your overworked mind rest. Walk away from the playground and turn it over to your subconscious, which will digest what you have for a while . . .

24. Being Aware of Your Muse's Favorite Activities

Make friends with your shower. If inspired to sing,
maybe the song has an idea in it for you.
—ALBERT EINSTEIN

Although they don't seem to do it consciously, writers put themselves into situations that foster creative thoughts and allow their subconscious to help out. When asked when they usually come up with bursts of original ideas, our mentors answered: While driving; showering; taking a relaxing bath; or performing any manual activity, such as shaving, putting on makeup, cooking, gardening, or exercising. They might be walking in nature, swimming, or jogging. It happens when they're reading, listening to music, sitting on the toilet, doodling at a boring meeting, and falling asleep or waking up—especially in the middle of the night. You'll notice most of these activities tend to free the mind to think, while their rhythms and routines put the body on automatic pilot. Put simply, these activities are just "disciplined inspiration." By making it a daily habit of just being aware of and prepared for these activities, you allow these heightened moments of inspiration to enter your consciousness on a regular basis.

Ron Bass: I get up very early. It used to be around three in the morning, now more like around four. But the "writing" starts before I get up. Right around the 3:15, 3:30, 3:45 of it all, I lie there thinking about the scene, I go there, and what happens is that there's so much there that I have to get up to write it down.

Jim Kouf: I do a lot of thinking about one hour before I get out of bed or before I go to sleep, but it can happen anywhere. I never leave home without a notepad.

Welcoming the Muse

Aha! Light bulb! Eureka! Out of nowhere, a great idea just struck you while you were pumping gas into your car. Don't let it escape. Do you have anything to record it on?

25. Recording Your Ideas As Soon As They Appear

Dig the well before you are thirsty.
—CHINESE PROVERB

Good ideas come and go quickly, so most of our accomplished writers don't let them escape. They record everything: random thoughts, observations, character sketches, overheard bits of conversation. Some use tape recorders, others notebooks, or whatever piece of paper is lying around at the time. Others feel self-conscious talking into a tape recorder, or they find it inconvenient to later transcribe their thoughts on paper. They'd rather write ideas directly on paper. Since the advent of cell phones, many find it convenient to call their answering machine, especially when an idea happens to strike while they're driving. Once again, it's an obvious habit that can eliminate a lot of frustration. The next time you get a wonderful idea and have nothing to record it on you may say to yourself, "It's such a great idea, I'll remember it." But next thing you know, life takes over, and your wonderful idea is instantly forgotten.

Steven DeSouza: I really believe in free association. I always carry a bunch of three-by-five cards where I write ideas that come to me, bits of dialogue, or odd observations. Eventually, a couple of them will collide to form a whole new idea or they will achieve a critical mass and a light bulb will flash in my head and I'll say that's a story.

Akiva Goldsman: I don't do anything. I just try to remember it. I believe good ideas stay, so if I forget one, it probably wasn't a good idea. The danger is that everything seems good in the moment. The question is: Does it last? Does it live with you?

Amy Holden Jones: I have several notebooks all over the place, and a scrapbook in my computer where I jot down ideas as they occur to me when I'm writing. I pop into it periodically and find that I forgot about a particular detail or line of dialogue. If I'm in the car, I try to remember it, but I often forget it. Small and forgettable ideas are meaningless. What matters are the big ideas of theme and plot and characters. If you suddenly get a solution that comes out of the blue, you will remember it if it's important.

Eric Roth: I write on a little note pad. I have one in my car and one by my bedside. But usually I can remember my ideas. The ones that can be easily forgotten are sense memories. You will have a sense of something that's triggered by something you see or smell and you want to write it down immediately so you don't forget it.

Raising the Idea to Maturity

Now you can let your left brain take over and judge what you've come up with. You also need to put it in some kind of order and know where you want to go before you start.

26. Outlining Your Story

Know where you're going.

—BILLY WILDER

Even three thousand years ago, Aristotle, in *Poetics*, said, "As for the story, whether the poet takes it ready-made or constructs it for himself, he should first sketch its general outline, and then fill in the episodes and amplify in detail." This is one of the most universally accepted habits among writers, although, as you will see, it doesn't have to be. Outlining is very much like constructing a human skeleton bone by bone before applying flesh, blood, nerves, and skin.

Ron Bass: When I feel I have enough critical mass, I decide to put an outline together. I take out three sheets of paper, act 1, 2 and 3, and I start to write down every scene, usually from the top down and the bottom up. I usually know what my first scenes are and what my act-out is, so then I figure out the scenes that lead to that. I don't necessarily know the order of all scenes but I try different ways. Then I start plugging in the numbers, see if they work, move them around. Eventually, I end up with a first act that has 15 or 16 scenes and I immediately page budget it to see how long these scenes will be. I can figure out which scenes will be two pages and which ones will be longer, so I get an idea how long my act is. If it is 67 pages long, I know I've got a problem. If it's 15 pages, I know I need more scenes. Over the years, I've come to realize my scenes average two and a half pages, so I have about 15 to 18 scenes. I do this with the second act and the third, eventually getting an outline in shape, with a number by every scene. From the matrixing stage, every idea has an empty circle next to it. Now I go back and look at all the notes I have from the matrixing stage and figure out if I want to keep them or get rid of them. If the note stays, I have to put a scene number in the empty circle because it has to go somewhere and be in the movie. If there's no place for it to go I get rid of it. There are no general notes. If I don't know which scene a note is going to, that's okay. I just write all the scenes it could go into on top of it. Now I do what I call "blocking," which is putting together everything I think I might want to have in scene 1. It could be anything—dialogue, setting, tone, or what the character is wearing. Once I'm done blocking and all the scenes are numbered according to my outline, I know when I'll start writing, so I make up my schedule. I have my little chart of all the days. I figure out, for instance, "Okay, today I can write scene 1, tomorrow I can write 2 and 3, they're really short, next day, I'll start 4, it's really long and I'll finish it the day after that and start 5, etcetera . . ." Then I start writing. Of course, my outline will change. The second it does, I stop writing and reschedule according to my new outline.

Gerald DiPego: First, I keep testing the idea in my head, trying to draw it out into a beginning, middle, and end, thinking about what it really means, what it's about. If it passes the test, I'll flesh it out in broad strokes, hitting the highlights of the story with the elements that have inspired me, that I've had in my head for a while. I'll think it through by running the movie in my head over and over so that each time I come back to the outline, it fleshes out more and more. So I may start with the broad strokes, which might be about two pages of outline, and by the time I have thought it through, including what my characters are like, I'll have a 12- to 15-page outline. That's when I'm almost ready to write because by then I've really seen the movie, scene by scene, in my head. But before I start to write, I'll do a character check, ask myself whether I really know these people, what they love, what they hate, what they're afraid of, what they want, how they move through a room, what their voices are. I don't want to start writing until I feel I have a unique personality, tone of voice, and pattern of speech for each character.

Akiva Goldsman: My process is similar whether it's an original or an adaptation. The difference is how one absorbs the source material. I used to do index cards but not anymore. Now I just do outline after outline after outline. With novels or short stories, you write your way in and write your way out. By that, I mean that the greatest short stories, for example, are a process of discovery in the writing, and the form of the story is the form of the discovery. I don't think it's true in a screenplay, which depends on structure. Screenplay structure is somewhat consistent, at least when it comes to Hollywood screenplays. It's very much like designing clothes. The clothing dummy always looks the same. Two arms, two legs, a torso and a head. You can dress it up all you want, but if you don't know what the body looks like, you'll be a terrible clothing designer. And the first thing you have to do is learn what the body of a screenplay looks like. Four acts, or really three acts, but the second act is really two acts, so we might as well call it four acts, and they're generally 30 pages long and they generally have cycles of rising and falling action. Or you can say something happens on page 30, something bigger happens on page 60 and something really depressing happens on page 90. And then something totally amazing happens on page 120.

Amy Holden Jones: It depends on the project. Sometimes you're given a book to adapt, sometimes it's an assignment and you have to come up with a story, and sometimes you get an idea of your own. For instance, *Mystic Pizza* started with the actual restaurant and I thought it would be a great title for a movie. So a title is a good way to start. I usually start with a theme, then I think about the characters. The reason I start with the theme first is because the nature of the characters will illustrate and reflect on that theme. A theme is not necessarily complicated. For example, *Indecent Proposal* explored whether money can buy love and its corrupting effect on love. I had always wanted to do a movie about a marriage over time and the violation of trust and friendship. After thinking about the characters, I start to think about the ending and I begin to outline in broad strokes with the basic three-act structure. It's the same process I go through to prepare for a pitch, especially for a book adaptation, because novels are not readily adaptable so you have to find a way to tell the story in a three-act structure. I outline before I start so I know where I'm going, but not as elaborately as I should. Instead, I create a sort of pitch or treatment, rather than an outline. I have to admit, though, that I often depart from it once I start writing.

Nicholas Kazan: Once the story fleshes out, I start developing an outline until I don't know what happens next and I stop. I go back to writing notes for a few more weeks until the story becomes clearer and then write another outline without looking at the first one. I start from scratch. If you've ever had the experience of losing a document after a computer crash and having to rewrite it without looking at the original, what you often find is that you've remembered the best stuff and forgotten what was problematic. That's why I try to do another outline from memory. Eventually, I go back and look at the original just in case I overlooked a minor detail. Once I have an outline that goes all the way through, I'll start getting anxious and ready to start. But I try to delay the writing as long as I possibly can because the more you solve before you start writing, the easier it is to have that free and automatic writing experience I spoke of earlier.

Scott Rosenberg: When I feel ready, I sit down with a legal pad and I number it 1 through 70 and I write a simple sentence for each beat of the story and I end up with an outline where I'll know what my first-act break and my second-act break are. Of course, this outline will constantly change, and I tool with it for about a week, and when I feel it's in good shape, I'll sit down and start to write. The cool thing is that you have this legal pad in front of you and as you write each scene, you check off these numbers and get this real sense of completion.

Michael Schiffer: When I know what the script will be about, I try to structure it scene by scene. I use note cards and stick them up on a bulletin board. Even though things always change when you start writing, this outline still gives you some of the markers that you're trying to hit along the way. If it's an assignment, sometimes the studio will force you to come up with the story prior to the research, so what you do is take your own real world experience, your sense of the truth, and you dummy up a good enough story to get the green light from the studio. Then when you do your in-depth research and reality-check it, and all your preconceptions get trashed, you tear up your note cards and start again. Once I feel confident with my outline and I can see a movie there, I start writing. Even then, I constantly go over to the bulletin board and shift things around in the middle of the work, but it's good to have visual reminders from these pinned-up four-by-six index cards. They help me remember where I am.

Tom Schulman: Once I realize the story works and it's got a beginning, middle, and end, a character I'm rooting for, and all kinds of interesting subplots, I will then go back, look at all my notes, take each one, and figure out where it belongs in the story. These notes become scenes and then essentially a fairly detailed outline for a screenplay, which will then guide me through the writing of the first draft.

Ed Solomon: I work in generations. By this I mean, I get the idea and I can easily fit it on a page, often even in a paragraph, then I stop. I start again a few days later and try to expand it to a few pages. Then when I feel I can tell the story, I try to develop a more detailed outline, always making sure I leave enough room to discover things. And then you get to that point of inevitability when you just have to start writing. It's not really a feeling that I want to write it, but more like I have no choice. It just starts itself.

Robin Swicord: Out of the preparation stage, almost magically it seems, narrative begins to emerge and I start taking notes, knowing that, like an architect, I have the freedom at any point to step in and correct anything that doesn't work. I like to just let the story unfold. I am not a fast writer. It takes me three to four months to develop an outline. The time you spend on this genetic code pays off enormously when you're writing a scene later on because not only do you have a very strong blueprint you can depart from at will, but every time you feel lost, you have something to look at. I'll have a lot of stuff on various pieces of paper and then I'll pull all these notes together, sit at the computer and create document files I call "Notes." Then from notes, I'll move to the outline. I have a template that has numbers 1 to 120 each on a separate line and I put down the blueprint of the foundation. Then I go back and put on the "plumbing and electrical." I know that if I give myself over to this experience, I will get to page 120 and it will have some kind of shape that is similar to what I've outlined. It helps to open up these channels where characters can speak through you. This is all an elaborate preparation for the moment you allow yourself to be taken over by the muse. Some people like to have a lot more discovery in the actual writing phase. I enjoy discovery at the earlier genetic code stage. By the time I sit down to write, I have a very detailed outline where I know what will happen on every page. I like to be able to look ahead to a scene I will enjoy writing, as if looking ahead to a great meal, a wonderful vacation, or an evening with my husband. But I still feel I have the freedom to depart from the outline anytime I feel like it.

27. Discovering a Few Scenes at a Time

Discovery consists of looking at the same thing
as everyone else and thinking something different.
—ALBERT SZENT-GYORGYI

Just as most screenwriters like to outline and know where they're going in the story, there are some who prefer the more organic and spontaneous process of discovering moments of narrative and character as they write. An analogy would be, for example, driving to New York from Los Angeles. You could map out all the details, pit stops, miles driven per day, touristy sights to visit along the way, and exact time of arrival. Or, armed with a compass and only knowing you must head east, you could just let the highways guide you, as you discover the United States. Either way is valid, depending, of course, on how much time you have. There's no right or wrong, just what works for you.

Jim Kouf: I usually start jotting things down, bits of dialogue, theme, character, key words, and try to build things until I have a rough outline.

But many times, when I'm just writing for myself, I'll just start writing a script, because for me it's the same process of writing an outline, except with an outline you think in broader strokes and in the script you have to think in details. So I figure I might as well write the script. I can always throw it away and start over, but at least I'm thinking through all the details that I would have had to think through anyway with an outline.

Eric Roth: I'm not a big outliner. I will outline just two or three scenes ahead, but I'll let the writing kind of take me in different directions sometimes. Let's assume I'm starting. The first scene I'll know backward and forward. You really want to grab the reader and bring them into some world they haven't been in before, that is unique, that will pique their interest and excite them. Then I know what the next three or four scenes are. When I get to the fourth scene, I'll know what the next three or four are. This leaves a little room for discovery. Sometimes characters take me to different places I wasn't aware of before.

•   •   •

Now that you're armed with a solid story, what are you going to do with it? Completing this creative process can be the most difficult step of all. An idea is just an idea until you take action and turn it into a 120-page screenplay. But first you need to think about . . .

CHAPTER 7
Creating a Writing Environment

28. Having a Favorite Writing Space

Appealing workplaces are to be avoided. One wants a room with no view, so imagination can meet memory in the dark.
— ANNIE DILLARD

It helps to create a space where you feel comfortable being, creating, and writing for long periods of time, and where you tell yourself, "I'm here to write."

Ron Bass: Whenever I can, I like to write outdoors, whether in my back yard or in parks. But if I'm writing indoors, I like a small space, a cozy kind of feel, like a cocoon. I've actually written scenes sitting in the passenger seat of my car, parked some place, like when I go to the park and it's too cold. Instead of going home, I'd sit in my car and finish the scene. Nobody bothers me, and since it's such a small confined space, I can't do anything but write.

Gerald DiPego: About three years ago, I realized a dream of having my own writing studio because I had been working in a makeshift office in a bedroom. So I took some backyard space and built a small studio. It's nothing fancy but it is my complete world with all my books, file cabinets, art work, a long table where I write, and only my favorite things that inspire me. I also collect toy soldiers, so I have a cabinet with my collections.

Leslie Dixon: My room is an old screen porch that is glassed in so it gets a really nice light, but I could work in a basement. When you're in that head space, it doesn't matter as long as nothing is distracting you like noise or music or kids pulling on your leg. I have written some of my best work in a crappy, smelly production trailer on a movie set. I have an old, beaten-up, roll-top, solid oak desk with lots of cubby holes from the 1800s, that came out of an old railroad station, where I sit when I'm on the phone or taking notes or reading pages. It has one of those very comfortable old chairs on a tripod base that tilts back. However, next to it, I have a modern, shiny stand with my computer and a separate chair where I sit to work on my computer.

Akiva Goldsman: Right now, I'm writing in my dining room. I always write on a laptop computer. I have an old, clunky one that I really like and a tiny one that I take on planes. Whenever possible I need to have a view and be able to see out. Even when I lived in Brooklyn, I could still look up at the sky over the top of the buildings. So I sit at my dining room table facing the windows that look out over the city and just tap, tap, tap.

Amy Holden Jones: I think it's pretty unusual: I have a zero-gravity chair, so I write completely relaxed in an almost horizontal position. My chair is positioned so that when I look out the window I can see down a canyon to the ocean. I write directly into a laptop computer that sits on a portable desk positioned perfectly over me.

Nicholas Kazan: I have an office about two blocks away from my house so I walk there every morning. I'd prefer not describing it because I don't want to jinx it. I don't understand why so many writers have their pictures taken in their writing environment, but I'll say that although a lot of people like to have a beautiful place to work, I like my space to be primitive. I feel that as an artist, you have to be outside of society. When you're a successful screenwriter, the tendency is to become part of the system, and as soon as you become part of any system, you lose your individuality, your perspective, and ultimately your talent. So my space is private and sacred.

Jim Kouf: I have an office, but I could write anywhere. I've written in airplanes and coffee shops. All I need is a piece of paper and a pen. But most of the time, I write in my office.

Scott Rosenberg: I can write anywhere, but not outdoors. I write directly into a computer. I have this huge bulletin board against the wall that has pictures of everything, from photographs of my family and friends to pictures of Steve McQueen, the southern sheriff from a James Bond movie, Heather

Graham, *A Clockwork Orange*, some quotes, basically different sources of inspiration that I can look at anytime.

Eric Roth: I write upstairs in an office in my home. It's fairly dark. I like it dark. I don't want to be distracted.

Michael Schiffer: I'm very fortunate to have a studio apartment that acts as my office on the ninth floor of a building in Venice, overlooking the ocean. I call it my writing module. It's very modest, nothing fancy, lots of natural lighting, a desk with my typewriter and another desk that I hand-write on, with a picture of Henry Miller behind me, and lots of reference books. I like to proofread in public, in a coffee shop with lots of ambient noise. I've generally been working so long at my desk at that point that I need the break. I need to be in some other environment to see what I've written clearly and objectively.

Tom Schulman: I write in a small office. It's got a kitchenette, a bathroom, a window on one side that looks out to the Palisades, which is a really nice view, although it's wasted because I never look at it. I have a desk, a computer, and my reference books against the wall.

Robin Swicord: It opens into a garden so I don't feel like I'm in jail. I have lots of natural lighting, a lamp on my desk, and my books all around me, which makes it easy for me to look up stuff. I know not everyone can have the luxury of having a room of their own to just write but I think it's important not to sleep in the room where you work. One of the hardest things for me when I was living in a one-room apartment in New York was that I could never sleep very well because my work would be right at the foot of my bed waiting for me. It's important to give the mind a rest, be able to turn it off, and go to another refuge, especially if you work at night.

29. Being Comfortable with Your Writing Tools

Nothing is more sacred to a craftsman than his equipment,
and no one can tell you which are best for you.
—Kenneth Atchity, *A Writer's Time*

All you need to communicate is something to write with—a pencil, a pen, a paintbrush, a computer, and something to write on—paper, a canvas, or a printer. No one tool means success. As you'll see, writers have their own preference. The important thing is that they're comfortable with them because comfort means relaxation, and relaxation means higher creativity. It doesn't matter what tools you use, as long as they help you write. You can even delude yourself into thinking you must have the latest screenwriting software in order to start your script.

Ron Bass: I write with pencil on three-hole punched paper, which goes in a loose-leaf notebook. In the notebook with my current script, there are two pencil cases clipped inside; one contains newly sharpened pencils, the other receives the pencils that become dull from writing. I never write on a legal pad because I like to be able to move pages around in the outline.

Gerald DiPego: I usually write longhand on notepads and notebooks and then give it to my typist who then gives me the typed pages to proofread and polish. Recently, however, I finally bought a computer, so now I often transcribe my hand-written pages into it.

Michael Schiffer: I still type with an IBM Selectric II typewriter and an associate puts things into the computer for me.

Ed Solomon: I like big white boards on the wall where I can write with different colored markers. I used to write on notepads and then transcribe into the computer, but now I find I can think more with my fingers on the keyboard, though I find it just as easy to procrastinate on the keyboard as I do on the notepad.

Robin Swicord: I love my computer. I write directly into it but I also have a notepad on my desk because often, when I want to write dialogue and I don't want to think about margins and the cursor flashing, I'll jot down what these voices are saying. Sometimes, there's a conversation going on and I just want my pen to fly on the page. Then I will go back to my computer screen and craft the scene with what I just jotted down.

30. Having a Favorite Time to Write

Now this is very important and can hardly be emphasized too strongly: You have decided to write at four o'clock, and at four o'clock write you must!
—DOROTHEA BRANDE

One could also say "regular" or "productive time" to write because the periods of time in which our screenwriters usually write may not necessarily be their "favorite." But it certainly is when their creative output is of the highest quality. The times differ widely among writers, although most prefer writing in the morning, starting the day with a fresh mind, cleared after a good night's sleep, and unencumbered by life's daily demands. Again, the writing time you establish should suit your individual creative style.

Leslie Dixon: I'm always better in the afternoon and best still in the evening, but I probably wouldn't be married if I wrote at night. Once in a blue moon when my husband is working at night, I'll rush to the computer and write. I would go to bed at three in the morning and sleep until ten if the world would let me. I become progressively more alert and clever with every hour after noon that passes. The minute the sun goes down, I am fully alive. That's why I generally do all the mundane things after I get up in the morning, like read scripts or get my e-mail correspondence out of the way.

Amy Holden Jones: I usually write in the afternoon and evening. In the morning, I exercise and gradually work into the writing by doing other things like reading the newspaper and play on the computer with e-mail and the Internet.

Scott Rosenberg: My best hours are between 11 and 4, unless the writing is going really well or I'm in production or I have a deadline, then I write all the time, whenever I can.

Eric Roth: I like to work in the middle of the night a lot when I'm sort of half-asleep. I like to go with the imagery that may come out of dreams. If it's interesting and applies to what I'm writing, I'll find ways to use it. But I usually write at the same time every day. I start at eight or nine in the morning and I find I can be creative for about four hours. In the afternoon, I like to hang out with my kids or go to the races, and then I'll start again at around nine in the evening and go until I'm tired or bored. Then I'll wake up in the middle of the night if it's going well. I'll write for about an hour and then take a little nap before waking up for the next day.

Michael Schiffer: I drive into my office and I'm at work between eight and eight-thirty. It's the first focused thing I do each day. I like getting the night's subconscious work or thoughts onto the page. When I sit down at the typewriter and begin, I have all the night's dream work still inside me. I find that if I do things all day long, I don't bring my insides to the table. If I can't work in the morning to start, the day is blown for original writing. The best I can do is edit what's already on the page.

Tom Schulman: I'm always writing by nine in the morning and try to quit at four-thirty. I write from nine until noon, watch CNN for half an hour as I eat my lunch, and then go back to writing from 12:30 to 4:30.

Ed Solomon: It's always changing. I love six in the morning but I'm never up for it. I know because it's always been great when I've done it. But my day usually depends on what stage of a script I'm in. If I'm in the outlining stage, I'll just work a few hours a day. I write longer in the writing stage, and in the rewriting stage I can go all day and night.

Robin Swicord: Now I keep the hours of a suburban housewife. I get up in the morning, get the kids ready for school, and then my husband and I go to our respective desks.

•   •   •

As you can see, even a well-developed, outlined story doesn't magically turn itself into a 120-page screenplay. It still takes hard work. Successful screenwriters are highly disciplined and, like any job, keep regular hours. Sure, you may think, that's easy for them, they've been doing it for years. How can I get some of that discipline to rub off on me? Let's find out.

PART III

Discipline

Applying the Seat of Your Pants
to the Seat of the Chair

*It is not the same to talk of bulls
as to be in the bullring.*

—SPANISH PROVERB

CHAPTER 8
The Writing Habit

31. Writing Regularly

*What's a writer? Someone who writes. Planning to write is
not writing. Outlining a book is not writing. Researching is not
writing. Talking to people about what you're doing, none of that
is writing. Writing is writing.*

—E. L. DOCTOROW

With most writers, there is a period ranging from 30 minutes to hours,
sometimes even a whole day, of fiddling around before facing the blank
page and tackling actual writing. You linger over breakfast and take
your time perusing the newspaper, catch up on e-mail correspondence
while sipping your morning coffee, straighten your desk, read a little,
whether it's work from the previous day or material from a favorite
author that may inspire you to create your own. This is fine, as long as
you write regularly. Even if it takes you a whole day to warm up only to
write quality work for one hour a day, it's better than no writing at all.
Working screenwriters don't wait for inspiration. Sure, there are times
when they stare out the window waiting for the muse to whisper, but
it's somewhat controlled. Rarely does it go on for more than a day,
because they know what's at stake and that their job is to write and
come up with material by a certain deadline. Many have likened writing
to a muscle: the more you use it, the easier it gets to use. So writing
every day on a regular schedule is the best habit you could ever develop.
The difference between successful screenwriters and dreamers is that at
the end of the day, successful screenwriters have more pages written
than the day before.

Ron Bass: The process of writing is so joyful, so satisfying, so necessary for me that I would do it even if no one else in the world but me was ever going to read it, let alone pay me a dime to do it. Aside from the pleasure I get from interacting with the people I love and care about, writing is the most intense pleasure I could ever have alone.

Leslie Dixon: The physical act of writing is sometimes a pleasure for me, satisfying would be a better word. It tends to flow in pockets and usually doesn't last more than a couple of hours at a time. I fall in the crowd who hates to write but loves to have written, like Dorothy Parker.

Akiva Goldsman: Writing is both a pleasure and a struggle. There are times when it is really aversive and unpleasant, and there are times when it's wonderful and fun and magical, but that's not the point. Writing is my job. I'm not a believer of waiting for the muse. You don't put yourself in a mood to go to your nine-to-five job, you just go. I start in the morning and write all day. Successful writers don't wait for the muse to fill themselves unless they are geniuses. I'm not a genius. I'm smart, I have some talent, and I have a lot of stubbornness. I persevere. I was by no means the best writer in my class in college. I'm just the one who is still writing.

Nicholas Kazan: I write every day, but not on weekends, now that I have children. However, if it's a first draft and I need the continuity, it's much easier to write every day, even if I work only a couple of hours and don't get a lot done. It's a way of visiting the world of this screenplay, so when I come back to it on Monday morning, there's no adjustment to make. If I start writing after two days away without contact, it's more difficult to re-enter the script.

Scott Rosenberg: It's just automatic pilot, a habit. You wake up, get your coffee, glance at the paper, sit down, and just go. Sure, you have bad days. I've had days where I sat there for an hour and a half and nothing came. Then, I just say, "I know better than to force it. Tomorrow's another day."

Michael Schiffer: I don't think writing is natural for me but I've developed a great endurance by working very hard for a long time. It's still a struggle every day but the repetition makes it easier. It's become a habit where my thoughts roll onto the page sort of naturally, but it's not like I was born to be a writer.

Tom Schulman: Writing is not a pleasure for me. It is something I like to have done instead of doing it. I hate getting started and I hate doing it. Words flow at times, and I could do it all day if I had to, but it is still a struggle.

Ed Solomon: Writing is mostly a struggle and occasionally, there's something nice that comes out and makes it worthwhile. You need to know when to *write* and when to simply *think* and then when (and how) to do both.

Robin Swicord: I always wrote and I always knew I wanted to live by my writing. I never saw myself as anything other than a person who wrote and brought stories to people. So for me, it was just a matter of simply pursuing that.

32. Facing the Blank Page

A pro is someone who can do great work when he doesn't feel like it.
—ALISTAIR COOK

Although some writers view this stage as a joyful opportunity for exploration, many complain about the mental torture of having to face the blank page every morning. Regardless, successful writers have learned to minimize their anxiety level by not leaving the page blank. They're either prepared for it—perhaps by having already developed an outline or a rough sketch of the scene the day before—or they read the previous day's work and the light rewriting of it gets them warmed up. Ernest Hemingway used to sharpen 20 pencils to get in the mood to write every morning, others read fine prose, while most, through force of habit, turn on the computer and just do it.

Ron Bass: One of the reasons writing is not a struggle, and I don't have what a lot of people call "block," is that I'm a great believer in preparation. I work 14 hours a day, spending 6 hours writing the script I'm working on, then I return phone calls and take meetings for 2 or 3 hours, whatever I have to do, and I spend 4 hours a day developing my next script, from the initial idea to all the other stages of it. So by the time I write "Fade to black. The End" on the current script, I set the current notebook aside (everything is in a separate notebook because I don't own a computer), I move over to the next notebook and I take out every page of notes. The first scene of that next script is already completely outlined and page-budgeted, with blocking and notes for every scene. I take all the notes for that scene and read them, put them down, and I write the scene. This way you never start with a blank page, because you have thought about this scene so much before you were even able to write it. It's important to remember that preparation is the key, because most people are eager to write that first scene; they can't wait, but they don't know what the rest of the script is about. You can't write that first scene without knowing the last scene, and the scenes in the middle, because it isn't just about what you think of that scene; it's where that scene has to take you, what that scene means to everything that follows. You're dying to get to the other script, but what keeps you from starting prematurely is that you're too busy writing the first script. Once you've finished the first one, you can't wait to start the second one, because you've been waiting for months. You've been thinking about it, kept jotting notes for pieces of dialogue, character sketches, thought about it in the shower or at dinner. When you're ready for that second script, all that preparation makes it a joy to start.

Gerald DiPego: I hear writers complain about the blank page all the time. I consider myself lucky because I actually enjoy it. When there's a story going inside me and I'm writing a screenplay or a novel, it's so alive in me that it feels good to get it out on paper.

Akiva Goldsman: I write in order and follow my outline, so when I start, I go back and read what I've done, usually the last 10 to 20 pages, just to get a running start.

Amy Holden Jones: Exercising before writing helps because it makes your blood flow and you feel more energetic to face the task at hand. But it's usually a struggle because I don't do enough preplanning. There are people who are great at visualizing ahead and they're better off. Unfortunately, my mind doesn't work this way. I usually work really hard on my first draft, which is like an outline, and when I know what I want to do, I'll start over again.

Nicholas Kazan: I love the blank page. It's a world of possibilities. I have no problems in the morning because I prepared the night before. I learned this trick from Hemingway who used to stop writing in the middle of a sentence because he knew his mind would work on what came afterward and finish the sentence the next day. Similarly, I try not to write to the point of exhaustion, where I've written everything I could possibly write that day. For instance, if I've written 10 pages and I'm satisfied with them and it's one o'clock and I still have energy to work a couple of hours, then I'll play around with the scenes I'll be writing the next day. I will rough them out, jot down images and bits of dialogue without any character names, without any capitals, in a really primitive way. Sometimes I'll look at it the next day and it's no good, but more often it's really good because there's no pressure on me. So there's no re-entry problem because I'm sort of rewriting and polishing what I did the day before. By the time I come to the end of the rough part, I have a lot of momentum and it's easy to keep going. But I only do this when I have the time and energy at the end of the day and only when I've had a productive day and it's too early to go home.

Scott Rosenberg: Starting with page one of a new script is definitely my favorite time because I always know what the first scene is in detail. I'm just excited to put it down. As far as starting with a blank page on a daily basis, if it's going really well the day before and you're leading up to a scene you're really excited to write, the best trick is to stop even though your instincts tell you to keep writing. Just wait until the next day, so when you start, you already know what to write.

Eric Roth: Mostly, I have something I've been wanting to write down, something I wrote in the middle of the night, a note or a sketched-out scene maybe, and then I just sit down and read the thing. All of a sudden, I'm immersed in it. Reading over your previous day's work gives you momentum and you also get to fix it as you go along.

Michael Schiffer: What puts me in the mood to write are desperation and fear. I had it when I had no money and no credits and now, I've got a family to support. I like writing first thing in the morning, starting with that first "Okay, I'm alive and awake and now I'm going to work."

Tom Schulman: I don't really think about it because it's become a habit. At nine o'clock, the computer is on, I'm ready, I say to myself, "I really don't want to do this today," and I just start. When I first started out, I was so naive and it was such a fresh process, I didn't realize how difficult it was going to be. After that wore off, it was just the understanding that it was the way it had to be. A teacher once said to me, "You have to go to work just like a grocer. You unlock the doors at whatever hour, turn the sign over, walk in, and start working." I walk into my office, turn the computer on, put my lunch in the refrigerator, open the drapes, make my cup of hot chocolate, launch the word-processing program, and up it comes at exactly the point I left it the day before.

Ed Solomon: I love the blank page. It's like arriving at Community Chest in Monopoly. You don't know what's going to be there when you turn it over. I don't know why writers complain about it. I find it harder to stare at a page that has words on it. The blank page is a big open invitation. The other great thing is not having a rigid schedule to write during the day so that I can just write in a more organic pace, and slow it down or speed it up as I need to.

Robin Swicord: I'm writing all the time. I have to put myself in the mood to do other things. My mind turns to what I'm working on the way it turns to my children or my husband when I see them again after a day apart. It's a reunion when I sit back down to the page.

33. Writing to Music

Music has the capacity to touch the innermost reaches of the soul and music gives flight to the imagination.
—PLATO

Many writers use music to put or keep themselves in the mood to write. Music undoubtedly has an effect on the brain. Studies have shown that it can help relieve stress and aid in relaxation. Fast-paced music with a heavy beat can have stimulating effects, increasing heartbeat and blood flow, while some studies have suggested that listening to classical music helps increase cognitive functioning.

Ron Bass: I usually write in parks, but when I have to write indoors, I play jazz in the background. How loud or how soft depends on how I feel at that moment. I like to play the same CDs over and over because I like the music to disappear. When I introduce a new CD into the mix, it can take my attention for a while, so I like to hear something that's so familiar I don't even know I'm hearing it. It becomes part of the atmosphere, creating a kind of warm, cozy, homelike feeling of relaxation. Human voice really distracts me. I could be sitting in Central Park with a jackhammer going close to me and it doesn't bother me at all. It disappears just like music will disappear if it's instrumental, but human voice always pulls me out of it.

Steven DeSouza: I play music all the time, usually soundtracks from movies similar to the genre I'm writing.

Nicholas Kazan: The last couple of years, I've started writing to music, mostly classical music or Gregorian chants. I don't like soundtracks because they're usually hyped up. I need something more constant and neutral. I find it's a wonderful aid that sort of massages the right hemisphere of my brain.

Scott Rosenberg: Music is a critical habit. I don't listen to soundtracks. It's usually rock-'n'-roll, and it's important because each script I write has a musical component to it, like a particular band or style of music. I will actually put the songs in the script so I listen to them all the time. For example, for *Con Air,* I was very influenced by the Allman Brothers and Lynyrd Skynyrd, all that sort of Southern rock. That's how I figured who the Nicolas Cage character was.

34. Writing in Silence

> *There are times when silence has the loudest voice.*
> —LEROY BROWNLOW

There are just as many writers who like to write in complete silence because music distracts them. Also, silence allows them to quiet their mind and focus completely on the scene at hand.

Leslie Dixon: I can't write with music on because I am musical. I'd start thinking how interesting the bass line is or how awful is that disco chord. I don't even have music in the car anymore because it's so distracting. I wish I could just enjoy it and not really hear it.

Amy Holden Jones: I write in complete silence, although I often leave CNN on in the background so that if I get stuck, I can look up at it for a little while.

Eric Roth: I don't listen to music while I write, but I'll listen to different kinds of music on a Walkman while I walk every morning. Sometimes a songwriter will articulate some idea or feeling that may apply to what I am writing.

Robin Swicord: I don't write to music because I'm easily swayed by it. It's such a higher form that it can be too distracting. Sometimes, I'll put music on when I'm sitting down, reading yesterday's pages and thinking about what I want to do today, especially if it's a piece of music I associate with the emotion of what I'm working on. It tends to unlock the door a little bit and helps you to focus on the business at hand.

35. Exercising

If you are seeking creative ideas, go out walking.
Angels whisper to a man when he goes for a walk.
—RAYMOND INMON

Exercise is a great way to get the blood flowing. We all know that aerobic exercise helps enhance creativity and sharper thinking. After all, your brain depends on efficient blood flow. Some writers exercise before writing, aware of its effect on their writing during the day, while others do it after writing, or else they'd be too tired to write. Still, since the effect of exercising lasts well into the next day, one could argue that they actually exercise the day before writing. As you'll see, walking seems to be a screenwriter's favorite form of exercise. Evidence shows that when walking, blood circulation increases, but the leg muscles don't need the extra oxygen that more strenuous exercises require. This means that walking oxygenates the brain more effectively than other forms of exercise. Perhaps this is why some writers say that walking "clears their head" and helps them think better.

Ron Bass: I try to exercise every day. I ride 30 minutes on a stationary bike as soon as I wake up, and I lift weights every other day. I also take long walks with my wife on the weekends.

Steven DeSouza: I try to exercise three times a week after I'm done writing, around mid-day. When I was doing television, and I'd hit a rough spot where my brain wasn't as sharp, I'd ride a bicycle around the lot until my blood started flowing again. I still do that if I feel sluggish.

Gerald DiPego: It's important to clear your head and restore yourself, so a long walk is helpful for regenerating ideas.

Leslie Dixon: I exercise after my kid goes to bed because the house is really quiet and nobody's bugging me. I don't take walks and I don't meditate, I wish I knew how, but I do take baths almost every night before I go to bed, which is sort of meditative, although I take them not to be relaxed enough to attract thoughts, but to make them go away.

Amy Holden Jones: I exercise in the morning. I walk, I golf, I do Pilates and yoga.

Nicholas Kazan: I exercise at the end of the day. I run, swim, and bike.

Jim Kouf: I exercise every morning before I write.

Scott Rosenberg: I exercise after I write. I go to the gym and do yoga, weights, and run on the treadmill.

Eric Roth: I exercise before I write. Usually, I try to walk four or five days a week.

Tom Schulman: Walking is best. Any physical activity helps. For instance, I'm often full of ideas the day after my wife and I go dancing.

Robin Swicord: I usually take a 40-minute walk in the morning before I write. The process of getting ready to go to my desk begins when I walk. If I do something more vigorous, like swimming or an aerobic class, I will do it after I write.

36. Taking Naps and Relaxing

I shut my eyes in order to see.
—PAUL GAUGIN

Taking a break once in a while allows you to park your mind in neutral and be in touch with your inner thoughts. Writers often feel blocked because of stress. Muscles are tight, energy doesn't flow smoothly. It's through rest and relaxation, meditation, or other distractions that they're able to recharge, focus on their thoughts, and often put their inner critic and racing conscious thoughts to sleep, thus freeing their mind to wander without pressures.

Steven DeSouza: I take naps, but not on a regular basis. Sometimes, I'll wake up at four in the morning for a call of nature and I'll have a flash of an idea, and I'm so excited that I don't want to wait three more hours until my official start time. So I'll start writing, but by nine o'clock I'll be fried. That's when short naps really help to get you through the day. I'm fortunate in that I'm one of those people who can fall asleep at any moment, like a light switch.

Nicholas Kazan: I do take naps about three times a week. Writing is so debilitating that I find it very productive to take a 15- to 20-minute nap in the afternoon.

Tom Schulman: I'm a big believer in naps. Mid afternoon, I usually lie down on the floor for about 12 to 20 minutes.

Robin Swicord: I take a bath at the end of the day. As to naps, I'm a very bad sleeper so I don't usually take them. I'd rather take a walk around the garden.

37. Being Nutritionally Aware

Food is an important part of a balanced diet.
—FRAN LEBOWITZ

Food, including all beverages and stimulants, is the most powerful drug there is, and if you know how it affects your thinking, it can be a good habit to cultivate. Our mentors are aware of the effects of food, drink, and drugs on their creative thinking. It doesn't mean their nutritional habits are the healthiest, just that they're aware of their effect, and adopt whatever works for them. Proceed at your own risk.

Ron Bass: I write on an empty stomach, never eat breakfast, even though it's my favorite meal of the day. I try to eat as little as I can, mostly at dinner. I know it's unhealthy, and I wouldn't recommend it, but I gain a lot of weight if I eat three meals a day, so I'm used to it.

Steven DeSouza: I'm not a junk food eater and I've never had much of a sweet tooth. But there is something that works like cocaine for me called Poppycock—sort of designer Cracker Jack. Interestingly, they originally sold it in film cans. I'm also a coffee drinker, so between the two, I could go all night if I had to.

Gerald DiPego: I don't like caffeine in my system. I've been free of it for the last 15 years. I used to have just one morning coffee years ago but I found it affected my attention span and I could never concentrate deeply. I have never smoked. My energy comes from looking forward to getting to my desk.

Amy Holden Jones: I don't drink coffee or tea, but chocolate around 3:00 P.M. usually helps.

Nicholas Kazan: I drink tea during the day. Coffee is too much for me.

Jim Kouf: Nutrition-wise, caffeine is the only thing to keep me going all day.

Scott Rosenberg: I have one cup of coffee in the morning to get started. I drink water all the time and try to have some carrot juice once in a while, but I don't snack or have any sugary things while I'm doing it.

Tom Schulman: I don't drink coffee. All I have in the morning right when I start is one cup of decaffeinated coffee with hot chocolate in it and I drink a lot of water throughout the day. I have a very light breakfast, usually a bowl of cereal with some fruit on top, and a light lunch, maybe a small sandwich and an apple. I find that if I eat heavy, I get tired in the afternoon.

Ed Solomon: I can't eat sugar during the day because I'll fall asleep. I've never smoked and I don't drink coffee anymore. It did help me write, but then I'd crash, so I only had small windows of opportunity where I could write. Same thing if I had a donut in the morning. By noon, I'd be physically unable to stay awake. So now, I try to eat light and healthy. No coffee, no junk food, no nicotine, no alcohol.

Robin Swicord: I usually drink one cup of tea in the morning and one cup after lunch, though I don't depend on caffeine to give me creative energy.

38. Writing Through Your Fears

I know I'm a writer because it meets my three tests: 1. When I'm writing, I never feel I ought to do something else. 2. It's a source of satisfaction and occasionally pride. 3. It's terrifying.
—GLORIA STEINEM

Writing is about feeling the fear and doing it anyway. In fact, a little anxiety can be a valuable tool in a writer's toolbox, one that can generate enough fuel to rev up the creative engine. We all have insecurities. It's part of being a writer. We ask ourselves, "What if I write something awful? What if I'm criticized? What if I don't have enough talent?" The only way to get through these doubts is to just write. Unfortunately, most aspiring writers try instead to cover these fears in all sorts of ways. Author Ralph Keyes, in *The Courage to Write,* calls them "false fear busters," a series of behaviors we all go through at one time or another to alleviate the fears of writing. Among them are buying new tools, such as a newer, faster computer or the right software; moving to a more pleasant setting or creating the perfect writing environment; attending writers' conferences instead of writing; thinking that a good agent will solve our problems; engaging in "necessary" procrastination, such as extra research, detailed outlines, or another draft; or finding excuses not to write—errands, walking the dog, house cleaning, and so on.

Gerald DiPego: It's very natural to doubt. As writers, we get many ideas and equally dismiss a bunch of them. We debate what will work and what's not worthy, and which ones make us feel anything. Then we start following an idea along and develop it in our head. We haven't even written a word, but we tell ourselves a story and start getting excited. By the time we're finished with this process, there's a story in our head that really inspires us. It makes us cry and laugh, and then the big doubt comes. Can I do it? Can I do it well enough? Can I transfer what's in my head to the page so that other people will feel what I'm feeling about this story? Can I make it sing? Can I do it justice? I think most of the fear comes at the very beginning, before we start writing. But after I bitch and moan to myself, this other voice comes in and says, "Will you just start?"

Amy Holden Jones: Everyone has doubts. You overcome them with perspiration, by being critical of yourself, and trying harder, and when losing perspective, by pulling other people in, getting opinions, and acting on them.

Nicholas Kazan: The best advice I got on writing a difficult scene was from Richard Curtis, who wrote *Four Weddings and a Funeral*. When he has trouble writing a scene, and I guess he uses a typewriter, he takes out five sheets of paper, writes one through five at the top of the sheets, he rolls in the first sheet and writes one possible version of the scene. Then he rolls in the second sheet and writes another version, and so on. He makes himself write five different versions of the same scene and then he sees if any of them are any good or if they can be combined in any way. It's another way of taking the pressure off yourself. Sometimes, if you're having trouble, a scene may be misconceived and very frequently, you may not need the scene at all. Another practical tip: I usually write during the day, but if I have to write a very emotional scene and I'm having trouble with it, I often try to write it at the very end of the day when I'm exhausted, or right before going to bed and all my emotional defenses are down.

Jim Kouf: My only writing fear is trying not to repeat what I've already done. I'm always thinking, "How can I do this better?" The toughest thing is to keep coming up with original ideas. You have to go through a hundred ideas to find the one that's right. That takes a lot of thought and a lot of trying. You just keep writing. The other fear is, "When will they stop paying you?"

Eric Roth: I sort of overcome doubts with a certain sense of confidence that came about with my experience of having enough of my movies made. The awards are nice, obviously, but then, I get a bit insecure if the movies are not successful.

Tom Schulman: I would not be a writer if I didn't have doubts. I wish I could find a way to enjoy the process more, because the fears are part of what makes it so excruciating. The only way you overcome them is by just writing and trying to make it better every day. I may not be able to make it great on any given day, but I can make it a little better every day.

Ed Solomon: Fears are the hardest part about writing, and the most debilitating is self-doubt. On the other hand, self-importance and over-confidence kill more creative souls than anything else, so you need to reach a balance between the two. I average being in the middle, because I spend so much time in the extremes. I'd like to live in that middle ground more often.

Robin Swicord: You always have doubts as a writer. You overcome them by just writing. It's healthy to question yourself. You're supposed to be humbled as you look at that blank page. My only big fear about writing is that I'm so odd, that what fascinates me, the things I'm giving myself to completely, will turn out to be of no interest to anyone else. It will be so personal and idiosyncratic that no one will think it's funny and no one will feel sad when they get to that part and I will be the only one to care. But then I say, "What the heck, I'll just amuse myself."

39. Silencing Your Inner Critic

If you hear a voice within you saying "You are not a painter,"
then by all means paint . . . and that voice will be silenced.

—VINCENT VAN GOGH

Since screenwriting is both art and craft, we write with both heart and head. The problem is that too many writers let their head dominate, and consequently, the voice of criticism within each of us, the inner critic, hovering, evaluating, and inhibiting our creative flow, is the reason we often struggle with our writing. Successful writers use their intellect before and after they write, not during. They know how to alternate between the two, letting their conscious take a break when creating, and getting its feedback during the editing and rewriting stage. In a *Writers Digest* article, writer J. Michael Straczynski quotes Harlan Ellison, who compares the process to dancing: "There's old Fred Miller, over there in the corner, *trying to dance*, tense, worried, and sweating, trying to remember the steps, muttering 'one, two, three' over and over to himself . . . and there, on the other side of the room, is Fred Astaire, who is simply *dancing*." In other words, don't think. Write from the heart. If the critic keeps bothering you, just tell him you'll let him have his turn when you're done creating.

Scott Rosenberg: I used to have this inner critic, but I got rid of him a long time ago. A professor once said to me, "Remember, no one will ever see what you're writing until you want them to see it." This really freed me up to just write. It's like playing jazz guitar and you're just riffing, and the stuff that sounds really good is the stuff you record. The rest of it just floated away up into the cosmos. You'll just be paralyzed if you labor over every sentence because it has to be perfect. I have friends who take six to eight months to write a script, and I think it's stupid. First, the chances of selling a script are so ridiculous no matter who you are, why spend so much time? Then, if you don't sell it, you'll feel devastated. Second, you're talking about 120 pages with a lot of white in them. How can it take you six months to write that? Especially if you have an outline. The reality is that if you can write three pages a day, and that's really low, that's 40 days, a month and a half. So, to think it has to be perfect is a dangerous habit. It should be vomited out as fast as you can manage to get it out. Nobody ever has to see it. Then finesse it, massage it, sweeten it, and do everything you can to make it better.

Eric Roth: I only know what is bogus and what is real, but my inner critic doesn't paralyze me. If something doesn't work, I just try something else. That's one of the main advantages of working with a computer, because I can switch things so easily.

Tom Schulman: I do have an inner critic, but I try to put him on hold. Once in a while, when I lose myself in the writing, I can't even hear him. But then, something will happen that takes me back to reality and the critic is suddenly watching over my shoulder, telling me that what I just wrote sucks. Then I have to go back and rewrite the scene, or at least emotionally get to the point where I know I can fix it later and move on. Then again, I've been in many situations where I thought a scene was terrible, only to read it much later and realize it wasn't all that bad. So I've gotten better at ignoring the critic a little bit. Now I wait until I read the work again to make a final judgment.

Robin Swicord: I don't let the critic write while I'm writing, but I move between the two boats pretty fluidly. When I go over my material, I'm reading critically. When I sit down to write after I've given myself notes, I send the critic out of the room and I do my writing without anyone looking over my shoulder.

40. Focusing Completely on the Task at Hand

Just remain in the center watching. And then forget that you are there.
—LAO TZU

Most people diffuse their writing energy in hundreds of random ways, due to anxiety, fatigue, doubts, or bad moods. But the successful writers who are able to focus their energy on the task at hand know their goal, concentrate on it, stay determined, and have the self-discipline to complete what they're doing, regardless of distractions. When writers cross that line from real world to fictive reality, when the words they see on the page or computer screen become characters that move about the scene and speak to each other, fully alive, they are focusing completely, and are experiencing what many call "flow." They're in that "world" they've created. Time disappears; they lose all sense of themselves, of their fingers striking the keyboard, and of their thoughts ordering them what to write. Instead, they are clearly observing, hearing the events and characters in their mind's eye, and writing as if taking dictation.

Ron Bass: It's hard to explain how to do it, but the honest truth is I just try to go there. It's about being there in the thing. It's like auto-writing. You're thinking about the scene (what else could you be doing?), but you're not thinking about it the way you'd think about solving a financial or math problem. You're there, you see it, you feel it, you are these people; you're both observing it and you're acting in it. And it kind of comes, it just happens. The characters say what they say. There's never a thought that crosses my mind, like "Wouldn't it be a good idea if she said such and such . . ." What happens is that she just says it. It just writes itself. It doesn't mean I don't think of the words before I'm writing them down, that the hand just writes and I'm surprised at what it wrote. I think of the words before and as I'm writing them down, but they're coming spontaneously. They're natural; they're not plotted in the original writing of it. In the rewriting phase, it gets much more analytical when you're looking at it. You're more removed, more objective.

Steven DeSouza: I can concentrate to an almost scary degree. I've been lost writing a scene, and then I'll see a hand waving out of the corner of my eye and realize someone has been literally shouting at me to get my attention.

Nicholas Kazan: I read somewhere that the two brain hemispheres switch off their dominance every 90 minutes, and I believe that bursts of automatic writing are triggered when the left hemisphere sets up the writing problem and then, just at the point it's set up, the right hemisphere takes over. This may explain my experiences where I can write for an hour and a half and after I get up, I literally don't know what I've written.

Tom Schulman: I find it very easy to focus when a scene takes me away and I'm lost in the moment of its world. Once I'm into it, nothing can really bother me. But if distracting things happen early in the morning, like the phone rings or the landlord comes to the door, it can often throw me off for an hour. It also depends on the draft I'm in. With the first draft, I usually can get lost for about two hours. If I'm rewriting, sometimes I'll notice noon is approaching and say to myself I'll eat in a few minutes, and next thing I know it's 4:30.

Ed Solomon: I get distracted easily. But I find that I can focus more when I'm working on interesting ideas, when the fantasy life is more interesting than real life. Sometimes, being able to focus is doing just that, focusing.

Robin Swicord: I'm not easily distracted unless I want to be. If the writing is not going well that day, I'm not the sort of person that quits and goes shopping. I'm such a Puritan, I'll sit there until four in the afternoon. I never take the easy way out.

41. Working on Several Projects at a Time

When I feel difficulty coming on, I switch to another book I'm writing. When I get to the problem, my unconscious has solved it.
—ISAAC ASIMOV

Having a number of projects going at once, though not necessarily being written at the same time, helps writers handle different problems. Dealing with rejection, for instance. Getting a project rejected is not as depressing because you're busy on others. Having several projects also helps keep the creative well fresh. When you run dry of ideas on one, simply switch to another. The most common habit among working screenwriters is to write one screenplay while developing and outlining a few others. It's all about preparation.

Ron Bass: The biggest mistake a beginning writer makes when he finishes the first draft of his first script is to start rewriting it. So many careers flounder because writers go through many drafts of the same script, trying to make it as perfect as they can, and it's still not great and it doesn't sell, and they feel like failures and they quit. Far better than rewriting your first script is writing your second script, and your third, and fourth, and just keep writing. Make them as different as you can. I rewrite every script as I write it, of course—you go back and forth—but when you're done with the whole script, and you feel it's the best it can be, and you've given your best shot at it, put it down, forget about it for a while, and begin your second script. It's probably the single most important piece of advice I have to give to writers. Always be planning your next project while you're writing your present one.

Gerald DiPego: It's important to have more than one project, because once you get a script out there, and it's in front of several decision makers, if you find yourself waiting, it can be very draining. If someone says they'll get back to you in a week, you can figure it will be more like two or three weeks. You can't count on anything when they are so busy. It's always best to put your heart into your next project.

Amy Holden Jones: When I have to, I'll work on one in the morning and one in the afternoon, or I'll work on each on alternate days or weeks. It can be good because you get to move away from stuff and come back to it a little bit fresh. But unlike other writers who can develop multiple projects at once, I can only work on two at a time.

Nicholas Kazan: When you're stuck on one project, it's okay to concentrate on something else. Many great writers are known to have written their best stuff when they were stuck on something else. So always pay attention when you're going someplace else. Follow it. Play hooky. It doesn't mean that if your brain wants to go to the beach, you go to the beach. If you spend your time at the beach, then you're not a writer. You're a beach bum. But if your mind goes to a different story, write some notes on that story. If you spend all day on it, and the next day, and you find yourself obsessed with it, keep going. You may end up writing a great screenplay trying to escape from the original one.

Tom Schulman: Starting your next project the minute you finish your current one helps a lot, especially when dealing with rejection. This way no one project can hurt you so bad that you quit. When I first started out, I used to make that mistake of finishing a script and then I'd live and die every day waiting for the phone call, until I realized I was wasting months sitting around. If you do it right, by the time the rejections come, you'll be a third of the way into the new one, which will be your favorite by then, and you'll just shrug off the rejections and keep going. I usually work on three or four projects but if I'm on assignment, I'll be writing that one while developing the others. Very often, if it's like 3:30 in the afternoon, and I'm tired of the one I'm working on, I'll spend an hour on another project.

42. Avoiding Distractions

Close the door. Unplug the phone. Cheat, lie, disappoint your pals,
if necessary, but get your work done.
—GARRISON KEILLOR

Because the creative muse is so fickle, it's important to keep interruptions, such as the phone, the newspaper, television, the Internet, research, or friends and family to a minimum. This is easier, of course, if you and your family accept that you have a "home office" (see Habit 28). In a way, dealing with your inner critic (Habit 39) is an interruption, because it forces you to jump between the creative right brain to the editing left brain. As you've learned, it's best to save him for the rewriting stage.

Steven DeSouza: The real killers for professional writers are the meetings, because people in this town are meeting-crazy. Sometimes, meetings are the only validation development executives have that their job is meaningful, because the reality is that a picture doesn't get made because somebody has done a great job on development, but because a star or a hot director becomes interested. Maybe their project fell apart and now they're available for this picture, or a director comes aboard and even though he wants to make a remake of *Psycho*, they'll make it, or a similar picture is a huge hit at the box office. I believe a lot of the development period is just a time waste, as are many meetings, but you've got to go. What I do is try to schedule a month's worth of meetings for the same day, and just lose one from writing.

Nicholas Kazan: I try not to answer the phone when I work, so I will return phone calls when I get back home, during that 3:30–6:00 P.M. period.

Jim Kouf: I'm surrounded by books—medical books, a lot of history, encyclopedias, dictionaries, etcetera. So I don't have to interrupt the creative process for too long. I don't like to have to get up and drive somewhere when I need some research done.

Robin Swicord: I try to schedule all my meetings on the same day. I have one special day, usually once a month, where I drive around to all my meetings. All my other days are sacred and devoted to writing.

CHAPTER 9
Time Management

43. Making the Time to Write

Realize that if you have time to whine and complain about something,
you have time to do something about it.

—ANONYMOUS

Unless you have a wealthy spouse or live off a trust fund, chances are that as an aspiring screenwriter, you're juggling a day job along with periodic bouts of writing. As you'll see, if you really want to write, you somehow make the time. Most beginning writers don't make writing a high enough priority. They intend to write, but their desire is not great enough to keep them from doing more pressing things. Professional screenwriters make writing an excuse not to do other things. They view their work as a job they get paid for, that has specific deadlines, and that demands a rigid schedule. A writer I know used to make herself write one scene per night before going to bed, until she finished her script in about eight weeks. Sometimes it would take her 15 minutes to finish a scene, and other times it would take her up to four hours, but she made herself finish the scene before rewarding herself with a good night's sleep.

Ron Bass: I realized this is what I really wanted to do with my life, even if no one sees it or pays me for it. I had a day job as a lawyer so I had to find the hours in the day, on the weekend, and in my vacations. I found time to do it because I needed to do it. When I was writing novels, my schedule was more like a hobby, writing in my spare time, weekends, vacations, dabbling in it in the evening, or waking up an hour earlier, before going to my day job. Instead of watching TV or reading a book, I'd be writing. Now, I usually do the writing first, because for me it's the most precious thing, and I want to make sure it doesn't get shortchanged. But I don't always write this way. It depends on the priority of a project. There are always many things to do, like reading, planning for pitches, and meetings. If I think another thing is going to weigh in my mind because it's a real obligation and I'm going to be preoccupied by it while I'm writing, then the writing will suffer, so I'll do it before the writing.

Scott Rosenberg: I always had a day job, so I always wrote nights and weekends. The pact I made with myself was that the minute I made dollar one, I would never again write nights and weekends. I'd have writing be my job, and it's pretty much what I do now. I wake up and I write between certain hours Monday through Friday. You try to keep in step with the rest of society because most of your friends have day jobs. It's only when I'm excited and it's going well or I have a deadline that I'll write nights and weekends.

Eric Roth: When I had a day job, I found the time to write. I'm awfully disciplined. I always say to people at seminars that if you write two pages a day, five days a week, you'll have 100 pages in 10 weeks. So if you can be disciplined enough to just do two pages a day, and I think anyone can find one hour to do two pages, even if you have to do them on a cocktail napkin.

Robin Swicord: There's a wonderful cartoon on the front of our refrigerator of two people at a party. One is a kind of dapper-looking gentleman with an unlined face and a nice big smile, and he's talking to a shlubby, smaller man with big bags under his eyes. And the dapper-looking man is saying, "A writer? I've always wanted to write, but I've never had the time." Everyone has the time to write. The question is, are you willing to turn yourself into the guy with the bags under his eyes in order to make that dream come true? Sure, it's very tiring to have two jobs, but it's a necessary sacrifice if you're a writer. There's no way around that. No one will pay you to write unless you have written something already.

44. Having a Schedule

I must govern the clock, not be governed by it.
—GOLDA MEIR

Whether writing to a schedule like nine to five, five days a week, or using a calendar to pencil in scenes to write, professional writers use their time effectively. Time to write is one of their most precious assets, and they don't like to waste it. They're able to prioritize and manage to seamlessly fit writing into their daily lives. Scheduling not only means fitting in what they *must* do during the day, but also what they *want* to do. Professional writers are a special case, because what they want and must do happens to be the same. By scheduling writing into your day, you can avoid procrastination and indecision, much like the way scheduled appointments or lunches with friends are often kept. Here's a quick view of what a day in the life of a working screenwriter looks like.

Ron Bass: I have a writing schedule, but I don't write to a schedule, like 9:00 to 12:00 every day, for example. Anytime you set up expectations for yourself about anything, you run the risk of feeling like a failure when you don't meet the expectations. What I do is draw a little handwritten chart of all the weeks spanning several months and enter what scene I think I'll write that day, all the way through to the end of the script. The important thing, though, is the second I don't meet that schedule, I change it. I don't like feeling like a failure because I'm four days behind. So I erase it and write a new schedule. If I get ahead of schedule, I don't like to feel too comfortable, so I also change it. With a schedule I know where I'm supposed to be, but I don't beat myself up when it's not right. I hardly write at night; usually I go from 4:30 in the morning to dinner. This is not straight writing, of course. There are meetings, lunches, and phone calls in between. Then I hop in the shower and go have dinner with my wife. After dinner, it depends on what's going on—housekeeping things like the phone list for the next day, reading I have to do, or proofreading. Actual writing at night is rare, unless I want to finish something or I have a lot of energy, but I usually let it all go in the shower and relax for the rest of the evening.

Steven DeSouza: I generally write in the earliest part of the day. I get up at 6:30, goof around for about 30 minutes, reading the paper over a cup of coffee. Jump into the Jacuzzi and wake up. Grab a bowl of cereal. Then I'll sit down and start writing until I'm burned out, which could be 5 pages on an off day or 12 pages on a great day. Then it's about 12:30. If it's Monday, Wednesday, or Friday I work out, grab lunch, and then spend the rest of the afternoon dealing with business stuff, phone calls, and meetings.

If it's Tuesday or Thursday, when I don't work out, I'll submit to that Hollywood hell, the lunch meeting.

Gerald DiPego: I've come to depend on that morning energy and use that well of creativity, so I usually get up early, have a light breakfast, scan the newspaper, and I'm at my desk by 8:30. I can go for about four hours and then, around 12:30, I take a long walk. That's what's great about living in California. You can do this any time of the year. In the afternoon, it depends on where I am. I have a home in the country, away from the city, where there's simply more energy. There, I can go back to my writing in the afternoon and even in the evening. Here, in the city, the afternoon is usually reserved for down time, like business calls, meetings, errands, or even doing nothing, putting your feet up or reading a book.

Leslie Dixon: I have tendencies, but I don't have ingrained habits anymore. My normal tendency was to stay home, try not to break up my concentration with business lunches, and I'd spend part of the morning figuring out exactly what I was going to write and the afternoon writing it. And I was pretty disciplined. Five days a week, no weekends. Every once in awhile, I'd have the wicked moment when another writer friend would call me and say, "Let's go to the movies and blow the afternoon," and I would do that sometimes, just so I wouldn't feel like a robot.

Akiva Goldsman: My writing ritual is not the healthiest, and I wouldn't replicate it if I were just starting out. I'm a little too driven. I just write. I write at home between 7 and 10 hours a day. There's nothing between me and the beginning of writing, no breakfast, no newspaper, just the task at hand. I get up around 8:30, put on my bathrobe, make my coffee, get my cigarettes. I'm in front of the computer by 8:45 and I start writing. I don't eat lunch, though sometimes I'll eat a can of tuna standing by the sink, maybe watch CNN for 15 minutes, and then I go back and continue to write until the end of the day, which is anywhere between five and eight. Then I'll either go to the gym or take a shower and go out for dinner. I also have offices at Warner Brothers, so sometimes I can go and be a producer and I don't have to do this all year.

Amy Holden Jones: I wake up at 7:30, read the paper and walk. I make phone calls and do errands like pay bills, go on the Internet, answer e-mail. Then, I'll generally rewrite what I did the day before. I take a break for lunch, walk around a little bit and then I work for two or three hours on the new stuff. If it's a first draft, I usually can't work more than three or four hours after lunch. If it's a rewrite, I might work all the way through until I go to bed, depending on my energy level. If I'm on a deadline, I'll work until midnight, seven days a week. If I'm not on a deadline, I usually spend the evening hours reading.

Nicholas Kazan: I usually write from nine in the morning until three in the afternoon. I take my kids to school, come back, read the paper, and have breakfast. I walk to my office, get to it by nine, work until noon, go to the store and get something to eat, bring it back to the office, eat lunch at my desk, work through until 3:30, come home, exercise, goof off with my kids, and after that it's just your typical home life.

Jim Kouf: I have several cups of coffee, look at the paper for a little bit, pay some bills, let the caffeine kick in, and then I go at it and try to do it all day.

Eric Roth: I take my kid to school, come back, take a walk, then I'll jump to the script and start reading from page one, make changes as I go along if I have to, finally get to where the new work starts, and by then I'll have enough momentum to start writing and I'll write for about four hours, and then pick it up again in the evening where I'll look at what I've done during the day.

Tom Schulman: I write five days a week, with the weekends devoted to family, but if a deadline is approaching, I'll sometimes do half a day on Saturday. During the week, I get up every morning at 6:15, shower, stretch, go downstairs, and help get breakfast ready for the kids. I get them ready for school, drop my teenage son at school by 8:15, and I'm at my office by 8:30. Then I take everything out of my briefcase, turn on the computer, and do all the little things you do when you first get to the office. I make sure that my all-important cup of hot chocolate coffee is ready, then start at nine. I don't answer the phone during the day, but I will make 15 minutes worth of phone calls at 4:30, then I'm back in the car and home at around five. I'll exercise from five to six, and have dinner with the family.

Robin Swicord: From the outside, nothing could be duller. I make a cup of tea, I sit down, and I don't move for six hours. I'm usually at my desk by nine and write until four. I eat a small lunch at my desk. I don't like to go out and be among people in the middle of the day, but when the writing day is over, I'll have social contact. In the afternoon, if it's going very well and the children are happily occupied and no one needs me, I'll extend myself and read over what I've done for the day. I'll think about what I want to do the next day, sort of get a running start for the next day. I will do this more often when I'm close to finishing something. Sometimes, if my husband is out of town or my children have play dates and I'm by myself, I'll have an evening writing shift until I feel tired, a festival of writing. If the writing is not going well, I'll say to my husband that I'm writing this weekend. This usually means that either Friday night or Saturday night I'll be writing until three or four in the morning. This can be good sometimes because it jolts your mind. By varying your routine, you attack the writing when it least expects it.

45. Setting Writing Goals

> *Great things are not done by impulse, but by a series of small things brought together.*
> —VINCENT VAN GOGH

Most professional writers set writing quotas. Whether it's the number of hours of actual writing, number of pages per day, or number of scenes, they produce a given page count on a steady basis. If you make a pact with yourself—reward yourself if you have to—that you won't leave your desk until you've completed a certain number of pages, you'll be surprised at how soon you'll have a completed screenplay.

Steven DeSouza: I give myself a quota. I tell myself I'll write six pages a day, every day. Sometimes I slip up and write four or five, but then I catch up the next week, and I do this until I'm done.

Leslie Dixon: I try to assign myself a certain amount of pages, and if I do achieve that quota and it's really quite solid, I will knock off a little early.

Akiva Goldsman: When I'm laying down the first draft, I try to write 10 pages a day, and then it's a matter of hours like a regular job. I generally don't write at night and on weekends, because the danger of writing is that you could be doing it anytime, so unless you build rules, you're never free of it.

Tom Schulman: I'm usually very precise at budgeting pages. If I have X number of weeks to finish a project, I'll be very specific as to when I want to be done and how long I'll give myself on each draft. I try to average 12 pages a day, but it depends on the day, because sometimes, I can do 12 pages in two hours. So for me, the goals are more like I want to be done with the first third of it by a certain date, the next third by another date, and so on.

Ed Solomon: Setting a certain amount of hours is irrelevant. For me, it's about getting through certain ideas and solving problems. It's not a number of pages or scenes. I'm done for the day because I run out of time. I wish I could have that freedom where I could just concentrate on the writing until I get tired, but because of my business schedule, i.e. meetings, phone calls, and the fact that I have a family, I usually write until I run out of time.

46. Working Even When You're Not "Writing"

The possibilities of creative effort connected with the subconscious mind are stupendous and imponderable. They inspire one with awe.

—NAPOLEON HILL

Writing doesn't only take place at the keyboard. Just like with Habits 4 (Being a Natural Observer) and 24 (Being Aware of Your Muse's Favorite Activities), you're always observing and your subconscious never takes a break. Though you're not typing, you're still "writing," even when you're sleeping, walking, cooking, playing video games, or just hanging out with your friends. When asked what they do that's writing related when they're not writing, this is what our mentors had to say:

Akiva Goldsman: When you're writing well, that place in your mind is constantly engaged, so sometimes I'll wake up, or I'm in the shower, and I'm still working. Sometimes, it helps to walk away because the mind is still working when you're not writing and it will solve problems for you if you give it a chance.

Amy Holden Jones: When you're out in the world, you listen to dialogue and think about other things while your subconscious is working on whatever the problems are in the script. Once, when I really got stuck on something, I took a weekend off and went to Santa Barbara. I wasn't thinking about it and woke up in the middle of the night suddenly understanding where I had gone wrong and what I had to change. Sometimes, your mind has to be released in order to get past things, like a muscle that knots up so tight, there isn't enough blood going through it. It has to relax in order for the blood to flow again.

Scott Rosenberg: When you're out in the world, you're observing and hearing people talk. Everyone who knows me and talks to me knows that if I hear a good line, it could wind up in a movie I write.

Michael Schiffer: What I learned as I got older was to stop obsessing about the work when I wasn't doing it. I try very hard not to think about the work when I'm not writing. But there are still times when I'm having real problems and this dark cloud descends over me, and I'm not a lot of fun to be around. But since I'm always working, I can't indulge myself and be this way all the time. So when I leave the office, I play back the problems in my mind while I'm driving home. But the minute I hit the door, it's over. I put the work out of my mind and try to make the transition to being alive and enjoying my life.

Ed Solomon: When it's going well, you have to drag me away. When it's not, it's hard to stay seated. Sometimes the best way to solve something is to force yourself to actively not write and not think about it. I've come to believe that the subconscious does a great deal of work if you allow it to. I will actually assign tasks to my subconscious, literally say to myself and type in the computer, "By Monday, figure out X, Y, and Z" and then just leave for the weekend. By Monday, I usually have it figured out.

47. Balancing Writing and Personal Life

If A equals success, then the formula is A equals X plus Y plus Z.
X is work. Y is play. Z is keep your mouth shut.
—ALBERT EINSTEIN

One of hardest things for aspiring writers with families or other significant relationships is balancing the pursuit of their dream, which is all-consuming at times, with the desire to spend time with their loved ones and the responsibilities of a day job to support them. I've seen many writers lose relationships, get divorced, lose high-paying jobs because they were too obsessed with making it as a screenwriter. Though you may think that our mentors have learned to balance their careers and their families because they are now successful, the reality is that, with a few exceptions, most had families and relationships when they were starting out, and they are still loved by the same people. They just had their priorities straight. In fact, one could argue that knowing what was important grounded them as human beings, which then made them better writers.

Gerald DiPego: I had a regular day job like everyone else. It wasn't easy. It depends on how draining the job is. When I was teaching, I used to get up an hour and a half earlier so that I could write before going to work. With other less mentally taxing jobs, I would write in the evening.

Akiva Goldsman: When I was married, I would have liked to juggle it better than I did, since I'm now divorced. This was when I created my rules of not writing at night and weekends. Otherwise, there would have been no life at all. When I had a day job, I got up very early in the morning and wrote for one hour prior to going to work.

Amy Holden Jones: I'd work when the kids took naps and after they went to bed. It was an effective motivator because I'd only be able to write about three hours a day, so I wouldn't fool around with doing something else. I just sat down and did it. In a way, I think it's harder to write when you have an unlimited amount of time stretching in front of you. But when you have a small window of opportunity, you don't waste it. It's good to actually have a day job or other responsibilities, like parenting. If you're really motivated, it can be done. You can work two or three hours a day and get the script done in no time. People who aren't serious generally come up with a million excuses for not having the time. If you really want to do something, you make the time.

Nicholas Kazan: The hardest part was making the transition from being single to having a family. It was a speedy transition. As soon as you have a baby, time changes. Prior to that, I'd go to the office, read the paper, day-dream, and ease into the workday. I don't ease into it anymore. I get to the office, turn on my computer, and start working, because essentially, if you want to work, you have to concentrate and make the most of the time available to you.

Eric Roth: I had a family for a long time before I started writing, so when I started writing, I just did it. I just made it part of the process. I used to work out of the living room with people walking in and out.

Michael Schiffer: In the beginning, I tended to overwork and drive myself too hard. When I sold my first book, I was writing around the clock, and a journalist friend of mine said, "You'll kill yourself at this pace. You can't work all day and night. You've got to put it down at six, or decide what your hours are, but write and then stop, and pick it up the next morning. It's a marathon, not a sprint." He convinced me to put a rhythm into my day. There's a Hemingway quote about writing, where he once said, "Knock off while you're still going good. The minute you're starting to crank out junk, you should stop. If you're afraid you won't be able to pick it up tomorrow, then you shouldn't be a writer." That's a paraphrased quote, but the message is clear. It's a delicate balance. You don't want to be lazy and stop too soon, like in the middle of the day, just because you hit a rough spot and want to quit. But if it's the end of the day, and you're feeling tired and you feel it going stale, then stop. Walk away from it. Pull the plug and come back to it the next day with fresh energy.

48. Procrastinating

You can't build a reputation on what you're going to do.

—HENRY FORD

When you're hungry, do you put off eating? When your favorite television show is on, do you put it off to a later time? Chances are, when you want to do something and you're not afraid of it, you just do it. Although many consider procrastination to be just another word for fear (see Habit 38), it can also be part of the incubation stage of the creative process, where ideas simmer in your subconscious. So it's not all that bad for you. In fact, all writers procrastinate in one way or another to alleviate the pressures of writing, or simply "waste time" puttering around in order to warm up into the day's work. The difference is that they control how long they procrastinate. So how do our mentors waste time?

Steven DeSouza: I know when I'm about to write when I become a neat freak and start rearranging the pens and pencils around, noodling things in my brain, and basically wasting time until I get that caffeine rush.

Leslie Dixon: I call them "stalling mechanisms." We all have them. Writers who are close friends will be honest with each other; they'll say, "Okay, I'm avoiding work," and next thing you know, you are having a 45-minute conversation. You waste time by checking your e-mail when you get up, drinking your coffee, or reading the paper. I guess you overcome that by feeling guilty and internally yelling at yourself to get on with it. In some cases, it's "Don't you want to get rid of this project? Aren't these people horrible? Don't you want to turn this in as soon as possible so you can go on to something else? Write!!" Procrastination can actually be a very interesting tool for success because, if you can control it, you have a leg up on the competition. If you're known as a person who can produce quality work in a reasonable period of time, they'll be much quicker to hire you over the writer who takes a year to write a script.

Amy Holden Jones: All writers are good procrastinators. Usually, it's easier once you're into the project enough and you begin to really care about it. When characters start to breathe and are really alive, it's much easier to write, because you care about them and take them places you want them to go. Before that, it's a very grueling and grinding process and that's why most people procrastinate. But then, you toughen up and think about your quota of pages. For me, if it's an original, it's three pages a day. If it's a rewrite, it's usually anywhere from five to 10 pages a day.

Scott Rosenberg: The phone is my biggest time waster, but a lot of it is business related, even though it is still wasting time when I could be writing. I also enjoy a very active social life. I don't overcome it. I just go out. It's a luxury you have of controlling your life. But I don't do it every day.

Eric Roth: I waste time great. As I said earlier, I like to go to the horse races, spend time with the kids, and read a lot. It's very easy not to write. But eventually, you get to a point where you have to move forward. You feel unprofessional. But it also depends on the material. If you're really excited about it, you really don't like to get away from it. When it's a struggle, it's a little more painful to look at it, so you avoid it a little bit more.

Tom Schulman: Excuses to myself are all right, but never to people that I work for. It doesn't matter to them what you're going through. Even today, I go through all the pencil sharpening, and I have one of the cleanest offices in Los Angeles. Starting a new project is always the hardest part. Some part of me will go lazy for the first few days, and I'll just sharpen those pencils, clean the office, and label. It's amazing how many things you can do when you're trying to avoid writing.

Ed Solomon: There are often so many things conspiring against you to write, but then I feel guilty, and once I start writing, it's hard not to write. To me, writing is like a shower in a bad hotel where the water is either really hot or really cold. You either can't seem to get anything done, or you just can't seem to stop. I haven't found that wonderful balance, like Hemingway, who could write for a couple of hours in the morning and then wander around Paris in the afternoon. I procrastinate by writing screenplays. Screenwriting is the way I procrastinate from actually living a happy and healthy life. The truth is I only have a certain amount of time to write. Sure, I "waste" time, but there's a big difference between putting off the work and not doing it. My procrastination is real life, all the stuff I *have* to do when I'm not writing.

49. Making Deadlines Your Motivator

I shall meet all of my deadlines directly in proportion to the amount of bodily injury I could expect to receive from missing them.
—PROCRASTINATOR'S CREED

As the saying goes, "Nothing makes a person more productive than the last minute." Deadlines are one of the greatest writing motivators, whether to finish a project on time or break through writer's block. And even better than a self-imposed deadline is one set up by other people. If you promise you'll let someone read your script by a certain date, it holds you accountable and keeps you moving forward.

Steven DeSouza: Deadlines are the greatest motivator I know; how could they not be? They're the reason I got my quota of six pages out of it. I realized I needed to write X number of pages by a certain time and I divided that by the number of days. The calendar is my best friend.

Amy Holden Jones: Deadlines can really focus the mind, but they can also do harm because they put pressure on the creative process. They can cause you so much stress and anxiety that you can't necessarily come up with an idea in the allotted amount of time. I think they work better for rewrites.

Scott Rosenberg: My goal is to finish a script, so it's not a matter of pages or hours, but more about a deadline. I won't allow myself to spend more than two or three months on a given script.

Tom Schulman: I can always think of a million good reasons why I shouldn't start a project on a given day, so I'll give myself a deadline. It's the only thing that really pushes me over, realizing that now, I don't have enough time to do it and I'd better get busy. If there's more time than I need, as much as I'd like to start early and have the luxury of stretching it out, I just won't do it. But when it's absolutely necessary that I start, I'll start.

CHAPTER 10
Writer's Block

This is probably the single most debated problem among writers because, while many do get blocked, the bottom line is that it's just a state of mind. Either you believe in it and try to overcome it with all sorts of tricks, or you don't believe in it and write through it (which is a trick itself). There's no right or wrong, and as you'll see, no matter what attitude you adopt, you'll keep writing in no time.

50. Combating Writer's Block

If you're going to be a writer, the first essential is just to write. Do not wait for an idea. Start writing something and the ideas will come. You have to turn the faucet on before the water starts to flow.
—LOUIS L'AMOUR

Sometimes, your mind gets foggy. No words or images come to mind. It's just a complete blank. Some writers panic at the first sign of block and rush to their shrink, while others believe it's only temporary and have a bag of tricks to overcome it. There are literally thousands of tricks employed by writers. The most common ones include Hemingway's favorite trick, stopping in the middle of a scene, leaving it incomplete, and knowing exactly how to end it. This way you start the next day looking forward to finishing the scene. Another one is writing out of sequence. If you're stuck on a certain part, skip over it and write a part you can't wait to get to. Revising material you have already written is another trick. Or the most popular: simply start typing stream of consciousness stuff. Even if most of it will be utterly unusable, just the simple act of writing gets the juices flowing again.

Gerald DiPego: Certainly, there are slow days, where your mind feels like it's made of honey. If I just can't seem to tap into the right creative energy, and I'm piddling around with it and staring at the screen or the page, I'll sometimes walk away. Sometimes, I'll use specific tricks. For example, if a scene isn't working, I'll shake things up by changing the setting completely, or I'll change one important element in the scene, and see what happens. But when something isn't working, it's usually because I'm rushing it. Either I'm not taking the time to stay with the core of the reality of the story, or I haven't individualized the characters enough and I've started writing these characters before fleshing them out completely.

Leslie Dixon: I've only had it once and it was absolutely horrible. It lasted two weeks and the reason was that I thought it was going to be an easy adaptation of a novel that just read like a dream. When I got into it, I realized I had to make big changes in order to turn it into a movie. I was in such despair that I almost gave the money back and said I can't do it. This was a job I really wanted and felt really passionate about, and I felt like a worthless idiot. So I called this shrink I go to once in a while, and said, "I never really experienced this before. Is writer's block a real thing? How long is it supposed to last?" And he said, "Between two and five weeks, don't worry about it." He just gave me this very specific answer, it was hilarious. Somehow, it gave my subconscious permission to provide me with the solution. By the way, the picture is shooting now. I guess he was right.

Amy Holden Jones: I've had it very seriously for about a year. I think it stems from depression more than anything else. It usually comes from the feeling that you're not going to control the work when it's done anyway, or that you'll never get anywhere with it. Sometimes writers suffer writer's block toward the end of a career, when they've said everything they needed to say. They've said it 20 different ways, and they haven't found anything new to say. Sometimes you just have to walk away from it for a while and sometimes you just have to keep grinding, and keep trying and trying, because writing is like a muscle. You need to keep doing it in order to strengthen it. If you walk away from it for too long, it'll atrophy. The way I got over it was to do a very easy project that was right up my alley, and I knew I could do. This gave me my confidence back. Confidence is important for anything anyone does. Whether you're a teacher, a doctor, or an artist, sometimes the best thing you can do is return to what you know you can do, or maybe do something simpler until you get your confidence back.

Nicholas Kazan: I believe it exists but I've never had any difficulty writing. I believe it was B. F. Skinner, of all people, who said that if he deserved any credit, it was for being at a location where certain processes could take place. As a writer, if you're doing your job well, you're placing your talent at a place where it can be worked by creative forces. I know it sounds mystical, but it's basically about putting yourself in a situation where you can tap into the forces of society and humanity, that collective unconscious, and write things that come out of yourself, relatively unguided and uncensored. Sometimes the writing is better than at other times. It's okay to say "I just don't have it today." But this usually happens in the early stages when I'm writing notes and I don't feel connected to it.

Scott Rosenberg: I believe in it, but it never happened to me (knock wood). I have the opposite situation, like in *Wonder Boys*, the 2,000-page manuscript. But there are days where it's not coming out, or you just don't feel like doing it. I just try to get it out anyway and often, that's when my best stuff comes out. There's a huge sense of triumph when it's really not happening and then you make it happen. There are times when I just can't seem to get through. It's usually around the end of the second act. Because I never use any stimulants to write, and only if I'm *really* blocked, I have this tradition, and it's always on a Friday night, where I'll get a cooler of beer, put it right on my desk, and I'll drink a beer and start writing. Five hours into it, I am completely bombed. I did this about two weeks ago. I was having a party for one, cranking the music, throwing caution to the wind, and writing like hell. I woke up the next morning with a huge hangover, and realized I wrote 35 pages and I didn't even know it. Now, you have to understand, 30 pages of it were absolutely terrible, but the 5 pages that worked got me through the bad part and allowed me to finish the script sober. I'm not recommending that you drink and write, but sometimes it helps to free up your inhibitions and take you over a bad spot.

Ed Solomon: I don't often suffer from this. I suffer from the opposite: too many things I want to write. But I know it exists for people. It also depends on whether you're talking about a chronic thing, or if you're just having trouble with a particular scene for a couple of days. One useful trick for me is to sit down and write about the problem I'm having. I will literally write "Okay, now I'm going to try to figure out why I cannot solve this problem. When I figure out how to do this, etcetera . . ." Actually writing about the problem often unlocks things for me and leads me to a whole new series of ideas. Another trick is to actively not write and trust your subconscious to work on it. That doesn't mean blow it off.

51. Not Believing in Writer's Block

Writer's block is a fancy term made up by whiners so they can have an excuse to drink alcohol.

—STEVE MARTIN

Some writers believe block doesn't exist! It's just another word for fear. Fear of failure, of being exposed as a fraud, or feeling your writing isn't good enough. This statement alone should help open your creative floodgates on days they'd rather be closed. The bottom line is there will be days when the words flow and days when they don't. On the days they do, you're happy to write. On the days they don't, you write anyway, even if you're not happy about it. The only trick is to get something on paper. You can always edit it later. When you adopt this attitude, block is no longer some evil, mystical phenomenon that paralyzes you for months.

Steven DeSouza: I never have writer's block. Not because I don't hit the wall like everyone else, but because whenever I get stuck in a scene, I just jump to another part of the movie. There's always another scene you can write today if you're stuck elsewhere. I always write what's clearest in my mind. I'd call it a "roadblock," not writer's block. What do you do when you hit a roadblock? You take an alternate route. You don't just wait there until they finish the road work so you can drive through.

Akiva Goldsman: Sure, I've had day upon day where I couldn't write anything particularly good, but you just write through it. Just write bad stuff.

Jim Kouf: I never had the situation where you just stare at the screen and nothing happens. Sometimes, I know what I'm thinking maybe isn't the best idea, but this usually leads me to something better, so I've never been completely empty. For me, it's like being on a jungle path. If there's a lot of stuff in your way, you hack through it. You don't whine, "Oh, it's too thick." You pick up the machete and chop. The trail might not be smooth or easy to take, but you're going to find something at the other end. And hopefully, that's a check. I have the opposite problem. I have too many ideas, and the frustrating part is not knowing which one to focus on. I don't know which one is better than the other. Then you commit to one, and people like the writing but they don't want to make the movie. Okay, so I picked the wrong idea. Let's just start over.

Eric Roth: I've never had it, but I believe other writers can get frozen. I think, in a way, it's about having the courage to fail. If you have no fear of failure, what's the difference? You have to force yourself to write through it, otherwise you'll never end it. So if a scene bothers you, just sort of sketch it in, blow past it, and then come back to it later. You might find you never needed it at all. If I get stuck on a difficult scene, I'll sometimes change the weather. For instance, if it's raining, it will open up a whole new world. Or maybe I'll realize I went down the wrong road, so I'll back up and go down a different road.

Michael Schiffer: A friend had a cartoon a long time ago. The first panel was a guy sitting at his typewriter, his head in his hands, looking really worried, with the caption "Writer's Block." The next panel was a guy wearing an apron, standing in front of a rack of fish at the fish market, with the caption "Permanent Writer's Block." I'd rather write badly than not at all. You can always throw it away, but at least you're in motion. You can spend a whole day, and if you get two good lines out of it, it really wasn't a waste. We all go through the occasional dry spells. When you're legitimately stale, you have to take a mental health day off and recharge your batteries. But if you find that you're doing this more than actually writing, then you have a problem. I have a simple philosophy: If I don't write, I'm not going to make it. If I don't make it, I'm not going to be a writer. If I'm not a writer, what else am I going to do? I can't lie about the task. There it is in front of me. Early on, I was trying to be a writer and my stuff wasn't good enough yet. I had to be honest about the cause and effect. It wasn't the world's fault that I wasn't writing well enough to get a movie made. I simply had to write better movies.

Tom Schulman: There are times in your life when you're more in touch with things and are more deeply resonant than not. Even when there are days when three out of the five scenes I write just stink, I never have this feeling of staring at the blank page and nothing is happening. If you can't write the beginning, just go to the middle. If you're having trouble with one scene, go to another scene. You can always write something.

52. Not Being Afraid to Write Terrible First Drafts

My best writing is done by writing rapidly and with few filters.
I then delete my way to excellence.
—RICHARD BACH

Most professional screenwriters have become comfortable with writing a lot of bad stuff in order to come up with a little good stuff. They often produce thousands of words before one line is fresh enough to jump off the page. To do this, they give themselves permission to write anything, no matter how terrible, because they know it can all be fixed later, thus giving them the power to free themselves sufficiently in the creative stage to write from the heart while silencing their inner critic.

Steven DeSouza: I especially like writing the first draft, which I blaze through as fast as I can, without even stopping for spell checking or fact-checking that might interrupt the flow. And I like the editing part of the printed first draft with my trusty red pen, though I hate all the retyping from the edited page into the computer. On the other hand, I never get depressed about what I write, because I know I'm going to rewrite it. I remember seeing an interview with George Lucas where he talks about a trick he learned from Francis (Coppola), which is not to read what he's writing until he's done with it. He writes nonstop, puts the pages in a file, and it's not until he thinks he's done with it that he'll find the nerve to look at his pages.

Nicholas Kazan: You should be able to write a terrible first draft. I used to think of my first draft as simply laying out the territory, and that all the work was done in rewriting. After finishing my preparatory notes, it would take me 32 days to write a script. I'd do a first draft in 10 days, take a day off, do a second draft in 10 days, take a day off, and then write a third draft in 10 days. This gave the screenplay a sort of velocity, but frequently, it also had built-in plot problems. Now, if I smell a problem, I no longer ignore it. I try to solve it before I go on.

Jim Kouf: You just write, blindly putting things down on paper. Just put something down, and then put something else down, because it's a process of thinking through all the choices. You have to be willing to throw it away. If you write something awful, you just say, "Okay, I tried," and sometimes you make it all the way through to discover it's not worth it. You've got to write. Don't be afraid to make mistakes.

Tom Schulman: Silencing that inner critic is important, at least through the first draft, because when will you have another chance to let it all out, if not in the first draft? I try to finish the first draft before rewriting it, and ultimately, I'll go over it about 10 to 12 times. But I usually go over the first third of the script and rewrite it until it's good enough because I feel that if it's launched properly, the rest will fall through.

CHAPTER 11
Rewriting

53. Finishing Your Draft Before Rewriting

Compose first, worry later.

—NED ROREM

Finishing what you write before editing it has a double benefit. It prevents you from tinkering with it too much, which could be a dangerous form of procrastination. Too many writers, sometimes laboring over the same opening 10 pages for years, take forever to finish their script. The other benefit is that it allows you to step away from it for a period of time, anywhere from one week to a month, so that you may come back to it with a fresh pair of eyes, able to look at it as objectively as possible.

Steven DeSouza: An art teacher once taught me to hold a painting up to a mirror to see its hidden flaws. But there is no equivalent to that in writing. If you hold up your script to a mirror, it's just backwards! The only way to get that perspective is time away from the material. So the trick in rewriting is to get away from it for as long as you can. Because if you try to edit yourself as you go, you might sit there anguishing over a sentence or a line of dialogue and at the end of the day, you may have a perfect page, and then maybe three weeks later, you realize it's a perfect scene that has no place in the movie. So I'll write a first draft as quickly as I can, and then go back and be a brutal editor. A lot of it is lousy, and I throw a good third of it away, but by the time I rewrite it over and over, it just gets better and better.

Akiva Goldsman: I try to build the story as cleanly as I can, make sure the structure works, then I write it really badly, as fast as I can, 10 pages a day of crap, sometimes actual dialogue, sometimes notes to myself about what people will say in the scene, just to get some feeling of the shape of the piece, trying not to rewrite it, unless I'm feeling I am so cheating myself. Then I go back and start rewriting. The truth is that writing is rewriting. I am by no means the first person to say this, but let me be the latest. And I go over and over and over, scene by scene, then act by act, then sequence by sequence, until it's as tight and clean as I can possibly make it.

Jim Kouf: The number of drafts depends on whether I'm happy with it. Usually I write about 75 percent of it and then go back and start looking at it. Sometimes, I write the whole script before looking at it and going through every word again and again. Sometimes you have to set it down for a while and get away from it. If I feel happy with it, I give it to my wife, and if she's happy with it, I give it to my agents, and if they like it, we do something with it. If they don't like it or if everybody is not thrilled with it, it doesn't go out and I just set it aside. You've got to have the ability to judge your own work.

Scott Rosenberg: I am all for dumping it out first, and then coming back to it.

• • •

If you choose not go forward until you feel a page is good enough, you may try . . .

54. Rewriting As You Go Along

It's like driving a car at night. You never see further than your head-lights, but you can make the whole trip that way.
—E. L. DOCTOROW

Gerald DiPego: There's a trap on either end of the rewriting process, whether you finish a draft and then go back to it, or you rewrite as you go along. You can monitor yourself so much that you almost have to squeeze the first draft out of you because you are so scared. Many writers feel they can't finish a page until it's perfect. The other extreme is to get it done by rushing through it. But then, what you dump on the page is often flat, hollow writing, and you just add to your problems by having to go back in there and work backwards. It should be a happy medium. If you've spent time outlining, you've already made many decisions, so the first draft should be well written. As many writers do, I read what I wrote the day before, and this helps me slide into the day's work, giving me a sort of momentum. When I start to write, I'm scratching and writing and polishing, so basically I'm rewriting as I go along. I've been doing this for so long now that my first drafts are pretty close to what I'll hand in, and what they need is just careful polishing.

Leslie Dixon: You often know when you're not hitting it, so I generally rewrite as I go along. But often, it's in your best interest to forget about it and get a certain volume of pages. I usually go back to the first 30 pages a number of times. If I get it to where it's pretty good, that gives me steam to go all the way to the end without stopping again.

Amy Holden Jones: I'm afraid to write terrible first drafts but I still write them, rewriting incessantly almost every day from page one. When I can make myself not do this, I'll try to write 20 pages at a time without going back.

Eric Roth: I don't subscribe to writing terrible first drafts and then rewriting them. I go back to page one every single day. I start and go over it, and keep refining and refining as I go through it. Sometimes I'll let things go in the first draft that I'll later come back to, because when you get enough experience, you know what will make or break a piece. But these are indulgences in the first draft I may leave for reading purposes.

Michael Schiffer: I don't mind throwing work away. I think that every pass at a scene is like an improvisation. You could improv it one time or 50 times. Even if you find one line of dialogue and the rest of the scene is no good, that's great. I roll pages a lot (I use a typewriter). I've got tons of crumpled-up paper all over the place. I read, throw it out, start again, read, and start again, as if I'm rehearsing a scene. I know a lot of people like using a computer to make changes because it's more convenient, but I find that with a typewriter, every time I'm forced to retype the whole page, it's like another rehearsal. It's like in the theater where actors rehearse a scene for six weeks before they go on stage. They begin to internalize their roles and the repetition is the act of creating the character. For me, the repetition of retyping a scene is part of writing really good scenes and good dialogue, constantly rewriting as I go along, doing it again, over and over, until it begins to form up and the energy starts to shape itself. But even then, it's never final. I could write a scene that feels really good for six months and then, two weeks before turning it in, I may find it stale, and then the director or star wants changes. A director once said to me, "You're never done with your film; they just take it away from you." I've done some teaching, and when I see a student write "Final Draft" on their script, the first thing I do is cross it out and write "Says who?"

Ed Solomon: I rewrite a lot more than anyone would think. I believe the difference between a professional and a beginner is that while they both write a lot of crap, the professional knows it and knows when to show it and when not to show it. It's just about editing more effectively. In theory, my method is to go all the way through a first draft and then rewrite. But in reality, I tend to look at it the next day. One way I avoid this is by creating files that are only 15 to 20 pages long. Once I reach 20 pages of a script, I close that file and start a new one. This way I go over a script in 20-page chunks. And I resist (as much as possible) the tendency to continue rehashing the first half of the movie.

55. Being Determined to Make the Script As Good As It Can Be

Only a mediocre writer is always at his best.

—W. SOMERSET MAUGHAM

Often the biggest mistake beginning writers make is submitting a script too soon, usually a first draft. They're too impatient, desperate for something to happen, because they've been at it for so long. Maybe they think it's good enough because it's better than the latest Hollywood flop they've just seen at the multiplex. Or the most common phenomenon: They think it's good just because the script is finally *done*. Big mistake. All they've done is burned a bridge to that one connection who was willing to read their script, because in this town, you only get one chance to shine. By sending an inferior script, they've only guaranteed that that producer, agent, or assistant will never read anything from them again. Whether a script requires only one or 50 rewrites, professional writers still believe it's not good enough. And even when they feel they've done their best, they still get a second opinion.

Steven DeSouza: I'm a pretty brutal editor of my own material. Whatever your craft as an artist, whether you're a painter, dancer, or writer, it's limited or unlimited based on your ability as an editor or critic. This process of seeing what works and admitting what doesn't is really what separates successful people from unsuccessful ones. In my experience, the people who work and keep working in this industry have a strong self-critical sense and a high standard of excellence. What you see when a script of mine says "first draft" has been rewritten 6 to 10 times. It doesn't mean that every page has been rewritten over and over, but I do rewrite a lot. We've all heard from our mothers that you never get a second chance to make a first impression. It's particularly true in Hollywood, where every executive is connected. When a script is covered, it's all over town in an instant. So the script you hand in better be as great as you can possibly make it.

Gerald DiPego: It's dangerous to submit an inferior script. You should always do the very best work you can. It takes patience. I wrote five scripts before I sold *Phenomenon*. Don't rush it. Don't depend on people filling in what you left out. On the other hand, don't fall into the trap of worrying so much that you don't let it out of your hands. Some say a screenplay is just a blueprint and the director will come and fill it all in. I disagree. A blueprint can't make you laugh or cry. It's a play for the screen.

Leslie Dixon: Being a tough self-critic is a hugely important thing. I'm harder on my material than anybody. If you can see your work with a laser eye, you're in a much better position, because if you can police your own work, rather than wait for somebody else to tell you what's wrong with it, you can be part of the process of how your script changes and therefore have more control about what happens to your work. Too many writers wait to be told what's wrong with their scripts.

Amy Holden Jones: It would help if beginning writers were critical of themselves. Too many people write something, and they think it's just great and then stop. They won't hear of it when someone tells them it needs work. When you read a wonderful script, chances are it's been written many times over. Good writers keep going over and over material, believing they can make it better. It's like many parts of life. People who aren't good at something but believe they are aren't as successful as those who have doubts and are self-critical, always striving to be better. If you paint a picture once, and look at it and say it's great, you won't be much of a painter.

Tom Schulman: You must make sure you can't think of anything to improve your script before you show it to other people. If you have any doubts about a scene, or you feel certain scenes are inferior or messy, then the feedback you'll receive won't be useful because people will be confused about what they read. You can't expose it too soon. Be patient. Put it away for a little bit and then come back, reread it, and be brutal. If you don't have a good enough inner critic, you need to get one.

56. Getting Feedback

Ask advice from everyone, but act with your own mind.

—YIDDISH PROVERB

Once you've done all you could on your first draft, you still need to get good, unbiased, realistic feedback on it. This may be why a family member, especially your mom, won't be as helpful as someone else. But they could be, as long as you trust their honesty, and that they won't sugarcoat their comments to spare any negative feelings.

Ron Bass: Like all writers, I used to be defensive and protective and get into arguments. During the week, I usually write in the backyard of a member of my creative team. So when I'm done with a scene, I have someone to show it to and get instant feedback. Also, since I do not have a computer, I have an assistant who types my writing, prints it, and then faxes it to my creative team, which then gives me immediate feedback, usually by the end of the day.

Steven DeSouza: I don't give a script to as many people as I used to, because in the amount of time it takes them to give me notes, I could have done two passes at it. Frankly, it's hard for me to find people who are as tough on my material as I am. But I would definitely recommend writers get good feedback on their material. I get a lot of writers who give me their script and say, "Here's my movie. I know you'll like it and I'd really like your notes because you're the best at doing action movies. The first act is little long and the plot needs some work and I'm not sure if the hero's buddy should be a guy or a girl, but here, read it." Now, if you know these things are wrong with this draft, don't give it to me now. And half the time they say, "No, no, I really want your notes so I can incorporate them into my next version," and I say, "I'm only going to read this once. You only get one shot. You have to make this as good as you can get it before you give it to me. Now go away."

Gerald DiPego: When I'm writing something, whether it's a script or a novel, my wife enjoys it when I read the day's work to her in the evening after dinner. It really helps me because I can hear it out loud, look at it again, and observe her reaction. She's the perfect audience because she loves film but she's not a student of it. Once I get a first draft I give it to my two sons, who are also screenwriters, and who give me valuable feedback. Not only do they know the craft but they also represent the younger generation. So between my wife and my two sons, I feel very lucky to get valuable feedback.

Leslie Dixon: I send my stuff to Robert Towne sometimes. Impressed? He sends his to Pauline Kael. But I don't have that many dead-ass, reliable, sources for feedback except for my husband, and occasionally my agent. I also have a couple of writer friends with whom I occasionally trade scripts. But I go more by my own gut than anything. I just try to please myself. Do I like this script? Would I pay $8.50 to see this? These are pretty big questions if you're honest with yourself.

Akiva Goldsman: I usually let a couple of trusted readers read it. Usually, they should not be friends or family, but they can be if you trust them to tell you what you wrote sucks, because better they say it sucks than Steven Spielberg says it. Then when you're at a place where you're okay with it, you let the world take a look.

Nicholas Kazan: When I finish a script, I show it to between two and 10 people before turning it in. I have a couple of criteria on the feedback. If one person says something, and I don't agree with it, I ignore it. If two people say it, then I start to worry. If three people say it, I have a real problem, whether I like it or not, and I have to do something. If I think it's a good idea conceptually, but I don't know how to do it, I don't worry about it. There are always ideas for a more brilliant version of any script, but it may not be the movie I want to write, or that I'm capable of writing. I frequently hear criticism from friends and say, "My God, if I could only write their movie." But I can't, so I don't worry about it.

Eric Roth: I don't get much feedback. Usually, I'll bounce it off my wife, or I'll start telling some scenes I'm proud of, trying them out on a friend. But this is more about trying to gauge a response, so it's not going to make a difference. I just rely on myself. I know by now what I think is good or bad, and I tend to be a little defensive when I get notes.

Scott Rosenberg: When I finish the first draft, I basically have four people that read it before I show it to anyone: a couple of friends, a girlfriend, and my brother. I give it to them and I don't think about it for two weeks while they read it. When they come back and give me notes, I read it again, sift through the notes, and make the necessary changes.

Tom Schulman: I have three people I show everything to. They're not writers, but I trust them because they always tell me everything. Sometimes, they can't articulate what's right or wrong with something, but I can tell by this sort of lack of response to a scene I thought was particularly good, or their enthusiasm for something I thought was particularly weak. I also find it necessary to ask a lot of questions, like: "Did you like this character? Are you really pulling for him here? What do you think this character wants out of life?" People often don't bring things up unless you ask them.

Ed Solomon: I try not to show a script in its early stages to highly critical people because they might kill it. Who you give the script to is a very important decision to make, especially when you're starting out. People who are available to you at your level are also young and vulnerable and have their own ego and self-image at stake. They often can be well intentioned on one level, but on a deeper level they can be destructive in ways that don't necessarily seem destructive. You need to be careful about what you take to heart. Be very skeptical about people's solutions to your script's problems.

57. Being Open to Outside Criticism

Don't mind criticism. If it's untrue, disregard it; if it's unfair, keep from irritation; if it's ignorant, smile; if it's justified, learn from it.

—OLD CHINESE SAYING

When faced with feedback on a script, no writer with an ounce of sensitivity wants to be told what's wrong with it. We often feel hurt and can't help being defensive. The reason is that a large part of us, our soul and sweat and tears, is on the page, and therefore, any constructive criticism of the material is destructive criticism of us, just as any praise of the material is a boost to our self-esteem. This is why it's so difficult getting honest feedback from friends and family, who know how vulnerable we are. A writer's group I used to moderate had as its first rule for any member receiving comments that they were not allowed to offer a defense after each criticism. Do you really want feedback? Because if what you really want is someone to pat you on the back and say your script is the greatest thing they've ever read, how will you improve your writing? Henry David Thoreau once said, "It takes two to speak truth; one to speak, and another to hear." You must be open to honest feedback. Listen, take it all in, and think about it. As the writer, you're free to take it or leave it. But first, you must consider it objectively.

Gerald DiPego: I remember how hard it was for me in college to take criticism. It was terrifying to put it out there for the whole class to comment because you put your soul and heart on the page. If someone comes at you with a very negative feeling about your script, it's easy to get defensive. It's something you have to get used to. It's a challenge, but it's worth it to stay as open as you can and be thoughtful about it. Don't dismiss it out of hand.

Amy Holden Jones: I've found that many people don't let others tell them what's wrong with their script. What they really want you to say is how wonderful and perfect it is. If you try to give them notes, all they do is defend themselves.

Nicholas Kazan: There's no such thing as constructive criticism. All criticism is destructive because it's felt by the author as destructive. All criticism says is (a) you didn't do this part well, and (b) there's something wrong with you. At least, that's how it's experienced. Because when you write, you put your whole self into it, and so what people criticize is you. It's very hard to absorb this. When people try to make their criticism constructive, the way they do it is often even more destructive. They try to make suggestions. They don't tell you, "It was slow in the middle," which is a symptom, and it's what you want. They say, "Wouldn't it be better if this happened?" And you wonder, "Why do they want this to happen?" Always ask people for the symptomatic feedback, not the suggestions. You have to accept that you're an individual, that you have idiosyncrasies.

Maybe you're really short or tall or skinny or fat, maybe you love cartoons or potty humor. You have a distinct set of tastes. In some areas, your aesthetic may overlap with a lot of other people's tastes. That's what you hope for when you write screenplays, that enough people like it so that millions will see the movie. But there are areas where you may not overlap with everybody, and the things you find funny other people may find irritating. Sometimes they're mistaken, but more often, they're not. As a human being, you're not perfect, and there are parts in your script you may have done imperfectly, so you need to be able to hear that. You don't have to like it. It's no fun. It's horrible. You want to kill your critics, but you need to listen. Recently, I've been taking my laptop computer to story meetings, and it's been very helpful because, whatever pain I feel, it just moves through my fingers and down into the computer. I'm just typing away whatever they're saying. Then, I go home and think about it, and often it's not as bad as my first impression. When you listen and analyze the problem, solutions present themselves.

Robin Swicord: What's good about giving your script to more than one person is that in the end, the notes are not so personal. If I give it to a few people, someone will like something. The most important thing is that if you hear something once, they could be wrong, but if you hear the same problem more than once, you have to pay attention. Notes are symptomatic, so you have to be good at hearing them in such a way that you can interpret these notes, and don't rush the process when there might be another solution.

• • •

Discipline is critical, but like a tree that doesn't make a sound if no one is there to hear it fall, a screenwriter without a great script won't get any attention in Hollywood. What makes a great script? Art and craft. Art is your talent. No one can "teach" it to you. But let's find out what our mentors can tell you about craft.

PART IV

Storycraft

Weaving a Great Tale

Nothing counts as much as the story, because it is the story that will attract the director, the actors, the studio, the money. The story is the thing.

—DAVID BROWN, PRODUCER

CHAPTER 12
What Makes a Great Script

In the planning stages of this book, I knew I didn't want to write another "How-to" screenwriting book. I even debated whether this chapter should even be included. But keeping in mind that highly successful screenwriters got their reputation because they've mastered the craft, I knew I'd have to include some habits related to the art of telling a great story, knowing it would be difficult to add any insights that have yet to be covered in seminars and books since Aristotle.

Despite the fact that it is a rare artist who can explain his art, at least 12 essential habits emerged while interviewing our mentors, habits any aspiring screenwriter needs to adopt when it comes to the art of screenwriting. I've included their comments only when they were able to share valuable insights on a particular habit.

58. Discriminating Between Good and Bad Writing

Do not go where the path may lead.
Go where there is no path and leave a trail.
—ANONYMOUS

The consensus among professional writers is that if the writing moves them in any way, if there's identification with a character, involvement, surprises, emotional satisfaction, anticipation, or catharsis, it's good writing; if it's unoriginal, clichéd, and boring, it's bad. Among executives, it is that they read so many scripts a week, they don't even think about what's good or bad. Their rule of thumb is if they *finish* a script, it's good. To paraphrase Gilbert Chesterton, "A good script tells the truth about its hero, but a bad script tells you the truth about its writer." As a screenwriter trying to improve your writing, you need to be able to discriminate between what's good and what's bad before anyone of importance (the buyer) makes up their own mind. As an unknown writer, you may only get one chance to impress.

Steven DeSouza: I'm guilty of what many executives do, which is to give scripts 10 pages to hold my interest, and they don't have to be in my genre. I can be enthralled by a historical drama—or even (gasp!) a chick flick—if it's well written. Sometimes, I'll just read the dialogue and then alternatively only the stage directions. Ideally, one without the other should not be able to get the story across. So a good test of dialogue is to just read the dialogue for a section of the script. If that leaves you hungry for more, that's good. But if I get the entire story with just the dialogue, then all that stage direction is just dead weight and useless.

Akiva Goldsman: You just know what's good or bad. There's no answer to this, and you're not always right. I was asked once by an interviewer why I wrote a particular line that was terrible. And I said I wrote it in the same way I wrote all the lines he thought were good. It's not like you sit there and go, "Now let's write some really bad lines." God knows we're not artists per se, but we are creative participants in the process. All we're doing is making stuff up. Sometimes we make it good, sometimes not. Making a movie is like painting a mural on the side of a wall at night, and your only light is a lightning storm. So there are flashes of light, and we're sort of painting really quickly, gradually doing the whole thing, and then morning comes and we get to see what we've done, and we either go, "Wow, that's great" or "God, what did I just do?" There are a few things first-time writers do that they could avoid. They don't really study the form, both in terms of structure and what it looks like on the page. There are definite formatting conventions that for some strange reason are often ignored by first-timers. You open up a script and see six giant paragraphs of text, or the dialogue goes all the way to the right, or there are way too many camera directions, and you can tell you're dealing with a beginner. Also, misspelled words blow me away, especially in this age of spell-checkers. All these mistakes are a sign of laziness, so you should be smart about it. Then, people try to write what they think screenplays sound like, rather than writing the way people talk, and really listening to what people say. Learning to listen is a big part of what a writer has to do, and you can feel it when someone doesn't know what voices sound like. Unfortunately, having a good ear can't really be taught. For example, I have a tin ear for music. If I studied music, I could probably be a little better, but I can't hear it. If someone asked me to replicate a pitch, there's just no way. But I do have a pretty good ear for dialogue. I sort of know what people sound like. I can look at a sentence and see its rhythms. Some of it is learned, a lot of it comes from reading and listening, and a little bit comes from the right set of chromosomes.

Amy Holden Jones: I can usually tell on the first page. Believe it or not, many people use bad grammar, and they are too lazy to correct it. They also don't understand that people who read a lot of scripts don't want to read elaborate descriptions, especially if it's in bad grammar. There's a certain quality in the dialogue, without straining to be literary, that tells you whether it's written by a writer or not. It's the kind of writing that pulls you in and just makes you want to know what happens next.

Nicholas Kazan: Good writing is usually idiosyncratic. The writing feels like a movie, rather than a screenplay. There's a specificity of detail and a sense of command. It's like when you're sitting around the campfire. One person really knows how to tell a story, and when it begins, you say, "This is going to be good!" When you read a screenplay, you want that same sense of anticipation. You don't know where it's going, but you know from the first page that it will be good.

Jim Kouf: You know bad writing when you read it. The dialogue is not sharp, the characters are not as interesting or as funny or as charming as they should be, the story is not as clever as it can be. Ultimately, good writing can't be boring. You've got to be clever. Why are we going to sit through it for two hours?

Scott Rosenberg: You can tell from the first page if someone can write, by its assuredness and its confidence. What this does is allow you to relax immediately and say, "Okay, you can write, now tell me a story." If, right off the bat, there are four-inch blocks of text, or it's not formatted properly, I know it's an amateur.

Eric Roth: The one thing I notice about bad scripts is that there's too much exposition. People talk too much and tell you what you've already seen. It's just tedious writing, telling you things instead of showing. I'm a very visual writer, so some of the exposition I write is just in the visual.

Subtext is very important. It's always terrific to write about something else and still tell the audience what's really going on.

Michael Schiffer: The first thing you listen for is whether the words move you in some way. The language itself speaks to you. As a writer, you hope that your words generate a feeling of excitement, and in a crazy way, that maybe there's something there. Initially, reality testing may tell you otherwise. But what you're looking for is that spark, hoping that others will see it too.

Tom Schulman: It's the old Harry Cohn thing, "you know a good script by how much you're squirming in your seat." The producer who hired me to write my first script also hired me to read scripts. For about four months, I was reading about five scripts a day. So when you pick up a script, you start by being optimistic, you want to believe this will be a great script. I think it's wrong to pick up something with the attitude of, "let me see what this kid can show me," but within a few pages, it either grabs you and sucks you in, or you find yourself having to just push and push into it. If by page 30 you have to fight to stay awake, there's something wrong. Sure, something great could happen on page 40, but it's too late. Today's executives usually don't give you more than five or 10 pages.

Ed Solomon: A script is good if I get emotionally involved. You can usually tell if it's bad writing when it doesn't affect you in any way. Also, I find a singular or interesting voice a more affecting and inspiring than a "perfectly" plotted or structured piece.

59. Understanding It Takes Talent and Hard Work

The only place where success comes before work is in the dictionary.

—VIDAL SASSOON

The most common and erroneous belief among nonprofessional writers is that writing a movie is no harder than watching one, and that because movies and TV shows are plentiful, relatively short, and frequently mediocre, there really are few rules, standards, or professional skills to worry about. In other words, screenwriting is easy. We all have access to a computer keyboard, and we all think we could write, if only we had the time, or the right software.

When asked why there are so many (the accepted percentage is 999 out of 1,000) bad scripts out there, our mentors responded this way:

Ron Bass: For some reason, there's a notion that writing is something anyone could do. Because everybody owns a computer and everybody knows the English language and likes to go to the movies or read books and think about stories, everybody thinks they could do it. The key is: Can everybody not only do it well but do it well enough that you'd want to pay money to go see that story? We all drive cars, but how many of us could drive at Indianapolis? Every woman in the world puts on makeup, but how many could become a runway model in Milan? Nobody can stop you from putting on makeup. You just never get to the runway, because someone has to ask you to model their clothes. It's the same with the desire to become a screenwriter. You don't need anyone's permission. It doesn't cost you anything. All you have to do is write 120 pages and print them. It's kind of a blessing in a sense, because nobody can stop you; so if it's your goal, why not give it a try? Starting is easy. Making it is another story. There's a certain ability needed to do anything, be it natural talent, intelligence, passion, desire, experience, whatever it is that makes people good at anything that needs to be done at a high enough level for other people to want to support it. When you get down to somebody spending $80 million to make a movie out of a script, do we really think anyone could do it?

Leslie Dixon: The only reason most scripts are bad is because most people can't write. Look at all the things you have to do to be a screenwriter. You have to be able to tell a good story. Most people can't do that. They haven't even read the great literature of all time, or seen the great films of all time, to see how it should be done. So where are they going to learn what a basic good yarn is? Because this is your first obligation as a screenwriter. You need some contact with your soul to create rich, interesting characters and writing talent to make them jump off the page. You need to have an ear for human speech, and you need to entertain the reader in a way that keeps him moving pages. Right away, this is a lot to ask.

Akiva Goldsman: Unfortunately, people believe that their first thing should be great. Writing is like anything else. You're not supposed to write a page and expect it to be good. You have to write a thousand bad pages to get to that one good page. It's as if we were training for the

20-yard dash, and instead of waiting until we'd trained before we ran, we invite everyone to our first practice, and of course, we fall flat on our face.

Amy Holden Jones: People don't know what they want to say and don't spend enough time learning how to say it. Too many try to write screenplays without doing the hard work. They have the mentality that it's easy, and the reality is that it's probably one of the hardest things they'll ever do. First, you need a strong commercial instinct. Many wonderful writers I know have failed because they didn't have this commercial instinct or were unable to deal with the collaborative nature of the medium. Many scripts would be better if writers were very disciplined, if they did the necessary research, and if they had some sort of sensitivity toward people in the way they really behave and talk to each other. Another reason why scripts fail is that the lead character's need, motivation, or goal is often not clear. You have to know what they want, no matter what it is or how goofy it is. And if you don't care about what they want, you won't be emotionally invested in the character.

Nicholas Kazan: There's a lot of bad material out there because there are so many courses and books telling everyone how to do it, and everyone does it the same way. If I tell you a story, and you've heard the same story in different versions five times before, you're not going to be interested. If I tell you a story unlike any other story you've heard, but somehow along the way it stops in the same places as other stories you've heard recently, you will be ultimately disappointed. But if I tell a story, and it's like nothing you've ever heard before, and it has a certain amount of narrative surprise, and there are idiosyncratic pleasures along the way, you'll love this story, even if you didn't expect to like it. When people follow their own instincts and truly get to something unusual and fun and unique, then they can write something good.

Jim Kouf: I don't read many beginners' scripts, but I have been told most of them are bad. It must be true, because I keep getting hired. I think the reason is that most people can't judge their own material objectively. They think their stuff is great when it's not, and they fail to get decent feedback. It's ironic that, despite this 99 percent statistic, almost every letter I receive from a screenwriter tells me what a great script they've written.

Scott Rosenberg: It's purely a numbers thing. Screenwriting is the only thing in this business that anyone can do in the privacy of their own home.

An actor needs lines and a director needs a blueprint. And we all go to movies and we're always disappointed in them. We walk out saying, "They should have done this and that." So basically, everyone with a computer can write a screenplay, and everyone does, despite the fact that they may not be qualified. I sometimes go to these seminars and see people who have paid thousands of dollars, and they all know each other, and they go to every seminar because they think we hold some magic pill, and you read some of their stuff and it's like, "My God! My grandmother on her worst day, who's never written a single word in her life, could write better than this." The level of windmills they are tilting on is enormous. Will they ever make it? Probably not. But if it makes them happy to do it, you can't blame them.

Eric Roth: I think people don't spend the amount of time necessary to rewrite a script and all the detailed work you need to really understand the characters.

Michael Schiffer: Hollywood is full of people who want to make easy money the hard way. People see a bad movie and say, "I can do that." Writing is incredibly hard, and most people trying to do it don't believe this is true. They are not working as hard as the task requires, and it shows on the pages. Since you don't break in by being bad, the question should be, "How do I get really good? How do I reach this level where my work is so unmistakably excellent that nobody can read it and not be impressed?" People ask me all the time how to break in. I honestly believe that if you get your work to the point where your writing speaks for itself, where it is categorically and objectively terrific and it moves the reader, you will get noticed. Readers will sit up and say, "Wow, that was well written." They may not want to buy the movie, but they will definitely want to be in business with you.

Tom Schulman: Too many aspiring writers push their first work too early. Dan Petrie Jr. once said that to become a doctor takes four years of medical school and four years of internship and residency, and to be a lawyer takes three years of law school plus so many years to work yourself up through the firm. Most people assume writing screenplays is something they can do in a couple of afternoons. The reality is that in order to be good at it, it will probably take you as long as any other profession to master the craft. So it is possible that this 99 percent of bad material we read comes from people who just haven't put in the time and effort, and it's their first or second script. Of course, there's always someone who can write a great screenplay right off the bat, but it's this 1 percent exception.

60. Trusting Your Instincts

Don't write what you know—what you know may bore you, and thus bore your readers. Write about what interests you—and interests you deeply-and your readers will catch fire at your words.
—VALERIE SHERWOOD

This is about choosing to write what excites you and never second-guessing your instincts. The common advice is to write what you know, but I feel it should be more like "write what makes you *feel*," what intrigues and fascinates you, because ultimately, the only thing you really know are your emotions. After all, doesn't everyone *feel* in the same language? Emotion, which equals great writing, transcends genres, ages, economic classes, and political boundaries. William Faulkner once said, "If you are going to write, write about human nature. That is the only thing that doesn't date." You shouldn't worry about trends, and you should definitely not write what you just saw in the theaters, because by the time you start, you're already two years behind. So no one knows what the marketplace is going to do (thank you, William Goldman). Second-guessing yourself will only kill your original voice. All you can do is be true to what you want to do, and hope other people will respond. Someone once said "writing is half magic and half perspiration." If you write for the market, you eliminate the magic, and all that's left is perspiration, and that's no fun.

However, with this in mind, you should still think about the *universality* of your script. Some people call it the "commercial" factor, and the argument of art vs. commercialism has been debated since the dawn of mass entertainment. The bottom line is about entertaining an audience. Unless you're writing to amuse only yourself, chances are you want millions to be moved by your story. And you'll only become a successful screenwriter if you write what people want to see and studios want to make. Amy Holden Jones has already mentioned that many good writers have failed because they didn't have this commercial instinct. This doesn't mean you have to be a slave to box-office statistics. It simply means you have to weave your unique soul into the universal themes that have been shown to be successful around the world.

Ron Bass: This is a big problem with my development team because I'd write a scene that I really like, then I'll get six faxes in the morning, and four of them will say they didn't like it. It tears at your confidence, but it forces you to look at the arguments in an objective way. Ultimately, if you really like what you wrote, you have final say. After listening to the comments and rereading the scene, maybe I'm wrong, but I have to listen to my own ear on this and trust my own judgment. You may be afraid, but it reinforces that feeling that you can't ever guide your star by other people's opinions. It also works the other way. If five people like it and one doesn't, but her argument makes sense to me, I'll go back and look at it, and find a different way of solving the problem. At the end of the day, you can only write to please yourself. Of course, you desperately want to please everybody, and hope everyone in the world will love it.

Steven DeSouza: I'm not sure that "high-concept" ideas are the best way to go. All those "How to play the Hollywood Game" seminars that teach you how to sell a script in 30 days, or how to get past the reader, contribute largely to this 99 percent of crap. With a few exceptions, the most successful films are the ones that break the mold. The market goes in cycles. What happens when a movie is successful is 20 to 30 months later, you see a whole bunch of bad copies of that film, and when these imitations fail, the trend is declared dead. For instance, last week it was just mentioned in the trades that the teenage ensemble movie trend is over. So you may have an absolutely amazing thriller with college students in it, but this week nobody will read it because that trend is now "officially over" . . . until it works again, of course. Write what excites you, or what you think you can do a good job of delivering. It doesn't have to be a high-concept idea. Look at *American Beauty:* An unpitchable sitcom about a dysfunctional family turned inside out, but amazingly well executed, original, and fresh.

Akiva Goldsman: The trick is to write what you know, and be connected to the material of your imagination, thematically and concretely. In the case of my first script, what I knew was emotionally disturbed children and autism. I felt I could write about that well. The other trick is to write what interests you, because if you're not fascinated and excited by the writing of the script, the reader won't be fascinated and excited by the reading of it. I don't know why this is true. If the fun goes in, it comes out in the same way. If you write cynically, the reader will feel cynical. I always say that even episodes of *The Love Boat* were somebody's best work. Somebody sat there loving what they were doing, and that's what gave it the energy to move forward. In my case, I knew autism and I loved thrillers, so I combined them. In the case of source material, be it a novel or a biography, you try to find something in it that speaks to your own life, something you think is authentic and true and compelling in the story you want to tell. People are too focused on that "high-concept" idea. By writing what you know, I mean write what excites you and study it sufficiently so that your imagination can reside with some comfort in the unique world of your story. If it's well written, it will sell more than the stuff written by writers who think they know what will sell.

Michael Schiffer: Too many beginners aim low. They think, "Hollywood never makes anything good, so I'll write some dumb comedy." That's not a good career strategy. I urge writers to aim as high as they can, to tell the most personal, or complex, or exciting story they can, to aim high so that the voice they bring is a worthy voice that will make a difference. So it's not a question of trying to be commercial, but writing the best possible version of your favorite kinds of movies. Without worrying about the market, write the kind of movies *you* want to see, and if they happen to be commercial, more power to you. It's fine to be a snobbish highbrow, but you've got to respect the fact that movies are a popular medium, and there's nothing wrong with writing movies that people like.

61. Having Something to Say

Art is a microscope which the artist fixes on the secrets of his soul and shows to people these secrets which are common to all.
—LEO TOLSTOY

The writing process is a search for meaning, a theme, what the story is *really* about, what gives it meaning and a purpose for being, besides making millions of dollars for stars and movie studios. Until you know what you're trying to say, your work isn't finished. All great writing is about something. With extrinsic motives aside, no professional screenwriter commits three months to a year on a script unless he has something to say. Because they're great observers and often sensitive souls, successful screenwriters are able to recognize and offer insights into the human condition. As writer Dorothy Bryant puts it, "We are the voices for the deeper, unspoken dramas in other people's hearts." The key is being careful not to make it so obvious that it becomes preachy. As Darryl Zanuck once said, "If I want a message, I'll call Western Union!"

Great stories have powerful themes, but they're told in an entertaining way. A good analogy is trying to sweeten a glass of ice tea. Mix regular sugar and it will sink to the bottom, making it bitter except for the bottom, which will be too sweet. Try it with Equal, and the tea will be sweet throughout. Sweetness is your message, and it must be completely diluted to disappear into the beverage of entertainment.

Gerald DiPego: Sometimes you can have something you might call "pure entertainment," and theme is not very important. But if you want more than just entertainment, if you want to entertain and enrich, inspire, or say something about the world and the human condition, then you have to think about what you want to say in order to subtly weave it through the story.

Amy Holden Jones: I write because I have something to say. Too many people want to be screenwriters but they have nothing to say, so all they can do is reference other movies.

Eric Roth: I think everything you write should reflect your theme. It's the first thing I think of and everything plays off of that. If your theme is "loneliness," for example, you try to show what makes these people lonely, how it affects them, how they behave in the world because of it. Whether it's intentional or unintentional, I think every story says something. You can have a teen comedy like *American Pie*, which says something about coming of age, or an action piece like *The Terminator*, which is more profound than most people would give it credit, that explores the whole idea of how you can undo history, amid its entertaining sequences.

Michael Schiffer: Whenever possible, I'd like to think my audience is smart, and I like to write not to the lowest denominator, but to respect my audience and think, "Wouldn't it be great to go to movies and see smart people talking about smart stuff?" So I try to write something that will flatter the intellect of my audience and be as meaningful as I can make it, while simultaneously entertaining them and sweeping them into the story.

62. Knowing What Makes a Great Story

*Tell me a story! Because without a story, you are merely using words
to prove you can string them together in logical sentences.*
                                        —ANNE MCCAFFREY

What makes a story great is entirely a subjective opinion. Each of the more
than one hundred screenwriting books has its own definition, though most
of them really say the same thing. Some tell the novice that great stories are
all about structure, with a clear beginning, middle, and end. Others teach
you that it's interesting characters doing unexpected things against clear and
compelling conflicts. Still others maintain that to make it in Hollywood you
need a high-concept, commercial idea. But I believe they all agree, some
more than others, that at their core all great stories must *move* an audience
or a reader in some way.

Ron Bass: What makes a great story is the level of your response to it.
Great stories make me feel in a way that's deep, original, and enjoyable,
and they stay with me.

Steven DeSouza: A great story is a delicate balance between foreshad-
owing and thwarting the audience's expectations. You get the audience to
anticipate a certain thing, and sometimes you deliver it, and sometimes you
take a different route. I'm also a firm believer in the three-act structure and
all the Aristotelian techniques that are part of any good story, like rising
tension and conflict. But basically, it's about giving the audience what it
expects, but in an unexpected way. Surprises and twists go a long way.

Leslie Dixon: To me, it's simply just wanting to know what will happen
next, all the way through. My husband was once a camp counselor where
he learned how to tell stories by the campfire. You learn quickly how to keep
the campers' attention, like throwing in a twist here and there and making
them wonder what will happen. All too often, writers never put themselves
in the position of the audience going, "This is boring the crap out of me."
They leave that to the reader who just tosses the script in the recycling bin.

Akiva Goldsman: What makes a great story is a resonance, and its ability,
through the vibration that occurs between reader and object, to transport
the reader from their life, and upon their return, give them some feeling
that they know their life better, that there is some relationship to that
which is common in human experience. This is why reading and watching

movies, when they work, is wonderful. By going away, you come back richer by the alchemy of art. You're transformed into someone who has a firsthand understanding of things that were really alien to you, and you're given a newer understanding of your own experience.

Amy Holden Jones: A great story takes me to a particular environment and introduces me to characters who face seemingly insurmountable obstacles and find ways to surmount these obstacles in a surprising matter. Humor helps a lot. Basically, anything that entertains me.

Nicholas Kazan: You have no idea what happens next, you're continually surprised, you're satisfied by the surprises, and ultimately, the pleasures of the narrative resonate with deeper themes.

Scott Rosenberg: I have to be invested in the characters. To me, the greatest action movie ever made is *Die Hard,* not because of all the stuff exploding, but because every time they cut back to Bonnie Bedelia's face, she knows that it's her crazy husband who's doing everything he can to save her. It was this connection between the two characters that made me care. Another film where you care about the relationship is *48 Hours.* With all the other ones, who cares? I despised the movies *Independence Day* and *Godzilla* and *Volcano.* I don't care what you do technically. If I don't care about the characters, I just don't care, period.

Eric Roth: Even though I think it's the weakest part of my writing, to me the exciting thing about a story is that it takes you to some place you've never been before. And it's got to follow dramatic rules, even if it's more incidental than the traditional kind of story.

Michael Schiffer: Nobody really knows until it's all there. For me, a great story, whether a comedy or tragedy, is an authentic cauldron for which there is no psychological escape for the hero. Stories often leak on all sides. They are so poorly constructed that there are a million ways they don't hold up. But when something is locked down tight, there's no way out and the stakes are real.

Tom Schulman: In the end, it's about some deep connection to something profound in us, touching us in some deep emotional way.

Ed Solomon: A great story is one that doesn't bore me, that makes me forget I'm sitting there, listening to a story, or that makes me lose track of the fact that I'm in a movie theater, watching a movie.

CHAPTER 13
Screenwriting Basics

63. Developing an Innate Sense of Drama and Conflict

All drama is conflict. Without conflict, you have no action. Without action, you have no character. Without character, you have no story. And without story, you ain't got no screenplay.
—SYD FIELD

This habit should also be obvious, as it's taught by every book and seminar on the craft. But I'm still astonished by how many scripts and pitches from beginning writers, with otherwise interesting elements, characters, or settings, simply fail on this issue alone, either because there's a complete lack of conflict, or not enough of it to warrant audience interest.

At its simplest, a story is about a hero we root for to achieve a goal despite obstacles standing in his way. Drama and conflict come from the obstacles. Without them, it wouldn't be a story. Conflict is what heightens interest from an audience and charges the air with tension by transforming boring events into compelling moments. It's what audiences want in a story, even though in real life, we try to avoid conflict and live as peaceful and conflict-free a life as possible. Then again, stories are not real life. As Alfred Hitchcock said, "Drama is life with all the boring parts cut out." And it doesn't matter what your main character wants to accomplish by the end of the story. What's crucial is that it's important to them, not easy to get, and that there are many obstacles along the way. "What do my characters want?" and "What's stopping them from getting it?" are two important questions you should ask yourself in thinking about conflict. Otherwise, what's the point in sitting in a dark theater for two hours?

Leslie Dixon: Conflict is simply having characters not get what they want.

Michael Schiffer: Good drama requires obstacles along the way, and if a section is very flat, one of the things a writer can ask is, "This is too easy for them. What could happen to make it absolutely difficult, painful, agonizing, impossible?" If you have a good story that goes from A to B, ask yourself what obstacles would make the journey from A to B more exciting and interesting to watch. The more legitimate and difficult the hindrance, and the more the characters care about reaching their goal, the more exciting the story.

Tom Schulman: Whenever I'm writing and my character gets happy, or everybody agrees with each other, I have a problem. I can only spend a couple of pages at that stage before I throw in some kind of conflict. You can spend a lot of time developing characters, but unless they come into conflict that will test them, there's nothing interesting happening.

Robin Swicord: You don't learn how to write a screenplay by just reading screenplays and watching. It's about developing the kind of mind that sees and makes drama. You can do this in a kind of holistic way by reading history and theology and psychology, reading great fiction and poetry, and plays. You develop an eye for the structures of everything and look for the patterns that help you become a dramatist.

64. Raising the Stakes

*I would never write about someone who
was not at the end of his rope.*
—STANLEY ELKIN

It is equally important for the conflict to escalate. The stakes must get higher and higher. This is another common element where most scripts fail. Something important must be at risk for someone. It's an even more interesting story if the characters are desperate to get something and really afraid of not getting it. This escalation is why readers read to the end of a story completely engaged in the drama of whether the character will accomplish the goal or not. Ask yourself what's at stake if the hero doesn't accomplish his goals? Usually, most stories are about one or more of the basic human needs being at stake for the hero. As outlined by psychologist Abraham Maslow, they are the things that drive us, that we need, and that, if unattained, cause us unhappiness. They include survival and safety (most summer blockbusters about saving the world, or thrillers), love (romantic comedies and love stories), belonging and self-respect (coming of age, or underdog stories), and the need to know and understand (mysteries), among others. Good stories are about raising the emotional stakes as the characters head for a crisis. This is important because if they aren't moved enough by the stakes to engage in all this conflict, how can you expect an audience to care?

Gerald DiPego: Whenever someone asks me to read a script, or I'm developing my own, I always ask myself, "What's at stake here?" If you lose sight of that, you'll eventually lose your audience. And not only do you need to know what's at stake, but it has to rise, things have to get worse during the course of your story. If you're in the middle in the story and everyone is having a great time with no conflict anywhere, how can you expect an audience to be involved?

Michael Schiffer: There are very few movies where nothing happens. You want the stakes, as the hero perceives them, to be as high as possible. The kind of movie usually defines the kind of stakes. For instance, in an action adventure, the stakes are physical jeopardy, or in a movie like *American Beauty*, the stakes are psychological, the survival of the spirit. Even in a comedy, the stakes are high and serious to the characters but funny to the audience. You want your characters to be at risk and have things of great importance to them to be at stake.

65. Realizing the Importance of Characters

The whole thing is, you've got to make
them care about somebody.
—FRANK CAPRA

All great movies are about characters trying to solve a problem. Look at the American Film Institute's list of the top 100 movies of all time and see how many of these classic films are character-driven. Well over 90 percent. What does it tell you? That you should only write character-driven screenplays? Not necessarily. Remember, only write what excites you. However, you have to understand (again, an obvious but often neglected element) that characters are the fuel that makes any story's engine run. Without them, a story could not be called a story. The questions you must ask when you develop your characters, then, should be these: (1) "Why will the audience care about them? (2) "Do they seem real?" and most important, (3) "Can the audience identify with my hero?" Psychologists call this "empathy," the tendency of human beings to feel themselves part of a situation portrayed before them. Used in connection with the relationship between audience and film, empathy means the sense of identification that the audience feels with the situations and characters on the screen. The more fully audiences can identify with the thoughts, emotions, and actions of screen characters, the better they will like the film.

Another reason why you should focus on characters more than anything: It's harder to get a movie made today, and because most movies get the green light when stars decide they want to make them, you should think about creating characters that actors would want to play.

Ron Bass: It's not surprising to hear a writer say that characters are important, and it's advantageous that they be complex and fully realized characters that the audience can care about and be intrigued by; it's not a new statement. But to me, there's no distinction between story and character, because most stories are about what happens between people. If the story is about someone climbing a mountain or facing some physical hazard alone, then that's different, but in most of the stories that I see, that I write, that I care about, story is what happens as characters interact, so character is story.

Gerald DiPego: Let's say you have an idea that starts out like, "I just thought of a great new way to rob a bank. I'm going to build a movie around that." If you don't throw your focus on who these people are, what their dreams and demons are, you will be on the road to a neat idea that ends up empty, because that's who's sitting in the audience—people. If you can connect them to your characters in a meaningful way, then the audience will have a complete experience with your film, and they'll still appreciate all the stunts, clever twists, and dialogue while operating on a deeper level, because they care about your characters.

Jim Kouf: Your characters have to be so interesting and compelling you can't wait to get an actor attached. After all, why do people sit through certain movies? Because the dialogue is great, and something about the characters makes you love them or hate them. It's just like life. Why do you sit with a few people and have a conversation, and other people, you decline when they invite you to dinner?

Tom Schulman: Aristotle was right. Plot determines who your characters are. But once you've figured out who your characters are, then they become more important than the plot. Without characters, nobody cares about the story. I always try to drive my characters toward a story.

66. Reading Your Dialogue Out Loud

If you read your work out loud, it helps to know what's bad.
—GARRISON KEILLOR

Professor Paul Lucey, in his book *Story Sense,* shares an anecdote about learning a valuable lesson on dialogue from his agent, who asked him to fan the pages of one of his scripts and notice anything unusual. Lucey noticed long speeches in brick-sized blocks of text. Then his agent asked him to fan the pages of an award-winning script. This time Lucey noticed the pages were white and airy, because the speeches used only a line or two of dialogue. The lesson? Use as little dialogue as possible. Audiences pay to see moving pictures, not illustrated radio.

The best dialogue is not that which just informs or pushes the plot forward or even reveals character, which are all things that it's supposed to do. The most memorable dialogue, in addition to revealing what people are *not* saying (subtext, off-the-nose dialogue), is dialogue that pushes people's buttons and causes an emotional reaction, whether it's to hurt another character, love them, hate them, or know them. Think about your favorite lines of dialogue and see if most of them fit this criterion. We remember great movie lines because of the feelings they evoked in the characters, and ultimately, in us, "You're not too smart—are you? I like that in a man" (Lawrence Kasdan, *Body Heat*). "I'm having an old friend for dinner" (Ted Tally, *Silence of the Lambs*). "Frankly, my dear, I don't give a damn" (Sidney Howard, *Gone with the Wind*).

Reading your dialogue out loud is a useful habit to test it. You'll be amazed at the difference between reading it and hearing it. You will not only hear what your lines sound like to other people but also see if the character's uniqueness comes through in that person's speech. Each of your characters should sound uniquely himself and not, as is most often the case, like the author.

Akiva Goldsman: Sometimes, I do read my dialogue out loud, especially when I'm brain-fried. It's a good way to test it, although I'm glad no one is ever around to see this. Ultimately, I've been really lucky to be on sets, so I often get to hear my dialogue spoken by professional actors. This never stops being a thrill.

Ed Solomon: Most people feel a great joy when they write something quickly, because they are unable to distinguish between the elation of transcribing their thoughts onto the page and the joy that comes from actually organizing thoughts in a way that will have some meaning for someone else. Most of the time, it's not the transcription of ideas that's meaningful; it's the way you organize these ideas that creates interesting substance and storytelling for the people. Sometimes, we feel something is great because it felt great to write it. Sometimes it's valuable to have a reading of your script, and listen to it with other people in the room. Further, if you're really serious about it, stage a few scenes from it, and direct them. Put yourself through what would seem like a ridiculous exercise. But it's a good way to get a feeling of how a scene really works. Those of us who've had movies made have had the benefit of seeing how some things work and others don't. Sometimes it's really painful to hear your words read.

Robin Swicord: I read my dialogue out loud all the time. That's how you know if someone would really say something. If you can't say it, cut it.

CHAPTER 14
The Most Important Audience

67. Realizing the Reader Is Your First Audience

It isn't what happens to people on a page—it's what happens to a reader in his heart and mind.
—GORDON LISH

Another important habit in the "obvious but not really" family is to understand that someone—a reader, assistant, agent, studio exec, producer, director, or actor—will read your script. And because there are so many scripts and so little time to read them, these readers want to like what they read. But more than anything, they want to be surprised and entertained. So, as you polish your latest draft, you must view the reader as an active participant in your writing process. Obvious, you say? Considering how many typos, spelling and grammatical mistakes, dense descriptions, bloated dialogue, and formatting errors I've seen in more than half the scripts I've read, I'd say this is an important habit to develop. Your script won't go anywhere if it doesn't impress the reader first.

Ron Bass: You definitely write a script knowing someone is going to read it. I'm probably more conscious than most writers of the prose descriptions between dialogue. It's something I spend a lot of time and care on because I feel that's when I communicate intent to the reader, who may be the studio executive, the director, or the actress. When it's not clear, I want them to know what my characters are thinking and feeling between the lines, because you can't see the actor performing. You're only reading the words. And without eliminating all ambiguity and irony in the scene, what you say between the lines helps the reader get the idea and the feeling of the atmosphere of what's going on, compensating for the fact that you're not watching the movie.

Steven DeSouza: The best piece of advice I got is "You've got to get them in the first 10 pages." You must keep in mind that you're always writing for the reader first, not a movie audience that will see the collaboration of 200 people a year later. Also, you learn over time to be less camera-happy in describing all the camera angles. I wince reading my early stuff—I'm actually recommending lenses!

Gerald DiPego: If you write with a sense that another artist is your audience, like "I'm writing it for the director, and he'll get it," you're fooling yourself, because your script is a selling tool. You have to think in terms of the reader, take them by the hand and walk them through your story.

Scott Rosenberg: Make it fun for me. I've started taking this novelistic approach that William Goldman invented and Shane Black popularized, which is a way of talking to the reader in a fun way. But you have to earn that. Don't wink at me if you haven't deserved it. I do it all the time because I know directors, producers, development execs, agents, and actors read like 30 scripts a week, so you have to make it fun for them. It's only going to set you apart.

Tom Schulman: I simply focus on making the story as interesting and exciting as possible, which includes the reader, who I imagine is actually watching the movie and I'm just describing on the page what they see. So I don't differentiate between reader and viewer.

Ed Solomon: Be careful, because the more you write a script like a final film, the more difficult it is for readers and studio executives to conceive of it as a film. What you get from a film when you watch it is a different experience than when you read a script. Edited film has a certain meaning when you watch it. The closer you get to writing a final film, the more difficult it will be to get it by the decision makers, because their gut feeling when they read the script is often different from the literal filmic translation. It is not always as satisfying when it is made into a movie. The same works the other way. If you took a great movie and transcribed it from the screen to a script and then tried to sell it to a studio executive, it wouldn't be as satisfying a visceral experience.

68. Avoiding Sin Number One: Being Dull

No one ever sold anybody anything
by boring them to death.

—DAVID OGILVY

You may think I'm repeating myself here. But whereas the previous habit of thinking of your reader is more about presenting a professional script and a positive reading experience, this habit covers a wider arena, encompassing not only the entertainment and emotional experience of an audience, but also an attitude in general. This habit originally was part of the pitching section in the next chapter (as in never being dull in the room), but was moved here when I realized that, for aspiring writers, it was more important for it to be included in the writing of a script, because most beginning writers fail to realize that what's interesting to them may be dull for a mass audience. Every time you sit down to write, you should be afraid of losing the reader at any moment. The worst sin in Hollywood is for the reader of a script or the audience of a film to say, "So what?" Again, I can't tell you how often I have thought these two words. No reader recommends a boring script, no executive green-lights a boring movie (unless, of course, a major star wants to make it) and no audience pays $8.50 to be bored for two hours. To paraphrase playwright William Gibson, "The first business of the screenwriter is to keep the audience from walking out."

Ron Bass: Has anyone ever advised writers to be dull? I'm sure most writers think about avoiding that. Sure, it's getting harder to make something interesting, but it's where the ability of the writer comes in. You're always trying to write something that's entertaining, and if it's boring, then people won't pay money to see it and you definitely won't earn a living writing scripts. It begs the question of what it takes to make something interesting. Sometimes, people fall into a false distinction between being honest and selling out. They feel they have an important story and, somehow, the fact that it's dull is ennobling; it's the hallmark of telling the story realistically, and you aren't cheesing it up with all the Hollywood tricks that people find entertaining, like extraneous suspense, action, comedy, or conflict. You aren't pandering to people's desire to be entertained; you are being honorable. You hear people say that, and it's bull. It's not a mark of nobility or integrity if your story is not interesting to people and they don't want to watch it. You can still write it for yourself and show it to anyone who wants to read it, but I don't think there's anything inherently great in the fact that a story is dull. There are fascinating and compelling stories in every genre imaginable that have been told by good storytellers. There's no kind of story that is beyond making it interesting if you're a good enough writer to make it interesting. And since you're not just writing for yourself, but trying to make a living to have your stories heard by others, then not being dull seems to be a crucial requisite that has nothing to do with selling out.

Jim Kouf: No one wants to sit through a dull movie, and no one in Hollywood wants to read a dull script. I write to entertain. I want to keep people turning the page, whatever it takes, so that they don't put the script down. I just want to tell a good story in the best possible way, and have someone become committed to the material based on the writing. The characters have to come alive. It's not real life we're putting down. This is heightened reality; people are a lot wittier, funnier, and larger than they are in real life.

Michael Schiffer: It's really cool if your characters are among the most vivid people you've ever known. We're not that vivid and colorful every minute of our lives. So what I try to do in successive drafts, once the story is sketched in, is wonder with each line of dialogue, "Is this the most interesting, vivid, and colorful way to say this? How can I boost this up so that the people I'm watching are people I wish I encountered every day in my life?" To do that you have to constantly question every line and every character and intensify every single boring moment in your script. Ask yourself, "Would I want to be at a dinner party with this person? Good guys or bad guys, are they interesting enough to be in my life?" If they're not, make them more interesting. You owe your audience the gift of good company.

Tom Schulman: Imagination and originality are crucial traits everyone is looking for in a writer because if someone has already seen what you've written, chances are they'll be bored by it. So when you conceive your story, characters, and plot elements, the key question is, "Is this something I've seen before?" and if so, you need to find an original approach to the material.

69. Evoking an Emotional Response

Find what gave you emotion; what the action was that
gave you excitement. Then write it down making it clear
so that the reader can see it too.

—ERNEST HEMINGWAY

It's difficult to believe that the single most important element in any story, the most compelling reason why people go to the movies, read novels, watch television, and go to plays is often the one element missing from most beginners' scripts. And that is the experience of emotions. The power of any story lies in its ability to connect emotionally with the reader, and ultimately with a movie audience. This is the habit I feel strongest about. To me, the emotional experience is the key to a great script. It's the essential ingredient for which producers will pay screenwriters handsomely. But the overwhelming evidence from aspiring writers leads me to believe they *think* too much and *feel* too little when it comes to writing their scripts.

I clearly remember my thoughts after experiencing Roberto Benigni's *Life Is Beautiful*, as I later analyzed its power on the audience. I realized I had just experienced the complete range of emotions, from laughter to sadness to wonder to suspense, love, anger, and so on. This is what we must do as storytellers. This is the job we get paid for. Although it could be argued that evoking emotions is the core of artistic talent and therefore cannot be taught (and I agree), this habit can be kept in mind as you write the script, so that you are thinking about it and asking questions like, "What does my character feel at this moment, and how can I show this so that an audience may be moved?" By answering these questions you will keep emotional content in the forefront of your script's action. I don't mean you must pander to the audience and manipulate them. But you must know what the characters feel, and show that. You don't state what emotions a character is experiencing; rather, you describe the situation that causes a particular emotion and let the audience feel that emotion. In other words, try to envision your words on paper as moments experienced in a darkened theater.

A quick perusal of newspaper ads for today's movies yielded the following descriptions from critics, which are promises of what an audience will feel by watching the movie: "Pulse-pounding, nail-biting, tension and excitement, seat-grabbing, electrifying, highly affecting, mesmerizing, powerfully seductive, provocative and intense, superbly gripping, exuberantly funny, fascinating, intriguing, harrowing, spellbinding, stunning, packs an emotional wallop, hugely satisfying, shriek-worthy suspense, ingenious plot-twists, heart-stopping, nerve-freezing terror, grabs you and won't let go, unrelenting in its purpose to thrill, challenge, and charm."

Can your script match these promises to a reader? Without a thorough commitment to developing this habit—in other words, writing script after script until you're able to evoke strong emotions in a reader—marketing your screenplays will be a futile endeavor.

Ron Bass: There's a bit of a cast to this idea that you're playing to the audience's response and you're thinking more about how the audience will respond than what your characters are feeling, like "This will make them cry; I think I'll write it to cause tears in the audience." This is something you never do. What you are doing is feeling the emotions that your characters are feeling, and finding the best way to express those emotions in the most powerfully felt, truthful, effective, moving way to yourself. If it moves *you* when you read it, when you think of it, when you say it, then you just have to hope it will move other people. So it's more about focusing on the emotional response of your characters to each other and your own emotional response to those characters than the emotional response of your audience. That's where the exchange is happening: between the characters with each other, and between you and your characters.

Gerald DiPego: Most movies that fail do so because they don't reach inside the audience. They feel empty because they're written from the outside and they don't ask you to invest anything or care about the characters, so it's not a complete experience.

Eric Roth: The drama of the story certainly dictates what's emotional, and you try to make your characters act in such a human way that's recognizable by an audience, and therefore universally understood. Even in the most outlandish situations, sometimes it is the little human touches that bring everyone together. If it makes me feel something when I write it, then I'm hoping that I'm translating that to the audience. For me, it's about setup and payoff. I try to set things up so that they pay off in a way I hope evokes a strong emotional reaction.

Michael Schiffer: Whether it's comedy or drama, our entire goal as writers is to make our audience respond to the emotions of the characters by pulling them through terrible situations that reflect their own conflicts. When an audience connects, they have a cathartic reaction. Their emotions are purged, because they all have stress and pain in their lives. When they can identify with actors who go through these things and triumph, they feel renewed and full of hope. It then becomes a communal experience that makes an audience know we all share a common bond.

Tom Schulman: All you try to do is involve an audience in the drama of other people's lives—their relationships, their obsessions, who they are, where they are—and if they're identifiable and they start out in conflict, theoretically, the audience should be hooked on that roller coaster. So emotion should be the result of what you've set up, not the other way around.

Robin Swicord: A great story needs to have some propelling forces, usually the great human emotions, because sometimes, a story can be very interesting on an informational level but what will make it into a drama is the emotional gravitational pull of the situation. What we do as an audience is enter the world of the protagonist and wonder what this story will allow us to feel. It's the big emotions that draw us into drama.

•   •   •

If you've studied and mastered all the habits up to now and written a great script, don't even bother with the next chapter on marketing. Why? Because if you truly have a great screenplay, you could literally drop it in a Beverly Hills park and it will get made. But since the odds are that your script is not perfect, let's find out how you can market your skills while writing your next script. You'd better be writing your next script! If not, go back to Chapter 2 and start over. You shouldn't even bother with marketing until you have at least three quality scripts.

PART V
Marketing

It's Not Who You Know,
It's Your Writing

The most important part in filmmaking is played by the writers. We must do everything in our power to keep them from finding out.

—IRVING THALBERG

CHAPTER 15
The Hollywood System

Because there is no one way to break in as a screenwriter, the habits presented in this chapter will attempt to give an overview of the industry and how aspiring writers may behave when marketing their writing services. Some habits will be controversial; they may go against the accepted, universal thought expounded by established "experts." But overall, you'll see that these are commonsense habits, whether they debunk or confirm the advice you've heard a thousand times from various sources.

70. Understanding the Rules of the Game

There are fewer stars for writers on the Hollywood
Walk of Fame than there are for animals.
—ALJEAN HARMETZ

Aspiring writers are generally sheltered from the realities of the industry; all they know from entertainment news sources are the "glamorous" articles and the sound bites about projects sold, dollar amounts, and players involved. It's only after selling something and being thrown into the system that they discover the realities they must adapt to.

First, you have to understand that, although a good screenplay is the hottest commodity in the industry, people in this business who don't know you aren't going to be impressed by the fact that you actually wrote one. It's an interesting paradox that writers are essential to the survival of the industry and yet are undervalued. This is an industry where your work is trashed, where you get rewritten, where you're fired without knowing it, where a stable of lawyers work diligently to make sure your payments are delayed, and so on. Until you sell a script, or at the very least win a major contest or are represented by a legitimate agency, you don't exist. If executives think your product will advance their career, they'll like you. If they don't, they'll ignore you. Remember the shock Robin Swicord experienced when she saw just how many scripts there were on just one executive's office shelves? Now multiply this by the number of offices in town and you'll only get the number of *current* scripts awaiting a decision. Based on Writers Guild statistics, you could safely estimate that, not including assignments, about 45,000 spec screenplays are written and registered every year. If you can't handle these inconsistencies psychologically, you won't make it too far.

Second, as many of you may already know, and at the risk of alienating sensitive artists, Hollywood only exists to make money. The industry is basically a collection of profit-minded megacorporations whose main product is the motion picture and who invest a lot of money to produce, distribute, and ultimately screen it in theaters and on television. Because this is more a business than an art gallery, no one spends $80 million on a piece of art without expecting in return to recoup all costs and make a profit in order to make more films.

Third, to justify their salaries, in addition to finding great material and attaching writers to it, most development executives believe they must change a script, even when it doesn't need any changing. They can't subscribe to the "if it ain't broke, don't fix it" theory. For development executives, it has to be "if it ain't broke, break it," and that's why the process you enter as soon as you sell a script is called "Development Hell." As writer John Gregory Dunne says, "writers are used and discarded like so many wads of Kleenex," until a star or a director becomes attached, and then it's a go-picture.

Obviously, I'm not saying this is the way it should be, just that it's the way it is, and you have to sink or swim in these shark-infested waters. There's an old joke of a man who wanted to win the lottery so bad he started praying to God that He let him win just once. And he prayed and prayed and prayed, but he just couldn't win. Until an exasperated God finally replied to the man, "Listen, son, help me out here . . . at least buy a ticket." Know how to play by the rules before you can break them. For more on the realities of being a screenwriter in Hollywood, see Habit 11.

Steven DeSouza: It's always the unexpected stuff that works, the one that breaks the rules, that is contrary to what "they" say. I think the biggest mistake studio executives make is not going to the movies enough in a movie theater *with an audience.* If you want to know what audiences want, what they like, go to the movies with an audience. You may see a lousy movie, but there's always one place in it where all of a sudden, the audience is on the edge of their seat. This may be a little hint of what your movie should be. Because things change. The audience is getting smarter and smarter and more savvy to movies in general, and so we have to be as sophisticated. If you can't surprise yourself, you won't surprise an audience. There are so many movies that get into the theaters, and you can just sit there and say this is borrowed from this movie; this is borrowed from that movie; this is one-third *Lethal Weapon,* one-third *Die Hard,* and one-third boredom. If you want inspiration, look at an old picture where Cagney and Bogart were the buddies. A 50-year-old picture might be a better inspiration for you than last week's copy of a copy of a copy of *Beverly Hills Cop.*

Nicholas Kazan: What you must understand about studio executives is that their prime job isn't to get your script made, but to keep their job. That's what they think about all the time, which means that, like so many people in our society, they're always thinking, "Can I use this person, and if so, how?" If you have a script that's kind of good, they can't take the chance. But if it's good enough, and they like you personally, they may take the chance to work with you and try to make it really good. The last thing they want to do, if you're an unknown writer, is walk into their boss's office and say, "this script is really good," and have their boss read it, and say, "this script is terrible, what were you thinking?" That happens three times and they're out of a job. So they only want to walk in with nothing less than a brilliant script that will make them look good. A good script is not good enough. You need a really great script with a subject that's idiosyncratic. But if you write a great script, and it's a "cop buddy" movie, quality may not be enough, because there are so many similar scripts. Another important thing to know is that executives are incredibly overworked. Between story meetings, and scripts they have to read, they need to make hundreds of phone calls a day. They don't have time to focus. It's a miracle they can work this hard and this long with any degree of efficiency. You can't expect to stay in their minds, especially if you're an unknown.

Scott Rosenberg: In the studio system, everyone's job is to say "no." Everyone is a gatekeeper, guarding the palace from the mobs out there. But the fact is that all anyone really wants to do is say "yes." Everyone's looking for that amazing project, and when there's an amazing script, everybody in town hears about it. I remember when *The Usual Suspects* was making the rounds. I heard about it. Everyone pricks up their ears when there's a hot new writer in town. The reality is all you need to do is write a good script. It's that easy. I promise you it is. I know it sounds so glib, but it's a reality. I know because most of my friends are the ones dying for great material. When I first came out here, I wasn't trying to push my script. I was just too busy to write because I was embarrassed. Everyone I met was a would-be screenwriter. I remember one time, I was invited to dinner at this executive's house, and he asked me what I wanted to do, and I said I wanted to be a screenwriter. He said, "My landscaper wants to be a screenwriter. And you see that guy over there? That's José, my gardener. He wants to be a screenwriter. And see that guy who's doing my pool? He wants to be a screenwriter and over there, that's my wife, Suzy. She wants to be a screenwriter." I was so embarrassed that from then on, when asked, I'd tell people I hunt Nazis. Anything to not be a screenwriter.

Ed Solomon: It's a hard world because there's a lot of duplicity. People say one thing and mean another. They use flattery as a kind of lubricant and it works because we are highly sensitive to it. We tend to blend people's opinions of our work with opinions of us. But most of the time they don't mean it, so we find ourselves confused. We don't really know what's true anymore.

Robin Swicord: My great disappointment was not understanding how unimportant the studio system of "perfecting" a screenplay really was. A lot of the so-called "development" is really about buying time for the studio. It's more about trying this or trying that. They don't always view the writers as the dramatic experts in the room, and that's a mistake because you end up having really good writers taking notes from people who don't know what they're talking about. So it was really a surprise to me that they would assemble these writers, who have been doing nothing for a decade except writing, and not listen to what they had to say, and then excuse them from the room when it came time to do the real work of casting, shooting the movie, editing, and so forth. It would be like asking I. M. Pei to design a building and when the blueprints are first laid out on the table fire him and bring in various subcontractors to make decisions about the building. It's amazing to me that this process still goes on the way it does. It's not a system that works to make good movies.

71. Learning the Business

In Hollywood, information is power. To make it in the entertainment industry, you'll have to know what's happening—to whom, where, when, how, and why. On a global basis.
—LINDA BUZZELL, *HOW TO MAKE IT IN HOLLYWOOD*

Quick! Can you name the heads of every studio in town? How about the directors of development at the major production companies? If not, you've got some studying to do. You need to know who the players are— the agents, directors, executives, producers, screenwriters (you now know 14 of them), where they are and what they like, and what movies they're associated with. This is the time to put on your businessperson cap and learn the market. Read as much as you can. Read the trades but not every day, or you'll become jaded and frustrated with the feeling that everyone is working except you. Several mainstream magazines publish a list of the 100 most powerful people in Hollywood every year. Make a trip to the library, where there are plenty of great books on the film industry and biographies of famous players. Do some Web surfing. Most studios and film production companies have gone digital and have informative Web sites. Television can be a good way. You can learn a lot watching shows like *Entertainment Tonight* and *Access Hollywood*. There are many films about the film industry. For example, some recent ones include *The Player, Get Shorty, Swimming with Sharks, The Big Picture, Bowfinger,* and *The Muse*. A few classics include *Sunset Boulevard* and *The Bad and the Beautiful*. And of course, as the best way to learn something is to be immersed in it, getting a job in the industry would be valuable.

Eric Roth: It's very helpful to know, as best you can, who holds the power and who doesn't. It's always better to work with someone who can say "yes" than someone who can't. Try to work with those who are highest at the studio, or with people who have some say over it when it's done. You'd rather work for someone who's more successful than not. But there are no rules. Don't misunderstand me; I'm not that Machiavellian. But there's a certain kind of material that appeals to a certain kind of executive, so you have to know these things. And you get to know this by being in this town a lot, or reading the trades, or paying attention to who's doing what. You sort of get a smell for what the market will do or not do.

Robin Swicord: You have to understand how the business works. Sometimes, I'm so mystified I can't believe this is a business. You have to understand that the tide comes in and the tide goes out. There's a constant shift of personalities. Some studios are more stable than others, and you have to note which ones are which. You learn this by picking up what my husband calls the "sports pages of the industry," either *Variety* or *The Hollywood Reporter*. The problem with reading the trades is that a lot of information is planted by publicists, so it seems everyone but you is making a big deal somewhere or they're associated with some wonderful project that's just been announced. You can't help but get into a state of envy. It's good to pick up the trades every now and then but not every day. Another way to learn is by talking to your agent or lawyer, or by going through horrendous experiences on projects, like one studio telling me, "We want to write a musical. We believe that musicals could be back in and Cher wants to be in a musical and if you can write the screenplay in six weeks and give blood every single day at our blood bank, you can be the lucky writer who writes a musical for Cher." What I wanted to know was, "Does Cher know she wants to do a musical? Has anyone talked to Cher? Let me talk to Cher's agents before I get excited." Check out the sources on everything that's brought to you, because you know you're the only one who'll do the hard work for the longest time. All these other people won't even have a job or get a paycheck until you say, "Yes, I'll write the script." So they'd better be ready to back it up, have the rights squared away if it's a book, let me have a reasonable period of time to write the script, or have a good enough reputation that agents won't run away from them. Always make sure you put yourself into the best possible environment.

CHAPTER 16
Networking

72. Living in Los Angeles

*Life is like a fishing trip—if you want to catch a big fish,
you've got to go where the big fish are.*
—OLD HOLLYWOOD SAYING, QUOTED BY PETER MILLER

This is one of the most debated topics among aspiring writers. Although a script can be written anywhere, making the necessary contacts to have it read can be difficult outside of Los Angeles. Human contacts are important. It's all about meeting people and having access to the buyers. Agents can represent out-of-town writers, but when they set up meetings all over town, it can become a logistical nightmare for both producers and writers. But aspiring writers should only move here after they've written a great script, preferably three to five representative samples of their abilities. All the screenwriters featured here live in Los Angeles. Sure, they may have other homes they escape to whenever they can, but most of the time, they're in Los Angeles because that's where business is conducted. So what do you do if you don't want to move? Don't bother querying agents and producers. Trust me when I say out-of-town writers are perceived as amateurs, especially when they send a query letter. Instead, I'd submit my very best sample to film festivals and screenwriting competitions. If you win a major contest, you'll be approached by agents and producers, and maybe flown into town for meetings. If you don't even place in the quarter-finals or above competing with substandard scripts, what makes you think you'll have a chance among the thousands of professional ones from major agencies making the Hollywood rounds?

Ron Bass: As a beginner, and even as an established professional, I think it's very useful, because of the meetings you have to take, and generally interacting with the people you'll be collaborating with. There's just so much that can be done over the phone, and I think it's harder if you're not in Los Angeles.

Jim Kouf: You've got to know somebody who knows somebody and you've got to be here. You can't do it from out of town. If you want to be in movies, in the business, you've got be in L.A. I mean I'm not here because I love it here. I escape to Montana as often as I can. But there's a certain amount of time that I have to be here. I've got to meet with them, see them face-to-face; you always have to work at being employed. That's a tougher job than writing.

Michael Schiffer: There are many advantages to living here, although you don't have to. You can learn an awful lot about moviemaking, and therefore screenwriting. You can take acting classes, meet other young writers, and share each other's scripts. I don't know where else, except New York, you'll find a higher concentration of creative people making this their life's work. And in the business, it helps to take meeting after meeting, because you have to knock on a lot of doors before you can find someone who wants to hire you, and it's harder to imagine working with someone from Minnesota.

Tom Schulman: You certainly don't *want* to live here if you're writing. But as far as marketing, there are only two places where scripts are bought, and that's primarily Los Angeles, and to a lesser degree, New York. So, unless you know someone in Los Angeles, it's just common sense to be here so that you can make the kinds of contacts that will help sell your scripts.

73. Knowing the Importance of Relationships

*Knowledgeable people know facts. Successful and
prosperous people know people.*
—JOHN DEMARTINI

The road to success for many screenwriters, in addition to well-crafted writing, has come through a network of supporters, mentors, friends, advocates, and champions of their work. It is well known that Hollywood is an industry that runs on relationships. As a result, many aspiring writers believe they must focus on making them. What they don't realize is that, when it comes to writers, it's their writing samples that get them assignments, not the fact they happened to be seen at a Hollywood party (see next habit). Although networking isn't as crucial for writers as the quality of their scripts, it's still an important habit to cultivate in order to create a network of supports that will welcome and champion your work when it crosses their desks. Networking should be seen as sowing the seeds for win-win relationships. It's all about helping other people achieve their goals, who in turn will help you achieve yours. You win when they provide access to your material. They win when you supply them the great material they so desperately need.

Gerald DiPego: It's very important to create relationships within the industry, but I'm not very good at it. I was very shy when I started, but I tried to push through that. I came out here wanting to write industrial films as a day job, while I tried to sell a script or get hired to write features, so every time I called an industrial film producer to see what was out there, I would also ask if they knew someone on the feature side, and I did this until somebody said they knew someone who was looking for scripts.

Leslie Dixon: Many relationships came to me because my first produced script was a hit. When this happens everyone wants to take you out to dinner or take meetings, so I met a lot of people from the get-go. But I've never been a schmoozing relationship chaser. There are people who shamelessly do this, and some of them succeed. It's a very male trait. Women don't tend to act like Sammy Glick type people. But I have to say the writers that do it will have more success than the ones who sit at home like the hermit. I recommend it. It's a quality I wish I had more of, but I'm just too proud to start up faux friendships, saying to myself, "I bet my career would be better if I were best friends with Steven Spielberg." Your hustle should depend on how much money you banked away. If you have a family to support and the well runs dry, you have to be responsible for your career. You can't count on your agent to do everything. You have to combine quality work with exhausting networking. There are writers who write script after script, then go to all the parties they can, they're out pitching every five minutes; these writers will tend to be more successful than the writer who just writes one script a year, and never goes anywhere. On the other hand, there's a point where this much activity can cheapen your stock.

Akiva Goldsman: I was very unconnected in Hollywood, but I had a friend from college who was an assistant at ICM, so I sent my script to him, and he read it and gave me notes. This process went on for months, and at one point, it was just lying on his desk and this agent picked it up and read it. Next thing I know, I get a call that they'd like to represent me.

Nicholas Kazan: Writers are writers because they like to be by themselves. Your impulse as a writer is to sit in a room by yourself. If you have some social dynamic, make sure you indulge it because not only is it important to have friends as a human being, it also doesn't hurt your career. Other people want to work with people who are enjoyable, who listen and understand them, and who are fun to be around. It's very important to have friends and to know development people because they'll be more favorably inclined toward your script. All you need is someone who'll look forward to your script, which may be the 15th in a pile of 30. The only way to gain an edge, no matter how small, is to go on top of the pile, or be taken out and put aside to read first thing in the morning because the reader knows you. And you get this edge because you met someone at a party, or it's a friend of a friend or whatever. It's a small edge over the competition. I came to Los Angeles in 1976 with a group of friends and just hung out with the same people, who gradually became more successful, and through these people, I met more people. I was single and made all kinds of friends in the first five years I was here. But I didn't do it consciously or in a calculated move in order to network. Anything you do in a calculated way hurts you. If you don't make friends easily, I wouldn't try to network, because you won't make *real* friends. They'll see right through you. You can't pretend to like people you don't like in order to help your career.

Eric Roth: I think a lot of the work you get is from relationships. I've always had the sense that relationships were a key part of a career, because my parents were in the business and also because of the nature of who I am. I recognize that people would rather work with someone they enjoy being with than not. But even though I wasn't consciously trying to make them, I wasn't afraid of relationships, so they kind of happened. Being savvy in who to work with or not, and being a gambler, I have a sort of street sense and try to put myself in the best position, where I feel the work has the best chance of getting done. Writers only get a certain percentage of their screenplays produced, so you try to limit whatever makes it hardest to get things done. It's a sort of educated and calculated choice. If I have three attractive projects to choose from, and they're all equal, then I'll go with the one that has the best chance of getting made.

74. Understanding Our Writing Gets Us Work, Not Our Charm

It all starts on the page.
—STEVEN SPIELBERG

Up to now, we've seen many obvious habits that are often ignored by beginners. There is, however, one habit that beginning writers mistakenly overdevelop, often at the expense of quality material, and that is the belief that networking will make them successful writers. You've just heard from established screenwriters that it is important. But the key word is "established." In other words, established writers have a reputation preceding them. If you're a beginner, no amount of networking will sell your script or get you an assignment, at least in legitimate circles. It may get you read, which is useful if your material is up to par. If it isn't, which is more likely, you're shooting yourself in the foot and burning bridges with the potential buyers you have spent time schmoozing. You only have one chance to shine. The screenwriter is lucky to be the only element in the industry that doesn't need to network, because his writing has to speak for itself. Focus on raising the quality of your material instead of raising the thickness of your Rolodex.

Steven DeSouza: When I was a story editor, I shared a suite at Universal with a writer who was obsessed with "networking." His first draft would always be his last draft. He never had time to do the polishing because he just had to have lunch with this person who just got promoted to that studio position, and so on. My bulletin board would be a set of three-by-five cards with the latest story I was blocking out. His bulletin board was full of articles from the trades about all the people he knew who got promoted. There was an inverse proportion of the amount of time he spent working the town to the amount of work he got, whereas I just kept my nose to the grindstone. To this day, I still meet people who've been around as long as I have and I've never met them because I don't go out much; I write. Networking is important in order to find out about opportunities, but at the end of the day, it won't make you a better writer or enable you to sell a weak script.

Networking is not a guarantee for a career. It's a guarantee to get a lot of Christmas cards and some invitations to premieres. I think it's better to know someone who's directing a play in some little theater and who's looking for material for a workshop. Even if you're writing a movie, you get out there and tell them you've got what they're looking for.

Scott Rosenberg: Here's the thing about me: I'm absolutely the most social screenwriter alive. I don't say this to brag. I'm actually a little ashamed of it. I go to these Hollywood parties when I'm here and I look around, and there's not one screenwriter there except me. Do you know why most of my friends are the heads of studios and agents and managers and executives? Because all the other writers are home writing. I was never conscious of the networking game, because it's just my personality. But the reality is that no one has ever said, "I'm gonna do a Scott Rosenberg movie because I hung out with him at a party last night." It's all about the writing. I've been doing this for 10 years now and I've never gotten an assignment through someone I met at a party. The exposure is too high. Why would they do that? I network because I find it fun. It's not even networking for me. It's just going out and hanging with people I like. My charm is never going to get me a job. Some of the most brilliant writers out here are the most low-functioning socially. You can't stand to be in a room with them, but their work is just brilliant.

Ed Solomon: Relationships are crucial. However, how people go about having solid relationships is often misunderstood. People think that by networking they make better relationships. This is not the case. By networking, you get your name out more, but you also establish yourself on a subconscious level as someone who needs to network. You have to be careful about maintaining a kind of cachet for yourself that involves people perceiving you as someone who has something to offer them. Often, people who have a lot to offer are not always out trying to sell themselves. If networking to you is about gaining information and understanding what's out there, I guess it could be valuable. But if networking is about getting yourself out there to sell yourself, you'll come across as just that. In a way, you're already networking simply by existing in this business. Your scripts are always out there networking on your behalf. As a new writer, my agents always told me to get out and meet a lot of people. However, in legitimate circles, no one will meet you unless they've already read your material. Your writing always precedes you. It all comes down to writing a great script, or showing real talent through a not-so-great but original script. People who go to parties only prove that they're good at going to parties. People only want to work with people who can help elevate their own personal career. Everyone knows that people you meet at parties usually can't. It's all about people searching for oil and assuming you have it.

Robin Swicord: The scripts I have written are my emissaries to the world, and if producers and studio executives and directors want to work with the sort of writer that has written these screenplays, I'm available. I've never consciously tried to meet people I thought would do my career some good. I'm not even sure that's how writers get hired. It's all about the work. I'm thinking of one writer who shall remain nameless, who mostly rewrites other people. He doesn't actually have original screenplays. He's the one who gets hired when the movie is already going into production and his job is to come in, walk all over the other person's script and make something scarier or funnier. He's like a short-order cook when it comes to writing. That guy'd better go to parties because he's the type of person with whom the director wants to hang out or be on the set with for four weeks. Their personality and their ability to connect with people and schmooze are what get them the job. The bottom line is a mediocre script will never get sold because you met someone at a party.

75. Not Isolating Yourself, Except to Write

I like living too much to be seated all day at a desk.

—Pablo Neruda

You know writing is a solitary task requiring hours of concentrated effort, and most writers should be comfortable with this solitude. Although there are some advantages to it, such as working your own hours, there are also disadvantages, such as loneliness and a sense of being cut off from the outside world. In addition, it can't be too healthy to sit in front of a computer screen all day. You shouldn't be afraid to go out once in a while. This would be one reason to join a writer's group, more for the social pleasures than for feedback on your writing, or get a part-time job in the industry where you're in contact with people.

Ron Bass: Although we don't meet as often, I belong to the "Thursday Night Group," a collection of the so-called A-list writers. It's a great feeling to know them personally and socially because writers don't really get to know each other. The reason is they don't work together. They're more likely to know directors and producers. We meet every month at someone's house, sit around and grouse about how badly writers are treated. We laugh and tell jokes and gossip about people we work with, talk sports and about our family, and then, at some point in the evening, we talk about what can be done for the cause, for writers in general. The Writers Guild is already doing a heroic job, but it can only do so much, and sometimes, people who are more visible in a smaller group can do things that may benefit everybody (i.e., the historic Sony Deal). We talk about how to win writers more respect in terms of credits or visibility, and making writers into name brands so people can identify individual writers. I firmly believe that only when writers are individually known by the general public will writers have actual respect. We need to be in a place where our faces, our names, and our voices become as well known as those of directors. When that happens, we'll have market value, and the studios will need to pay us the respect they pay to directors.

Steven DeSouza: Attending conferences can be a good idea because of the validation a beginning writer can get by interacting with other writers who will share common experiences and tips. You get encouragement by hearing other people's stories and it's an opportunity to get out of your little closet of solitude.

Tom Schulman: You can't be a hermit. A writer is an observer, someone who writes about the world, so you have to experience it. Certainly, I applaud and admire the writer who can spend many hours alone doing the work, or can go off into the woods for months at a time. But you need to balance it by getting out of your cocoon, talking to people, seeing movies, and interacting with the world.

Michael Schiffer: I get up in the morning and then leave the house to go get a cup of coffee. It's always exciting to get to my desk after getting a taste of the world, just getting the light and the energy of the world inside me. As a writer, you get so cut off. You spend so many hours alone, and if you also live alone, it is even worse. I need to connect with the outside world, but not so much that I blow my focus and energy.

76. Gaining Value from Every Opportunity

It is one of the most beautiful compensations of this life that no one can sincerely try to help another without helping himself.
—RALPH WALDO EMERSON

Since the familiar saying, "It's who you know," can be true for writers as well, any relationship, no matter how trivial it may seem, is a resource and link to any opportunity. The genesis of this project is a good example. As an executive attending a pitchmart, I had the chance to help a writer I didn't know with a particular take on the story she had just pitched me. I didn't think anything of it. She was one of a hundred writers there that day. But apparently, I had made such a strong impression on her that she recommended me to a friend, who happened to run a major screenwriting conference and who asked me to serve on a faculty panel. At that conference, I was introduced to a book editor who inquired about various projects I was working on. So I pitched this book's concept, and she liked it and asked me to send her the proposal, which I did, and her publisher later accepted it. Everything was a chain of events sparked by the fact that I helped an anonymous writer at a pitch conference. Every chance meeting is an opportunity. Don't dismiss them so easily. And be nice to everyone you meet.

The first order of business is to get out of the house. There are thousands of opportunities to make legitimate contacts in this industry. It's the old "six degrees of separation" idea. And if you're in Los Angeles, it's two degrees of separation. Everyone knows at least someone who knows someone in the industry. By attending screenings, seminars, industry conferences, award ceremonies, charitable functions, or just spending time in dog parks you can always meet someone who may be a link to an appointment, referral, idea, tip, or bit of advice. As Woody Allen says, "Eighty percent of life is just showing up."

Or you could get a job in the industry. Internships have become an effective way to get a foot in the door. Many producers, who have to hire quickly, don't have the time to look at resumes and instead turn to colleagues for hiring recommendations. The most common entry-level job for writers is a script reading position. As a reader, you'll be seeing your competition. Realizing just how many scripts there are out there and how much better than yours these scripts are and still not getting bought may make you quit in discouragement. Or perhaps it will inspire you to take your writing to the next level, which is the logical choice if you're serious about becoming a working screenwriter.

Steven DeSouza: If I were starting out and had a choice of a high-paying job at a car dealership, or a crummy-paying job that was remotely related to show-business, I'd take the show-business job in a heartbeat. Any way to get in is smart, even if it's a nonpaying job. It's a great way to make contacts. You'll meet people, anybody who works at that studio will walk by your desk, you'll hear about other opportunities. I know so many people who started out as gofers somewhere, which ultimately led to assisting jobs, which led to better opportunities down the road. Anybody who complains they can't get their first break is just too narrow-minded in their definition of exactly what defines a show-business job.

Gerald DiPego: I would recommend that aspiring writers just get any job in the industry because they'll start meeting people by that alone. Both my sons started out as production assistants.

Akiva Goldsman: Everyone knows someone who knows someone who knows an assistant. If your script is truly great, it will rise to the top because there's so little great writing out there. It doesn't mean you don't have to still be ingenious when it comes to getting it seen. Everyone starts with, "Who do I know who knows somebody in Hollywood?" That's part of the job. It's how you break in. Joel (Schumacher) used to say, "If it was easy they'd hire their relatives."

77. Having Mentors

Those who seek mentoring will rule the great expanse under heaven.
Those who boast that they are greater than others will fall short.
Those who are willing to learn from others become greater.
Those who are ego-involved, will be humbled and made small.
—SHU CHING, 2,500 YEARS AGO

The word "mentor" comes from classic Greek mythology. Mentor, a wise teacher, was asked by Odysseus to watch over his son while he embarked on a long voyage. As a surrogate parent, Mentor gave to the young child support, love, guidance, and protection. Today, we have come to know mentors as those who gently guide and nurture the growth of others. They act as teachers, counselors, and advocates who show newcomers (their protégés) the ropes, share with them their wisdom and experience, and offer insight to support their dreams. A good mentor can take years off the learning process for any aspiring writer. But notice I said "take years off the process," not replace it. Writers still have to pay their dues. Mentors just make it a little easier.

Steven DeSouza: I learned a lot from the people I was working for. They allowed me incredible access to all the different facets of filmmaking, like letting me into the editing room. They taught me about rewriting myself and reading my own dialogue out loud, and especially about the business of show business. I found that most of the people I've learned the most from, even though they're not writers now, started as writers.

Akiva Goldsman: I've had a bunch of them, Joel Schumacher, first and foremost. I was living in Venice with my girlfriend. My first script, *Indian Summer*, had been bought but not yet produced, so I was in development at Warner Brothers. I got a meeting with Lorenzo di Bonaventura, who was then a creative executive and who had read *Indian Summer* (filmed as *Silent Fall*) and liked it, and he said, "I can't sell this to the studio, but here are some projects that have been forgotten and have no priority. Do you want to rewrite one of them?" So I picked one I liked and got the assignment for scale, which was a lot of money for me, because I had exhausted all my money writing my script and only had a couple of hundred dollars in the bank by the time it sold. I always say never come to L.A. unless something is meeting you here. Write the script first and then come out. So I was writing this project in Venice and then one day, I heard these voices coming from my window, which was fascinating because I was on the third floor. I look out and see Joel Schumacher on a crane platform, scouting a shot for *Falling Down*. We had no contact whatsoever. He was sort of outside my window, and it was strange. Some months later, I get a call from Lorenzo asking me if I had read *The Client*. They were about to start production, the script wasn't working, they were looking for someone to rewrite it, and did I want to go meet with Joel. So I read the book and I read the script, and on a Saturday, I went to Joel's house and we had a conversation. We just talked about life and the book, and how he had read *Indian Summer* and quite liked it. As I was leaving, he said it would be really fun to do this together, and I was thinking, "Well, this didn't work out." So I went home. I didn't have a car phone, and there were six messages on my machine. I'm about to play the messages when my phone rings again and it's Lorenzo saying, "Congratulations, you've got the job. You've got to meet Joel at his house tomorrow morning. He's going to Cannes for *Falling Down*. Ride with him in the limo so you can go over the notes for *The Client*. You've got to fly out to New York and see Susan Sarandon." So it began from this odd encounter with Joel, and through karma or kismet, I ended up working with him. Then he said, "Why don't you come to Memphis with us to shoot," and then *Indian Summer* came together, so I finished *The Client* and went directly to the set of *Indian Summer*. And then Joel calls me up and says, "The script for *Batman Forever* isn't working . . ." And so it went.

Amy Holden Jones: Martin Scorsese was the first person to help me into the industry after I won a film festival where he was a judge. I wish I'd had a mentor as a writer, but I have mentored other writers extensively. Some have done extremely well and others have not. Generally, the difference has to do with how much they persevere, how critical they are of their work, how able they are to pick themselves up from a large amount of failure and keep going, and how realistic their plan is for getting ahead in the movies. But the single biggest contributing factor is whether they are able to write, not just a great script, but a script I would define as "a movie," which is a very narrow range of things.

Jim Kouf: A sort of mentor was Dorothea Petrie, who really got me to focus on rewriting. For very little money, she got me to rewrite and rewrite and rewrite. And I think that was the most valuable lesson I ever learned as a writer, the value of rewriting, to be able to go over your work again and again and again.

Eric Roth: There are a couple of people, whose work I respect a lot, who were kind of a mentor to me and took a particular interest in me and gave me advice, mainly in maintaining a high standard of quality, but most of my advice came from people I worked for, especially directors.

Tom Schulman: My only mentors were the screenplays of the great writers I read when I started out: Robert Riskin, Paddy Chayefsky, and Billy Wilder.

CHAPTER 17
Getting an Agent

78. Getting the Right Agent the Old-Fashioned Way

We do not employ the writer; the writer employs us.
—LEE G. ROSENBERG, AGENT

At some point, aspiring writers wonder whether they need an agent. That depends on how much of a hustler they are, how many people they know who can take their script and champion it through the studio mazes, and how good they are at selling themselves. Scripts can certainly, though rarely, be sold directly to producers without the involvement of an agent. But because most writers aren't very good at it and, more important, because having an agent validates them as professionals in the eyes of the industry, the question becomes not whether you need an agent, but how do you get one?

First, the bottom line is: a great script always finds an agent. Always. Guaranteed. No exceptions. It's all about money. Agents know a great script will sell in an instant, maybe even generate a bidding war, and if they can make money from your script they'll represent you, period. That's why it's a good idea to enter a legitimate and respected screenwriting contest. Winning one or placing in the final rounds is the drop of blood that entices the sharks to swim your way.

But what do you do if your script is not so great yet? You keep rewriting until it is! No one wants to represent so-so material when his or her reputation is on the line. Your script must be great to even get a meeting, let alone an assignment. But let's assume your script is good enough to attract an agent. What do you do? I know your first inclination may be the shot-gun approach of writing hundreds of query letters to WGA-franchised agencies, hoping one or more will respond. Big mistake

(see next habit). The consensus in the industry is that clients come to agents
through referrals. Someone they know, whose taste they respect, has read
your script, liked it, and put his or her stamp of approval on it, recommending you to them. It's that simple. Sure, there are a few isolated exceptions of writers getting represented off a query letter, so I'm not saying it's
impossible (they still had a great script). What I am saying is that 99 percent of legitimate (read: too busy trying to get work for their clients) agencies don't read query letters. So you've got to play the odds. When asked
how they got their first agent, here's what our mentors said:

Ron Bass: It was easy for me because I was already an entertainment
lawyer. So I called up a guy I knew, a really good friend who was an agent,
and said that I'd written a novel, would he take a look at it, and he said
sure. I had the great luck of being in the industry already.

Steven DeSouza: I got my agent through my aunt who referred me. But
I still had to have great writing samples to impress him. The only thing you
can do is make your script the best that it can be, because there's no such
thing as a perfect script. Every year you get all these critics listing their top
10 best films of the year and they're all different. What's best and what's
not are subjective things. The perfect script is the one where you've done
every possible thing you can think of that absolutely represents your best
work. *That's* the perfect script. It doesn't matter what anybody else says.

Gerald DiPego: I attracted an agent because I had the beginning of a sale.
I had sold an option on a screenplay just by networking on my own, and then
I happened to be at a gathering where I was introduced to a woman who was
an agent's assistant. She asked me what I had done and I said I just optioned
a script, and I guess that legitimized me because she said she'd talk to her boss.

Leslie Dixon: When you're starting out, it's best to get little agents who
are just building their client lists, and are wildly enthusiastic about your
work—better than the larger ones who will never return your calls. With
our first script, my friend and I split up the work, he was pounding the
pavement trying to find us an agent, and I was doing all the typing. I don't
know how he did it. He was pretty resourceful. He found little tiny agencies that were barely on the map, flirted with the receptionists, anything
that would get results. But I'll say this: Without an agent, you've got
nothing. All your efforts once you move here should be on getting an agent.
It's a validation and an umbilicus to the inside. Otherwise, you're just
scrambling on the outside, looking in.

Jim Kouf: You have to write a good script that gets somebody's attention. Period. If you write a good script, you'll get an agent, it's that simple. I'd gone to school with a friend whose father was a sound man who knew a writer who wrote a lot of TV stuff in the '50s, and he introduced me to her. She knew what it took to make it and she said, "If you want be a writer, you've got to write something. Pick out a show on TV and write me a script for it." This was the first advice I ever received. So I picked out *M*A*S*H*, which was my favorite show at the time, and wrote a script for it. She looked at it and said, "Okay, you can write. Now write me another one." So I went back and wrote another one. And she said, "Okay. That's good. Now write me another one." And those were the first three scripts I ever wrote. Then she said, "Okay, now let's see if we can get you an agent." So I got an agent based on those three scripts. They never sold, but they helped get me started. As to my first deal, I started in show business at the same time a friend of mine started, but he wanted to be a producer, so he eventually wound up at CM. He introduced me to Dan Petrie Jr., who at the time was also in the mailroom, going to be an agent, and he optioned my script to his mother, Dorothea Petrie, who was a producer. So my first deal as a writer was his first deal as an agent.

Scott Rosenberg: I had a very Zen approach to the whole thing because I had friends who, when they came out here, immediately did that mass mailing of query letters and no response. So I always had the attitude that when I was ready, they would find me. And it's pretty much what happened. I was just constantly writing and getting better until I placed in a contest, and I had my pick of agents. Besides, you don't necessarily need a fancy agent right away. The hardest part is to go from no agent to agent.

Eric Roth: I got my first agent as a result of winning the Samuel Goldwyn Award at UCLA.

Michael Schiffer: I got my first agent simply by sending out my best writing sample, and having somebody respond to it, through a referral by a friend.

Tom Schulman: When I came to Los Angeles I didn't know a soul. So I did what all aspiring screenwriters are told to do, which is to go to the Writers Guild and get the list of signatory agents, and write those query letters. I must have written over one hundred letters, and I didn't get any response, except one man who called me and said, "I got your letter. It's a nice letter. Why did you send me this letter?" And I said I had a screenplay and he said, "I'm not a literary agent, I'm a talent agent. The people next door to me are literary agents. But you wrote a good letter, so I'm going to recommend you." And sure enough, they called me and they became my first agents. All because this total stranger referred me out of the blue. I'd also recommend that you get an entertainment attorney before you get an agent because a lot of them will take you on a contingency basis without any kind of fee, and most of them know a lot of agents. So if an attorney likes your script, he or she will recommend you to a number of agents.

Ed Solomon: I hate to say this, but if your script is genuinely good it will attract agents like a magnet. The sad truth is that most scripts probably aren't that good.

Robin Swicord: Finding an agent is the one part of networking that's really important because you must have someone who'll represent your work to the marketplace. That's the way the system is set up. When I started out, I was looking for a theatrical agent because I wanted to get my plays produced. I was so completely naive when I came to New York, I didn't even have a clue about how to meet an agent. So I put up this play with some friends, and an agent happened to see it, and asked to represent me. She is still my agent to this day. If you're starting out, I'd recommend you get the agent that loves your work over the one who says, "I think I can sell this and I could probably get you some meetings." You want the agent who says, "You are so great, I'm gonna give you such a career!" I'm very lucky that I like my agent, that we can call her as I would call a family member. Agents can be very destructive to writers and totally erode their confidence. Often, they represent you because they feel they can sell a project, and when it doesn't sell, they forget about you. You want someone who'll travel the long road by your side and who's hungry enough. The agent with the big office and three assistants will not read your script, but their assistant, who will be an agent one day, will be hungry enough to read it. So it's very important to choose the person that really loves your writing.

79. Never Writing a Query Letter Again

Of all the habits explored in this book, this will probably generate the most debate, because for the past 20 years, it's been the most frequently given advice in conferences, seminars, magazines, and books. But my personal experience, and that of my colleagues in the trenches of the industry, disproves it. As you've seen, none of our mentors got an agent or sold a script because a producer responded personally to a query letter. This is the reality: No *legitimate*—therefore overworked—executive, producer, agent, assistant, or manager reads them. If you worked 16-hour days making and returning over a hundred phone calls; taking meetings and lunches; attending screenings, staff meetings, negotiations, and functions; being pulled in several directions by demands from bosses, clients, clients' managers, other agents, producers, development executives, and lawyers; and then spent your entire weekend reading 10 to 30 scripts, while trying to have a personal life, would you spend even one rare minute reading a letter from an unknown writer? Probably not. So why worry about it? Why are you spending your money on paper and envelopes and stamps, clogging the postal systems with 200 query letters begging agents to represent you when they're too busy getting work for their clients? Take the words *query letter* and burn them out of your memory bank. Replace them with the word *referral*. This is how the town works, and if you hear one more person tell you how to write a query letter, run out of the room and ask for your money back. Even if a legitimate executive or agent tells you they'll read them, they're either lying or they're not that busy, which means they won't help your career anyway. I'm sure every writer has an anecdote about a writer who broke in with a query letter. There are exceptions to every rule. If you're still anxious to send one, query letters should only be sent to small agencies that are looking to expand their business. I'm just telling it like it is. All our mentors agree, and Jim Kouf puts it best:

Jim Kouf: I get a lot of query letters. Is this a new thing? Is this what the books and seminars tell you to do? Because nobody reads them. I certainly don't. I literally don't have the time to sit down and read them. If you really want to be a screenwriter, you've got to get in there and be there with the people. You have to get a job on the set, meet producers, directors, actors, assistants. You can't do it through the mail. Here's how it works: My ex-brother-in-law, who's a fireman, calls me and he has a fireman friend who's written a script. So he asks me whether I would read the script, and I say, "For you, as a favor, sure, I'll read it." So I take the script and I read the first few pages and I say, "Okay, it is well written enough." But I don't have time to read the whole thing, so I send it to the agency, and they read it and they like it, and now I'm trying to see if my agent wants to handle this guy. All because of my ex-brother-in-law. That's how it happens.

CHAPTER 18
Pitching

Pitching is a fine art that takes years to perfect. In a nutshell, pitching is pretending you've just seen a great movie and you're so excited about it that you tell your friends what it was about and share the best parts of it. You want them to experience the high points so that they'll go see it. Since pitching is about convincing an executive that your story is worth $80 million of their money, learning sales techniques can be valuable for the introverted writer who has difficulty pitching. But there are also some worthwhile habits you can develop to make the process a little easier and more effective.

80. Believing in Your Work

Some of the world's greatest feats were accomplished by people not smart enough to know they were impossible.
—DOUG LARSON

Hollywood is full of stories about projects that took years to sell because the writers or producers believed in them—they never took "no" as a final answer. You *must* believe in your story, because a studio only worries about selling the movie in seconds, whether it's 60 seconds in a trailer, or 10 seconds with a newspaper ad or poster. You have to adopt the attitude that you've got the best movie they'll ever hear about, and they're lucky to be given the opportunity to hear it.

Gerald DiPego: That inner love of your story is an important measuring stick. If it makes you laugh, if it makes you cry, if it touches you in some deep way, then you've got to trust there are other people out there who will feel the same. You may have to go through a hundred before you get to the one who will feel that way, but it's important to hold on to that.

Ed Solomon: The most important thing in preparing for a pitch is believing in the material. Your belief in it and your ability to lean on the story, *not* your reliance on pizzazz, flash, or hook, are the key elements. If you're telling a good story, you naturally have a hook.

81. Rehearsing Your Pitch until It's Flawless

Life's a pitch!

—DAVID DWORSKI

Since pitching is a verbal presentation, and therefore a performance, rehearsing it is a common habit among working screenwriters. Every chance they get, they pitch their story to friends and family, to their pets even, so that it flows naturally. They pay close attention to what parts in the story people respond to, and what questions they ask when certain parts are unclear, allowing the writer to embellish and rehearse the story until it's a good yarn.

Ron Bass: Preparing is very time consuming. When I started out, going around trying to get jobs, I had six to eight stories all worked out. I never write anything down because then it becomes too mechanical. So I say it to myself over and over many times, developing it as a sort of speech, pacing around alone until I get it the way I like it. I repeat it often enough until it reaches a point where it's not completely memorized, but close, where I can say it so casually that it doesn't sound memorized, more like I'm speaking fluidly.

Gerald DiPego: Pitching is a skill you need to learn. I prepare for it by trying to distill the idea into its essence, making it exciting and clear and finding ways to put my enthusiasm into the storytelling. I pitch it to myself a couple of times, then I pitch it to my wife, which really helps because the first few pitches will be awkward.

Amy Holden Jones: What's useful is to start telling the story to your friends in 30 seconds first, then in five minutes. Pay attention to the first time they get distracted. If their eyes glaze over, you have a problem. If you keep telling the story, and refining it until you can tell from your audience that it's worth pursuing, you'll have a complete story with interesting characters. If you never reach this point, you'll probably have a story that will never interest anyone.

82. Knowing the Story Inside and Out Without Rehearsing

When it comes to preparing for a pitch, there are just as many screenwriters who don't rehearse the story for fear of losing spontaneity and enthusiasm in the room. Rehearsed or not, they're always prepared by knowing the story inside and out. The most important thing is to keep the bored executive from falling asleep, and engage their imagination and interest.

Akiva Goldsman: I don't rehearse, but you certainly need to know your story well before you can pitch it. I'm lucky that I'm social because it's true that pitching is a social art. Relationships are irrelevant, because you can go into a room with someone you have a relationship with and not sell it. To all the introvert writers who have a tough time pitching, my advice is to not worry about pitching. Concentrate on the writing, because you won't get to pitch unless you've written well in the first place. If you're lucky and get called in to pitch, get a best friend or producer who'll help you practice. You don't have to be a great pitcher if you're a great writer. I know brilliant writers who are terrible in rooms.

Nicholas Kazan: I don't enjoy doing it and haven't done it in a long time. I don't rehearse. I try to keep it as spontaneous as I can. It's important to be enthusiastic. You try to give them the overall concept, even some scenes so they can visualize it, and the ending so they can have a feel for the movie. The most important thing is tell a good story and control the enthusiasm in the room.

Scott Rosenberg: I don't rehearse it consciously, but the thing about me is that, when I get an idea that really excites me, I love pitching it to my friends.

Eric Roth: I don't pitch very well and I do it as infrequently as I can. I was never any good at it. I don't bother to prepare, but I'll come in knowing what the material is about, even though I may not know the story per se. I will say this is an area I'm interested in, these are the people that are involved, and then I'll give them a sense of what the movie could be like, the general tone and main values. And I've been fairly successful, so they know I can always back up what I have to say with my material. Many times, the executives will say they need to know more, and then I'll decide if it's worth giving them more or not.

Tom Schulman: My way of preparing for a pitch is, unfortunately, to write the story. A lot of people make the mistake of thinking they can go in and pitch their story in general terms, whether it's because they haven't worked out the story or because of the sheer commerciality of the idea that they think someone will buy it on the spot. The reality is that most executives want to know the whole thing. It's like sitting around the campfire, saying "Once upon a time . . ." and getting the people involved in your story so that they can't wait to hear what will happen next or what will happen to the main character. The story controls the room. If it's interesting and you're excited about it, your enthusiasm will come through. If you have doubts and problems with it, it will also show through. Once the story is written, I'm prepared. I don't really rehearse it. I just go in and tell them the story. But I find that when you talk about your story to other writers as you're developing it, you can sense where your weaknesses are by their reaction to it.

83. Keeping the Pitch Short, Simple, and Exciting

It never gets better than the romance and the blush.

—SYD FIELD

Because pitching is a performance, it should be viewed as an emotional and mental seduction of a listener. And because the listener is most often an overworked and stressed-out executive with a very short attention span, the key is to keep your story as short and simple as possible, while still communicating the passion of the story with energy, enthusiasm, and excitement. Matching the pitch to the genre also helps. If it's a thriller, make it thrilling and suspenseful, and keep the listener riveted. If it's a comedy, make it fun.

Ron Bass: Since you only have a short amount of time to tell your story, you only stress the key elements of the story, the entertaining, interesting parts. It's a performance. It should be engrossing, compelling, and exciting.

Steven DeSouza: I pitch off my three-by-five cards, because if I go deeper, I have too much detail. You need to keep it simple and short, and you've got to be entertaining. But if you're starting out, it's probably better to spend your time writing than pitching, because nine times out of 10, if a studio buys your pitch, they'll get rid of you and hire a more established writer to write the script. They don't want to waste time on an untried writer, and have to wait 12 weeks to know something they already know, which is that they'll get rid of you anyway. I can't tell you how many times I've been hired to write a script based on a pitch by a first-time writer. The writer pitches, the studio tells him to go write an outline, he or she comes back with five typed pages, the studio says, "thank you very much," and then they hire me because they know I can deliver an acceptable script in 12 weeks. So if you really want to write the story, it's a risky proposition to pitch it. You're better off spending the extra time writing the script.

Leslie Dixon: Basically, be enthusiastic, make it short and, most important, don't be desperate. They'll either sense it's a movie or they won't. It helps to have more material prepared than you actually present, so if they ask questions like, "What happens here?" you can answer them.

Scott Rosenberg: You have to know what to pitch and who to pitch to. In terms of what to pitch, I'd never pitch *Beautiful Girls*, but I could pitch *Con Air* in 15 seconds. The key to a good pitch is trying to do it in under five minutes. Know what to leave in and what to leave out. Also have the answers to every question they may have. You may not have said it but you know it, so you allow them to have this question and answer session, and if you can answer all the questions and be done with the pitch in five minutes, you're golden. Executives want to know the act delineations, the general beginning, middle, and end of the story, and they want to know your characters. It's important to always let them know where they are in the script because you could've been going on for 20 minutes and yet you're only on page 20. When you finish pitching the story, they should be able to see the poster. They need to quickly see the movie in their head because all they're thinking about is how they're going to sell the movie. If they can see it and it's exciting, they'll buy the pitch. Another tip is that I always cast my characters so executives can see them right there. So instead of "Fred and Bob duke it out," it's "Nick Cage and Kevin Spacey duke it out." It makes it easier for them to visualize and follow the story better.

Michael Schiffer: There are no secrets to pitching. Just be energetic, concise, and, most importantly, not boring. I try to know what I'm feeling and thinking, and then speak directly. I try to tell the story in a simple fashion, but energetically, keeping it lively so that I don't get bored with it. Another simple rule is never take the couch because you want your energy up. The couch will rock you back and put you to sleep. You want to be able to move, not be so far back on these soft cushions that you can't get up.

Ed Solomon: Genuine interest in what you're pitching is by far the best thing. Being able to tell your story in extremely short, short, medium, and lengthy versions is also important. You need to have several versions prepared, so that if you need to, you can tell what your story is about in 30 seconds, in three minutes, or in 20 minutes.

84. Overcoming Nervousness and Not Showing Desperation

Fear cannot be banished, but it can be calm and without panic; and it can be mitigated by reason and evaluation.

—VANNEVAR BUSH

If being dull is sin number one in Hollywood, then showing desperation is sin number two. It's like that old commercial advises, "Never let them see you sweat." Chances are you're not nervous when you talk enthusiastically to your friends or loved ones about a great film you just saw. A film school professor used to teach his students how to pitch by having them pitch their favorite film of all time, to show that, when you're excited about a story and familiar with it (assuming they've seen it multiple times), telling the story with enthusiasm is a natural act. Pitching, like telling your friends about a good movie, is simply about sharing the highpoints of a story to get someone excited enough to see it. Sure, there may be more at stake. Writer Bo Zenga calls it the "Two-by-Four Theory." If you put a two-by-four on two cinder blocks and ask someone to walk across it, no problem. But if you put the same two-by-four across two buildings, it's a different story. Same two-by-four, same distance to cross, but the stakes are higher. But when it comes to pitching, there shouldn't be anything at stake if you have a great story to tell. If you're nervous, tell the executive. Don't hide it, or you'll lose the energy you need to think about your story. Have fun! After all, isn't that one reason you love the movie business? This is simply an attitude, a mind game you have to play with yourself before you enter the room. And as you probably know, nothing succeeds in Hollywood like the appearance of success. You have to believe you have the upper hand, that the executive is the lucky one for getting to hear your incredible story, not the other way around, where you go in as a sacrificial lamb and grovel because they gave you an opportunity to tell them your story. The bottom line is that they need material to survive and you are their main supplier with lots of buyers to choose from. In other words, they need *you*.

Ron Bass: Not memorizing your pitch is important, because if you fumble or get confused and have to make unexpected decisions during the pitch, you'll look very uncertain. The way you present yourself has a lot to do with how much the buyer has confidence that you'll be able to write what you're pitching.

Gerald DiPego: Once you're in the room, you will be nervous. You need to take a breath and take the focus of the room. It helps if you're in love with the story, because your enthusiasm and passion will help sell it. It's a challenge if you're shy. And you hope they'll give their undivided attention, that they won't take phone calls, or that the secretary won't come in the middle. You have to be prepared, and not be thrown by that (see next habit).

Leslie Dixon: You just have to know what you're doing, and it helps if you have an entertaining personality. I'm pretty social and outgoing; I'm not afraid of people. Most of the writers I know in this town have big personalities. I think the bigger your personality, the more of a tool you have, and a very strong voice will come into your writing. Pitching is basically sitting in a room and talking. That's the least intimidating thing for me. Sitting in front of a bunch of people and playing music, now that's really scary. So after that, pitches are nothing. Shooting my mouth off and babbling is natural for me. Being a charming, self-confident person in the room and having a lot of ideas goes a long way.

Scott Rosenberg: It's the old acting exercise where I have to get $50 out of your pocket. I desperately need the $50, and you desperately don't want to give it to me, and what the teacher tells you at the end of the exercise is that the best way for you to get the $50 is to imagine you already have $50 in your pocket. In other words, have this attitude that you don't need the $50. Don't seem desperate. You have to walk that fine line between arrogance and confidence.

Michael Schiffer: I view a pitch meeting as a creative process, much like a story meeting, an opportunity to share my story with someone who'll comment on it and maybe make it better. So I'll sometimes take notes of what's said to me during the pitch. I'll even interrupt my pitch to write things I haven't thought of before if it would make the story better. Executives are filmmakers too. They hear a million pitches, and they usually have good instincts. They'll probably even be your editor in the development process, throwing story ideas along the way, so don't be shocked if it starts at the pitch meeting. In fact, that's a good sign. If they sit there and have nothing to say, either you've hit a grand-slam home run or you've bombed.

Ed Solomon: What's important is taking a moment to focus and think of your pitch as a performance in the same way an actor or a musician would. Focus before you go in and think about what you're trying to get across. If you're good enough, you can certainly sell crap and pretend it's good, but that's a much lower-odds game than if your story is really good and you believe in it. I've also found that not needing to sell it is one of the best ways to sell it. Quiet confidence that what you have is of value is far more persuasive than the need to sell it. Explaining to someone why they'd like what you have to offer only insults them more, because they know their business better than you. At the very least, they know whether it's a movie or not, and if they can make money off it. Also, remember that you are communicating several things at once: your story—it must be interesting—and who *you* are, that's an equally important part.

85. Adapting to Any Situation

Question: How many development executives does it take to change a light bulb? Answer: Does it have to be a light bulb?
—OLD INDUSTRY JOKE

You shouldn't be unnerved by interruptions and often mind-blowing suggestions by executives to make your story more commercial. An executive's phone never stops ringing, and it's always a good sign when they instruct their assistant to hold their calls. At the other extreme, I know of a colleague who has a little buzzer that tells her assistant to walk in with an important phone call of Spielbergian caliber she "must" take should the pitch be of no interest to her. Because you never know what to expect, you need to be flexible, adjust to any unusual circumstance in the room, and be prepared to pick up where you left off.

Ed Solomon: It's not as important to have the perfect pitch memorized because frankly anything can throw it off, a phone call in the middle of it, someone asking a question, another only wanting to hear parts of it. What's more important is knowing what your story is about and having the confidence that it's the real thing.

Michael Schiffer: Don't have a canned pitch because you can always count on being interrupted by an "important" phone call. You want to be talking to a human being. Your pitch will vary according to the executive's body language, their facial signals, how fast or slow to go, if they're following you, or if their eyes glaze over. And they will ask you questions in the middle of your pitch, so you have to know where to pick up again. If a canned pitch worked, you might as well tape it and send it around town. I had a pitch meeting once, where I thought I had someone in the palm of my hand, until she got a phone call in the middle of the meeting, and then my pitch turned to ashes, I didn't understand what happened. Later, I found out that in the middle of my pitch, she had gotten fired. When she returned to the office, she just sat through the rest of my pitch without saying anything, while I was fumbling. In that case, I wished I was on tape.

Tom Schulman: I've had just about everything you could ever imagine go wrong at a pitch meeting, like starting with, "This is a story about a 50-year-old guy," and within seconds, the executive interrupts with, "Could it be a 70-year-old guy?" and you go, "Well . . . let me go on with the story." And they go, "Why couldn't he be 70?" because, unbeknownst to you, they've just signed a deal with Paul Newman and they're trying to squeeze him into your story. Or they try to change the gender of your main character, or the executive seems absolutely distracted by everything in the room except your story, and then you're surprised when they buy it. And the opposite, where you're just on a roll and they're riveted and they give you great ideas on the story, but they're just not interested.

CHAPTER 19
Acting Like a Professional

There are no rules about how to behave professionally, just common and generally accepted customs that separate amateurs from professionals. The following five habits fit the criteria of these accepted customs but are not set in stone. Take them or leave them at your discretion.

86. Not Being Paranoid about Your Ideas Being Stolen

It used to be executives could spot an amateur by the look of their script: the page count, the number and quality of brads used, or whether a WGA registration number, draft number, or date were printed on the cover page. Now, it's the second a writer utters, "But how do I know you won't steal my idea?" Why? Because it's a useless worry for something that rarely happens in legitimate circles. There are two important reasons why executives almost never (it's still possible, but very rare) steal ideas. One is financial. It costs a lot less to buy an idea from a beginning writer than to fight a lawsuit in court. The other is interpersonal. Because relationships and appearances are crucial to executives, they won't risk embarrassment and losing their jobs should they be faced with a lawsuit. It's just not worth it. This is why executives are so careful to avoid even the slightest potential for a lawsuit by avoiding reading unsolicited material and making sure that release forms of all kinds are signed or that submissions come through legitimate channels such agents, attorneys, or people they absolutely trust. A common scenario is of the paranoid writer who never lets go of his "original" idea, only to read in the trades that another writer has just sold the very same idea. "How could it be? I've never told anyone about it," claims the shocked amateur. It's the universal consciousness: as soon as you think up an idea, at least four other people around the world come up with the exact same thing. What's important in Hollywood is not just the idea, but also the unique execution of the idea that the writer brings to the table. So if you think you have such a unique idea (doubtful, but possible), develop it into an outline, treatment, or script. Otherwise, relax and free your energies for other worthwhile habits. Professional screenwriters, who also have attorneys and agents, protect their developed work by registering it with the Writers Guild or copyright office, and they keep detailed records and logs of phone calls, meetings, business lunches, and memos.

Ron Bass: It's something I've never worried about, maybe because I used to be an entertainment lawyer, and you know that in legitimate circles, it just doesn't happen in general. It's relatively rare when someone feels that the best thing for them to do is steal your idea. I'm sure it can happen, and has happened, but you can't really function in the business worrying about it. You have to get away from that paranoia, especially if you've registered it with the Writers Guild.

Gerald DiPego: Beginning writers tend to be overly cautious and paranoid about their ideas being stolen. That is not to say that if you have a really great hook or high concept, that someone couldn't easily borrow it and do it their own way. In that case, I wouldn't blabber it all over town. Developing a script from the idea is always your best protection.

Michael Schiffer: Most professionals in the business will bend over backwards to avoid even the slightest impression that they've borrowed your idea. The last thing they want to hear is anything remotely close to what they're developing, so they'll stop you. On the other hand, nonlegitimate and desperate people who hear your idea at a coffee shop could run out and sell it, so be cautious in public.

87. Not Pitching in Social Situations

> *Talking about an idea squeezes the juice out of it.*
> —ERNEST HEMINGWAY

First, as one mentor said, in general you shouldn't worry about pitching, because you won't even get to pitch unless you've either sold a script or made a movie that made money. But if you happen to meet an executive at a social function, your first inclination shouldn't be to pitch your ideas. Executives constantly get blitzed by unsolicited material—valets leaving scripts on their car seat, amateurs throwing them over fences into their backyard, people pitching to them at weddings, bar mitzvahs, in restaurant bathrooms, you name it. When they meet you, the last thing they want is to hear another idea. In fact, it's such a typical occurrence that they'll probably be dreading that you'll launch into one at any moment. Screenwriter Les Bohem calls this the "Nashville Handshake": No one ever shakes hands in Nashville without putting a demo tape in your hands. But if they are genuinely interested and ask what you've done or are currently working on, then by all means, do so. Otherwise, don't be afraid to ask for an official meeting, and say you'll have your agent or attorney set it up. This will make a more favorable and professional impression.

Jim Kouf: Nobody wants to go to a party and listen to somebody's idea. This usually happens from someone who has no other access to them, so they're immediately considered an amateur. Professional writers set it up through normal channels, like an agent or attorney. That's the way to do it.

Eric Roth: You only do it if someone asks you what you're working on and wants to hear what your story is about; otherwise, no one wants to talk business in social situations.

Michael Schiffer: We're constantly cranking out stories, working on characters and plots, and my rule is, when I leave my office, to think about being alive in the world. I don't want to think business outside business hours. If an executive wants to hear your pitch, they'll give you signals and ask for it. But pitches out of context become triply boring because you're imposing characters and settings on someone who's usually not in the mood.

88. Not Working for Free

There are a lot of hustlers in Hollywood, who call themselves producers even if they have never produced a single thing in their lives, except business cards with the title "Producer." Since they don't have development deals, they don't have the inclination to pay writers to develop scripts for them, especially when so many writers are willing to do it for free in order to break in. This is a judgment call. You either trust them or you don't. The general consensus among professionals is that if these so-called "producers" can't pay you even a little money, they're not in a position to get anything made, or they don't value your work enough. First, you're risking spending months out of your life for something that may never get made. Second, chances are you won't own the material anyway. Bottom line: if a producer values your work, they should put their money where their mouth is. If you still want to do business with this producer, write the script on spec, and then let them decide whether they'd like to option it.

Ron Bass: It's fine to work for free for yourself only when you write speculatively. First, working for free is in violation of the Guild. Even if you're not a Guild member, there's still a good reason why this rule exists. If someone doesn't want to pay you anything for your work, chances are this is not a good person to be working for, and it's not a legitimate situation that will result in something good for the writer. Then, you can end up with a conflict over who owns the work, and the other person claiming you can't use it. If you're willing to write it speculatively, just tell the producer you're writing it for yourself and you'll show it to them when it's done, and if they like it, they can make you an offer for what they think it's worth, and if not, you can always go somewhere else with it. At least you'll own it.

Eric Roth: If the producer and the writer are both out of college and starting out, then I don't think there's anything wrong with a handshake agreement. But if a producer *hires* you, then you shouldn't do it for free. In that case, you should sign a partner agreement with the producer so that you equally split any future rewards, which means in a sense you're writing a spec script. Never give the work away for free. No one takes a writer seriously if he's doing things for free. It's not professional. There's a sense that you're getting less.

Tom Schulman: When I started out, before I was in the Guild and had any hope of selling anything, I'd meet a lot of aspiring producers, but I always got them to pay me something. Even if it was a small token, like a small option on a script, it got them motivated because they had something invested in the project.

89. Not Being "Difficult" to Work With

*The greatest lesson in life is to know that even fools
are right sometimes.*

—WINSTON CHURCHILL

I know of a writer who argued with executives for 45 minutes over the color of a minor character's dress! This is what I'd label "difficult," and most executives, producers, and directors don't like working with difficult writers. I'm not saying you should take everything with a smile. Obviously, if you believe in something strongly enough, and it isn't as trivial as the color of a dress, then by all means, you should voice your opinions. One extreme is thinking your script is perfect and notes are just a waste of time. The other is taking everything they say verbatim like a secretary. The ideal attitude is somewhere in between. Many writers have said that the best trick in dealing with studio notes is to shut up and listen. Then you say, "There are some interesting ideas here. Let me explore some of them," you thank them for their valuable insights and leave the room.

Ron Bass: I've walked out of many projects before, but it's not like, "I'm out of here!" in a storm of fury. You talk with the executive or the director about what they don't like and what you're doing, and you say to them, "I agree, this is the time to bring in someone else, because I don't think I'm the guy that can make it work; I don't know how to make it work." You have to understand this other person, your boss, is only saying the same thing you're saying. They have to make the same movie to their vision, and they think you're wrong. Sure, I've been in millions of arguments and screaming matches over specific scenes, but ultimately, when it comes to parting company, that person isn't getting rid of you because they don't like you. They just have a different vision they don't think you can match. Maybe you like their way and try to do it their way, but they don't think you did a good job. What else can they do but get someone else?

Gerald DiPego: As writers in the development process, we constantly need to be on the alert to fend off bad ideas that people don't realize would hurt the material. At the same time, we have to stay open enough to embrace the good ideas. That's a real challenge. It's a whole other skill from writing. If you're the type of person who gets mad quickly, starts yelling, throws a script across the room, and walks out of a meeting (anyone can be pushed to that point), you won't last too long. Generally, it really pays to be a good listener and to consider thoughtfully what comes at you. Even if you think it's really stupid, and it might be, politely explain why it won't work.

Leslie Dixon: Do really good work. Be self-critical and make changes they don't expect you to make. If you can take their notes in your own way, you'll both be happy. If a director gets on the project, try to understand the director and become someone he or she likes to deal with. If you don't like the notes, or you are defensive and arrogant about taking them, you're not going to last. You have to figure out a way to make them feel you're working with them. They are paying you. If you realize the project is becoming the movie you didn't want to make, and you don't think it'll work, it's perfectly okay to walk away. I've done it.

Nicholas Kazan: Being cooperative doesn't mean you're a puppet. When people say to me, "I hear you're difficult," I thank them. It's a compliment because to me, being difficult means I stand up for my opinions. If they're making a mistake, I tell them so. I support it passionately and vehemently, but I don't throw things. Everyone wants to have a good time working on a project. I like to create and make things, so the people I work with generally have a good time working with me. When they say I'm difficult, it's because they ask me to make a change, and I tell them it won't work. There are some writers who will do anything they're asked, and I don't think those writers are very good. If you do what people tell you to do, you're not writing from the inside. You're writing from the outside and it shows. You always want to have an enthusiasm for the work and the process, explain your reasons to people, and be agreeable. If you simply say, "I can try to make that change, but it will have the following four effects that I don't think you want," they'll consider it, they'll hear you. But if you threaten people, or are unpleasant and sour, you won't work again.

Michael Schiffer: We all lose control of our work sometimes. The key is to be open-minded. If I've structured the story, told it really well, and have it locked down, even if they bring another writer, in many ways, all they're doing is changing the colors of the curtains. They can change the dialogue here and there, they can change a few jokes, but the architecture of the piece is exactly the same. So when the director comes in, all he does is the interior decoration of the monument you've built, and that's all right. Sure, it sucks; you want to say, "Why don't you let me change it from blue to green, I can do that." But often they don't want you to, because people like to work with associates they've come to trust over many years or projects. Ultimately, it doesn't matter, because when the movie comes out, it's not the colors of the curtain that dazzle people, it's the story and the character conflicts, and if you're the original author and get it right and bulletproof, it's very hard for people to mess it up.

Ed Solomon: You have to choose your battles. As a screenwriter, you're never in a position to win a fight. You can only argue your position. And it's true that "difficult" writers often get fired, unless they're really good. But if they're really this good, people don't tend to argue with them that much, because they respect their opinions. If they pay you money to write for them, they view you in the same way you view someone you hire to design a kitchen. I'm not saying I like it, but that's the way it is. I've taken stances where I've argued successfully, and other times I've been fired for it. I think the position of the screenwriter in the industry, that they are perceived as expendable and fired so easily, is detrimental to the quality of film.

90. Not Burning Bridges When Fired

Getting fired off a project is a common practice in Hollywood, even among highly successful screenwriters. What's also common is being rehired to fix your script after others have failed to make it better. So always be nice to your employer, even if your first instinct is to slash their Porsche's tires or burn their Malibu cottage. Understand that when you get fired, it's usually because of the work. It's not personal, even if it seems like it. Remember Habit 57 about being open to criticism? It's tough to disassociate ourselves from our material. If we get fired, we can't help but be hurt by it. It's okay to be angry. Just be professional, put on a fake smile, go home, and then cry or throw things. Chances are you'll get rehired on the project when the 12 rewriters they'll hire won't even get close to the magic you wove in the original draft that made them buy it in the first place. And even if they don't rehire you on this project, it's such a small town, chances are they'll consider you for future assignments.

Ron Bass: Not burning bridges is always a healthy attitude to adopt in anything in life, as long as it's not a euphemism for not being true to yourself. If you're in a situation when you feel you have to end a relationship because of the way you've been treated, you won't feel right if you don't. But that aside, and I don't think that happens a lot in our business, you want to know that even if an experience went badly, if you've decided you want to work with that person again, you'll be glad that you haven't burned the bridge, especially when getting rehired on the same project is common. But I have yet to be fired off a project for a personal reason. You're taken off a project because somebody feels that right now, they need someone else's writing on it that you weren't able, or willing, to deliver. It's really about the work, not me personally. Sure, you're disappointed and hurt, and you wish you could still be on the project, but unless the person has been abusive to you, being furious at the person who felt you weren't doing the job is a foolish and misguided emotion in most circumstances.

Gerald DiPego: It depends on how you've been treated personally. If you feel you've been really abused by someone, you'll probably not want to work with them again. I'm not for yelling and screaming, but sometimes it's really important to clear the air and tell them how you feel, and if they've done wrong by you, tell them why you think that's wrong. So you're not exactly burning bridges, but you're not just shrugging and walking away either. Everyone knows how writers are treated in Hollywood. And I think that if writers are fired off a project for what is no good reason but just someone's whim or an insecurity, or this trend that any writer will do and of getting a fresh look from someone else, it's important for writers to go on record that this is not a good way to make movies and that there is such a thing as a writer's vision. Directors would never allow this to happen to them. It would be outrageous for a director to be replaced once he hands in his cut. I'd love to see what they'd think when someone says to them, "Don't take this personally, we're just bringing in another director for a fresh look, maybe a little reshooting." They'd go through the roof, and yet that's exactly what they do to writers.

Amy Holden Jones: The thing about rejection is that you should never make the people who reject you feel particularly guilty about it. Often, when they move on from you to someone who doesn't work out, if you haven't made them feel guilty, it leaves the door open for them to bring you back.

Jim Kouf: You never know when you'll work with these people again, so it's a good habit to cultivate. I had more of a temper when I was younger, but it was never about the people I was working with—more like the project. I've always stayed on pretty good terms with everybody because it's a small business, and more than likely, you'll run across the same people again.

•   •   •

The journey to screenwriting success is full of obstacles and disappointments. As if writing a quality script out of nothing weren't difficult enough, trying to market it may seem like an impossible task when faced with constant rejection. To keep the dream alive, in addition to thickening the layers of emotional skin, you need to adopt the four Ps: Patience, Persistence, Passion, and Practice.

PART VI

The Four Ps

Keeping the Dream Alive

Nothing in the world can take the place of Persistence. Talent will not; nothing is more common than unsuccessful men with talent. Genius will not; unrewarded genius is almost a proverb. Education alone will not; the world is full of educated derelicts. Persistence and determination alone are omnipotent.

—CALVIN COOLIDGE

CHAPTER 20
Patience

91. Adapting to the Hollywood System

Everything comes to he who hustles while he waits.

—Thomas Edison

A screenwriter's life in Hollywood is a long waiting game—between handing a draft to your agent and getting feedback, between pitching and decision, or between dealing with attorneys and finally getting paid (one writer told me there are studio executives whose only job is to creatively delay payments to talent). Even when a project is green-lighted, it can take over a year and a half from preproduction to wide release. You need patience and you need to pace yourself. At first, a lot of people act in desperation out of impatience and a need to succeed. Don't be angry or discouraged if it takes an agent, producer, or development executive a long time to respond to your script. Some say you should give them two weeks. The reality is more like two months. It's just a matter of priorities. A "hot" spec up for a bidding war will get read over a lunch hour, whereas reading a "recommended" script from an unknown writer will depend on the relationship between producer and agent.

Steven DeSouza: Be patient, keep your fingers crossed, and believe your ideas are viable and valuable. Even though "they" don't want what you just wrote this week, the tide will turn, believe me, and it can turn on a dime. Michael Crichton told me he had the script for ER in his drawer for 18 years! He wrote that script as a pilot for a network series but had the dumb luck of turning it in right after a movie of his flopped. Unable to come to a decision based on the merits of the script, the network executive decided to pass. So Michael kept this script in a drawer and concentrated on his novels and big movies. Then he heard that Spielberg was looking for a medical show, so he took the script out of the filing cabinet, and thought he'd have to rewrite it. But to his surprise, he did not have to rewrite the characters or the dialogue, but all the equipment and technical jargon the doctors were using 18 years ago that have since changed.

Akiva Goldsman: It's very hard to be patient because you put so much energy into something, and it's your first priority for so long, but it's someone else's 200th priority. That's painful. You have to have wisdom and empathy and understanding. Also, you don't want to be out here if you don't have to. Don't come to L.A. until you're ready. Don't write your script here. It's one of the worst places to write anyway because you're so isolated from real experience. Write it where not everyone you walk into is also writing a screenplay. It will drive you insane. Better to write it in Des Moines or Brooklyn, and figure out how to get it into the right hands. Then start writing another one. Eventually, if you're good, one will hit. Also, don't waste your energy staring at the phone. I'm speaking from experience. You get into this bizarre, unbelievably anxiety-ridden, codependent marriage with an inanimate object, and you're scared to leave your house because, "What if it rings?" What if they finally call and tell you they like it or they don't?

Scott Rosenberg: You can't count on anything, and you'll make yourself sick if you do. Anything that happens is gravy, and you should just feel happy to be part of this crazy business. A long time ago, my father said to me, "Do whatever you want to do, go after it with all your heart, and then figure out a way to get paid for it." And I think it's so easy to look at others who are doing better than you, and have this "grass is greener on the other side" attitude that's so endemic to this business. There's a lot of envy in this town, especially among screenwriters. I just say be happy you're making a living at something you love to do and essentially living your dream.

Michael Schiffer: This business is unbelievably and heartbreakingly slow, and often, when you think a script is done, it's years before it's fully realized. There are hundreds of films, now considered classics, that have taken close to 10 years to reach the screen. I think it's because there's an incredible friction between art and commerce, between a piece of work everyone loves and recognizes as great and a million ways to ask the question, "Will I make my money back if I make this movie?" They can love the script but still pass on it, and then some day, where either the times have changed or the world feels different, someone reads the script and they do see a potential for profit. As a producer, I try to option material for the longest possible term because it's unrealistic to believe you can set up a movie quickly in this town. Everyone is afraid to commit to anything that's financially doubtful.

CHAPTER 21
Perseverance

92. Handling Rejection

If you have made mistakes, even serious ones, there is always another chance for you. What we call failure is not the falling down, but the staying down.

—MARY PICKFORD

Since rejection is a way of life in Hollywood, even among successful screenwriters, survival is simply a matter of the thickness of your skin and the ability to get up after being kicked down, dust yourself off, and keep going. Novelist Barbara Kingsolver has a wonderful psychological trick for handling it. She says, "Don't consider your project rejected. Consider that you've addressed it 'To the editor who can appreciate my work,' and it has simply come back stamped 'Not at this address.' Just keep looking for the right address." So how do our screenwriting mentors handle rejection?

Ron Bass: I handle it terribly, but not with anger at the other person. I try to realize that anger is an expression of your own insecurity, that the person is rejecting you, not to hurt your feelings, but because they don't like what you're doing. So I don't feel terribly angry, more like hurt and insecure and sad. But I have to go home and start working again, and it eventually wears off, especially when you have multiple projects. That's why it's a good habit to have several projects at the same time because when one is going badly, there's still a chance that the others could be doing all right.

Steven DeSouza: I just go back to something I'm working on. I just had a pitch meeting the other day. I don't know how it's going to turn out, but I just got back and started working on my current script again. When you get rejected, you try to put it out of your mind. Sure, it hurts a little bit, but then you remind yourself that every great success has been turned down before. Look at *Star Wars*, which was rejected by every studio. *Forrest Gump* took 10 years to get to the screen. I can't think of any reasonably successful movie that wasn't an uphill battle.

Gerald DiPego: You have to believe in yourself and in your idea. You have to know that not everyone will like everything, but it still hurts when they don't. If it doesn't hurt maybe you just don't care enough. You want people to embrace your work. You can't shrug it off, so you just have to get through the disappointment and go on. I've been doing this for almost 30 years, so when I put my hopes on a project, and the bad news comes, I mourn it no more than a few days and move on.

Akiva Goldsman: I used to handle rejection poorly and get depressed. I'd climb on a bed under a blanket and go through a fugue of self-pity that generally would last a couple of days. Now, I wait. What I've learned about moods is that they pass. It's okay to feel sad, it's okay to feel loss and hurt over it. You have to mourn things. If you wrote something and put real energy into it, and it doesn't work, you have to dignify that by regretting its loss. Mourn it. You'll be a better writer. If anything, it will redouble your efforts to be good. I wish I were more like the guy who says, "It's good, they're wrong." But I'm the other guy. I generally think the script is terrible and then I'm surprised when they like it.

Amy Holden Jones: Even the biggest screenwriters get rejected all the time. I handle it badly. That's why it's good to have another project to go on to as you finish one. When you're disappointed with the one you just delivered, it helps to turn your attention to the next.

Nicholas Kazan: Successful writers have an overwhelming determination, and an ability to accept pain, humiliation, and rejection and to persevere in the face of towering evidence of lack of talent. (I don't mean that good screenwriters have no talent. Just that screenwriting requires diligence, and until you are good, you are bad, often very bad, and that may appear to be lack of talent.) The easiest way to handle rejection is to take out a contract on the people who rejected you, but that's expensive and risky. Seriously, it's always shocking when people don't like something. The fact is, you don't need every executive in town to love your screenplay. You only need one person at the right level, with the right degree of confidence and courage to champion your work. But how do you know when to stop, and when to keep going? If you can read your script after it's been rejected a hundred times, and it still reads great, keep going. If it doesn't, you've got to be honest with yourself and believe that maybe they're right, maybe it's ordinary. So you forget about it and try to write an extraordinary screenplay, something you love, that's unusual and different, that will set you apart from other people.

Jim Kouf: I don't worry about it too much. That's one good thing about having several projects going on at the same time. When one door closes, you jump to another open door. The same goes even if your movie gets made. The public is either going to love it or reject it, some critics will love you and some will hate your guts. You've got to have a thick skin in this town because one way or another, everyone will comment on what you do. What else are you going to do? You can't become a writer and not have to deal with people's comments.

Scott Rosenberg: Rejection happens all the time, but my philosophy is that I feel bad for the person who rejected me. But again, it depends on the project. I have this one script I love. It's the best script I ever wrote, and it's amazing that nobody likes it. I can't get this movie made. So when I hear the next person or the next star turns it down, my attitude is, "You poor bastard, do you know what you're doing to your career?" So you basically shift attitudes. I also have bad scripts that get rejected, but I recognize they're bad. So you deal with it one of two ways. Either my material isn't good anyway, and I can understand why you're rejecting it and it's okay, or the material is so good that if you're rejecting it, it's your loss. When you first start out, and you get rejected left and right, self-doubt can creep in. It's easy to ask yourself, "My God, what am I doing?" But the great thing about this business is that when one person rejects you, there are a thousand other people to go after. If one agent rejects you, there are many other agencies. And even if all the agencies reject you, guess what? There's a whole other level to explore. They're called producers. And if *all* the producers reject your script, then it's got to be really bad. But then the best part is that you can write another script, and then another. So the numbers are in your favor. Unless you have some serious personal rejection issues, you can always start again with something better.

Eric Roth: I have thick skin, but I do get upset like everyone else, and it will usually last a day. It's not a rule but what seems to happen. After a while, you develop an antenna as to what might or might not happen. But no one ever calls and says, "This is terrible." It's more like it might be too long, or they don't quite see it.

Michael Schiffer: I have a 24-hour rule. I tell myself no one is allowed to make me feel miserable for more than one day. Rejection sucks and failure hurts. Anybody who tells you it doesn't is crazy. But if you're letting it go on too long, then you're the loser. If you get hit, you go down, but you can't stay down. You have to pick yourself up and start something new. It's like boxing. The referee is counting to 10. If you stay down, the fight is over.

Tom Schulman: Rejection is painful and it's a shock every time. In order to be good at what you do, you have to be enthusiastic about your writing, so when people read it and they don't like it, it hurts. But I found that, over the years, I've gotten over it faster and faster. The first set of rejections probably took me days. Eventually, I got to the point where I'd lie down on the floor for about 15 minutes. I'd think for the first five minutes, "I'm through, I'm out, I've got to find something else to do, I can't take it, blah, blah, blah . . ." and then five minutes of "What else am I gonna do?" and then five minutes of "What can I do to make this better?"

Ed Solomon: It's a very fine line because you need to believe in yourself and keep pushing, but sometimes your stuff just isn't good enough. So how do you know? You have to really look into your gut. There's a difference between hearing creative criticism and getting abject rejection. If you get a rejection and people are saying, "it's not for me," you say, "fine, it works for me." But if they're saying, "I just don't find the central character worth following," and someone else says, "I have trouble liking your central character," then you need to look at it. Be very aware of the kind of rejection you get. Some of it is good, because it tells you something is not working.

Robin Swicord: It depends on when the rejection comes. People can reject my ideas left and right, and it doesn't bother me because at that point, it's all in the realm of the possible. If a person doesn't like the idea, maybe someone else will. When I feel the most wounded is when I've done an enormous amount of work and the studio keeps changing the rules so that, no matter how well or how hard I work, it doesn't make a difference.

So when the movie doesn't get made or when they fire me off my precious material and put on people who are not very good to do all kinds of terrible things, it really hurts. I come in to do a certain kind of work and I hold myself to very high standards, much higher for me than anyone else, and it hurts when people don't share your values or enthusiasm. I've had movies be destroyed, which is another form of rejection, movies that were made so badly, I felt I was watching my child being dismembered. It takes a while to recover from that. You need a period of mourning, however long it is. Often the writing helps, because it's a sort of refuge, but if you're really not over it, you have to take care of yourself for a day or two with some other thing that gives you joy. It's like being able to love again. You can't just force yourself to sit there at the table. It helps to just go away to a special place. We have a summer home where I go sometimes with my husband or with friends, where you can sort of heal yourself by walking and looking at trees, or reading a wonderful book by the fire. You just make yourself whole again, like a child who goes to her room after she's been punished severely for something she didn't do. It takes a lot of strength of character to survive what this business dishes out.

93. Not Being Afraid to Fail: Finishing What You Start

Never regret. If it's good, it's wonderful. If it's bad, it's experience.
—VICTORIA HOLT

What would you do if you knew, with 100 percent certainty, that you couldn't fail at something? Whatever it is, it should be what you really love to do. I hope it's writing great screenplays because, with few exceptions, you'll need to write several before you reach that high standard of craft demanded by the industry. Unlike many aspiring writers who become psychologically paralyzed and quit after writing the first 20 to 30 pages, successful screenwriters finish what they start because they believe in it and are not afraid to fail. Each script is a learning experience.

Scott Rosenberg: It's very important to finish what you start. I remember a professor who showed me a drawer full of scripts, 75 sets of the first 20 pages. He wrote the first 20 pages of 75 different screenplays and went no further. This paralyzed me. Even if I just start something that sucks and is wildly uncommercial, or an exact movie comes out, and I know I'll never sell it, I'll still finish it. Every script you finish, you learn.

Eric Roth: The most important thing is to finish what you start, even if it takes forever or it's painful. There are no secrets, no mystery. Some people are better at it than others. Some have different things to say, but finishing is the key.

Michael Schiffer: The act of finishing something is absolutely critical. People who say they wish they'd make themselves write, or that they'd write more if they had more time, are not writers. If you don't write, you're not a writer. Every writer I know is incredibly hard-working; they work their tails off every day. How are you going to compete unless you do the same? The only chance to break in is to outwork the competition, and never give up. If I had an impulse for a story, any story idea that seemed to have a beginning, middle, and end, and some sort of commercial appeal, rather than play Hamlet and wonder, "should I write this, should I not?" I'd sit down and write the story and see where it took me. I'd make myself finish it. I did this over and over, until I finally got a strong writing sample that opened the doors for *Colors*.

94. Not Giving Up Easily

Sticking to it is the genius.

—THOMAS EDISON

There's an old folk tale about a young woman who wanted to be a dancer. One day she learned that the greatest dancing teacher of all time was to pass through her small town, so she practiced and practiced in the hope she could impress him. When the day arrived, she managed to be introduced to him and she asked, "Oh, wise teacher, would you tell me if I have what it takes to be a great dancer?" The man asked her to dance for him, and she danced like she'd never danced before. It was her greatest performance yet. But unimpressed after only 30 seconds, the man said she didn't have the talent and that she should quit. Devastated, the young woman ran to her home in tears, threw her dancing shoes in a trunk and forgot about being a dancer. She got married, became a housewife with children, and led a happy life for 20 years, until she had a chance meeting with the same dancing teacher. She couldn't help asking him how he knew within 30 seconds that she didn't have it. He responded, "I couldn't tell, but if you quit so easily because I told you to, then you weren't a real dancer." Bottom line? If you're passionate about your goal, nothing will stand in your way, no nay-sayers, no statistics, no experts. If someone tells you you'll never make it, if they try talking you out of it by listing all the logical reasons you should quit, you keep going, more determined than ever, because you love it and it has meaning to you. As Marianne Williamson says, "If you want to give up, then perhaps you should give up. The real writer doesn't consider that an option. Courage matters as much as talent."

So when should you stop trying? Common sense dictates that if you're doing this because you love it, then you should quit when you're no longer having any fun. When you've done the best you could and the process just brings you more depression than joy, you should re-evaluate your goals (see Habit 96).

Akiva Goldsman: Just truly persevere. It's so frightening how many wonderful writers stopped writing because they couldn't take the pain of rejection. What you have to remember is that great writers are just stubborn. There is a persistence of vision over time because being a writer is a life led. It's not about having written a single thing. A writer writes. Everyone says it. It's true. A writer spends a life writing. And if that's what you must do for a living, then you will. If it's just fantasy and the rejection knocks you out, then it should, because it's not work for the squeamish.

Nicholas Kazan: I wrote a play in college that a professor gave to a theater director, and we never heard back from the guy. Months went by and I just assumed he didn't like it. I was depressed and didn't think any more of it. The professor later ran into the same director again and asked him what he thought of the play. He said he didn't remember it, that he probably lost it, and to send it to him again. So the professor did, the director liked it and he ended up producing it and a number of my other plays. This is a case where the writer's psychology, which is to be timid in the face of the world, to be paranoid, to see rejection everywhere and be emotionally infected by it, all of these worked against me. Had I not had this persistent advocate, my plays would never have been done. It's like Faulkner, who showed *The Sound and the Fury* to every publisher in New York and nobody would publish it. Likewise, you could show your script to 100 people, and it could be great. There's always 101. But if a lot of them tell you it doesn't work, maybe you should go back home, because all that may be waiting for you here is frustration, rejection, and heartache. Certainly, these things are waiting for you even if you are a success, but if rejection is your sole diet, it can be very difficult. I began writing short stories before I wrote plays, and I enjoyed writing them, but people didn't think they were any good. Then I wrote plays and had some success and then I wrote screenplays and didn't have much success at first. But I wasn't even conscious of whether I had talent or not. I was just so passionate about the process that I kept persevering in the face of contrary evidence. I wrote 15 scripts before I sold my first one.

Jim Kouf: I don't think you can ever give up, because the older you become, the wiser and better you become. There are many instances, though less true in Hollywood, of people making it later in life. You never know. If you really love doing it, you ought to keep doing it, and if you're truly talented, you'll probably get discovered. You can always *not* do it, then you know for sure what the outcome is.

Scott Rosenberg: The best quote I ever saw was from Steven Soderbergh—he said that he felt that luck equaled talent plus perseverance. And I really believe that's true, because you can be supertalented, but if you're not willing to really gut it out for a long time, you'll have a difficult time. I have friends who were wildly talented writers when I first got here, and after two or three years, they were like, "You know what? I want to get married, I want to have a family, I can't deal with this anymore." Now they're selling computers. I remember watching an episode of *Taxi* where the actor character says, "If I don't make it by my 30th birthday, I'm quitting." I had that in the back of my head, but the actor in *Taxi* doesn't quit on his 30th birthday, he just tacks on another five years. The problem for me was what else was I going to do? IBM wasn't going to hire me. You have to believe in yourself, and in the process have a strong support system around you. I was lucky that no one, not even my parents or my girlfriend, ever said to me, "Why are you wasting your time when you could become a lawyer or something?" or "Stop loafing around. I hear there's a cashier opening at Wal-Mart." They were always completely supportive.

Michael Schiffer: I came to town and gave myself a five-year plan. I had written hard for five years with no sales, then I came out here when I was 35 and I said, "I'm going to work every day, all day, and I'm not going to look back once for five years. And if I haven't broken into the business by the time I'm 40, then I'll just get a day job, I'll quit, walk away from it, become a teacher somewhere or find a job in business." But for five years, I wasn't going to second-guess myself. I wasn't going to fail for lack of hard work or effort, so I worked really hard for that time, and I wrote 14 scripts in three years before I got *Colors*. Sure, they weren't all good, but I made myself write everything from beginning to end and forced myself to rewrite everything at least once.

Ed Solomon: I was very lucky to somehow land a job (as a staff writer on *Laverne & Shirley*) when I was a senior in college, but I almost gave up once, right before we sold *Bill and Ted*. I had gone about a year and a half without working after my first job, and I thought the script was funny but my agents wouldn't send it out, so I finally left them. I walked out of the agency with no agents and no deal. Then, I began to think maybe they were right, maybe the script was no good. And at my lowest moment, we found someone who believed in it and got it set up.

95. Changing What Doesn't Work

I can't control the wind, but I can adjust my sails.
—ANONYMOUS SAILOR

There's a saying that insanity is doing the same thing over and over, and expecting different results. As an aspiring writer, persistence is good, but you must also have the flexibility to change what doesn't work. Different actions lead to different results. Successful screenwriters adapt to failures and learn from their mistakes. Their attitude is, "There is definitely a way and I will try different routes until I get there." Thomas Edison is known as one of the most persistent scientists, perfecting the light bulb after 1,000 tries. When asked why he kept going after 999 failures, he responded, "They weren't failures, just 999 ways not to invent a light bulb. Every wrong attempt discarded was another step forward."

Leslie Dixon: Things have changed for me now. I woke up one morning, really bored with what I was doing, and decided to do a dramatic book adaptation on spec. It was a book in the public domain that I've always liked, and it wasn't a comedy at all. I sold it, got *The Thomas Crown Affair* off of it, which was also not a comedy. So I think it's a really good thing to shake up the way you work from time to time and try different methods.

For the adaptation, I started doing more research because it demanded it, but I didn't use an outline. I tried to go in more by my gut and my unconscious. I realized that was a new resource I hadn't really jacked into, like I've spent all those years writing from the front part of my brain and not really relaxing, letting things pop into my mind more. Your subconscious is a very valuable ally. It can solve problems without driving you insane. So suddenly, my habits changed, the hours I worked, the way I worked, and I was pleased not only with the results but with the reaction to the results. I also had no idea I could write any other genre than comedy. It was a revelation that got me all excited to be in the business again. I really believe I'm a better drama writer than a comedy writer and I never knew that. So as much as you can get all these answers about writers' routines, like "This is what I do, this is where I buy toilet paper, this is where I place my cup next to my computer," changing your routines once in a while can be a good thing.

96. Re-evaluating Your Goals Regularly

A job is what we do for money; work is what we do for love.
—MARYSARAH QUINN

Even though there's something admirable in the stubborn refusal to take no for an answer, there are still people who've struggled for over 20 years without even a positive comment on their work, and who are so bitter and jaded by their experiences that they may not realize they are wasting their time. I don't mean to be presumptuous in judging what people do with their lives, but when it's clear screenwriting brings more depression than joy, you wonder about their choices. The demarcation line should be in the joy of the artistic pursuit despite the temporary setbacks. Every so often, take a moment to ask yourself, "Am I having fun trying to make it? Am I doing my best? Do I still love writing screenplays?" If you answer "No" to all these questions, maybe you should re-evaluate your aspirations, and focus on what you truly love to do.

Gerald DiPego: It's hard to discourage people, because you want them to follow their dreams. But it goes back to getting that feedback from people you trust. If the feedback keeps coming in more negative than positive, if you haven't broken through, or if nobody is embracing your work, it has to tell you something. You can persevere and take more classes and try to get better, but if you don't see the improvement, it's a big indicator you need to re-evaluate your goals.

Nicholas Kazan: If you feel you must write, and your real triumph is reaching the end of a screenplay, keep at it. But if you're making up your screenplays, and people don't respond, if you don't take joy in it, if the act of writing movies doesn't transport you, quit. If you're not getting the compensatory joys and satisfaction out of the process itself, then it's too difficult.

CHAPTER 22
Passion

97. Paying the Price

Success is simple. First, you decide what you want specifically;
and second, you decide you're willing to pay the price to
make it happen, and then pay that price.
—BUNKER HUNT

Think of the life you'd live if you weren't pursuing this "silly" dream of becoming a screenwriter—going out with friends, dating, getting married, having children, traveling—in other words, a *normal* life. If this seems more attractive to you than years of starving, struggling, and honing your craft, quit now. Because you have to be willing to pay the price of entry into Screenwriting Land. Frank Darabont speaks from experience when he says, "There are potentially more talented writers and directors than I, working in shoe stores and Burger Kings across the nation. The difference is I was willing to put in the nine years of effort and they weren't."

Sure, there are exceptions, with first-timers gaining entry with their first script. But the general consensus is that the journey to professional screenwriting will take time and effort, money, obsessive personal involvement, diligent follow-through, constant rejection, personal pain, social sacrifice, and a persistent belief in yourself, no matter how overwhelming the obstacles. Are you prepared to pay the price?

Gerald DiPego: To me, writing is very close to an obsession. Those who are serious about it are driven, so paying the price goes with the territory. You will have obstacles and disappointments, and if you hit those and you give up and walk away, then maybe you weren't as driven, as inspired, or as obsessed to begin with. And that's not a bad thing because you learn how much you can take.

Jim Kouf: There's no other way. And there's no guarantee that any particular way will be successful. Everyone has to find their own way into this business. It's not like you can go and apply for a screenwriting job. They just don't exist. You have to write something that is good enough that people want to buy, and at that point, usually, if the script is good enough, they'll ask you, "What else do you have?" or "We'd like you to rewrite this script" or "What ideas do you have?" But until then, you're paying those dues, and there's no guarantee you'll ever break into this business. And even if you do, there's no guarantee that you'll ever sell another script. So you really need to have the talent and the desire, but it's not as if you can tell people how good you are. You have to let other people tell you how good you are. I could think I'm the greatest writer in the world, but it doesn't matter what I think. What matters is what everyone else thinks, and what I can deliver on the page.

Scott Rosenberg: I wrote 10 scripts before I got my first agent, wrote another two before my first sale and another three before anything got made. That's the most important advice I could give to anyone starting out: Write a lot of scripts. I get this phone call at least once a month: "Hi, my mother met your mother at a wedding and I just graduated college, and I'm out here and I really like your work and I wrote a script and I'll be happy if you would read it." And I say, "Okay, how many scripts have you written?" and they say this is their first. "Are you sure you want me to read it? Because I'm very busy. I'd be happy to read your script, but if it blows, which it will because it's a first script, I'll never read another one." I look back at all these 10 scripts I wrote, and they suck. Sure, they have moments of great stuff, but who am I at age 22 to think I'm going to write the Great American Screenplay? It's just wrong. I didn't have the life experience and I was just learning to crawl, learning my process. And these kids, with their lottery mentality, think they just wrote *The Terminator* and it's ridiculous. The one thing I'm most proud of in my process is that I was always writing. When people talk to me about "paying your dues" and I think about these lean years when I had no money, I was sharing a room, sleeping on mattresses on the floor, driving the worst car, working in the worst jobs, it didn't feel like I was paying my dues. I was still living my life, going to the movies and having a girlfriend and watching sports, and all of a sudden, I look back at those years and I realize I was living like an animal. But there was a kind of innocence to that time that I long for.

Tom Schulman: There are two kinds of dues you have to pay, before and after you make it as a professional writer. So you're always paying your dues. If you continue to write, and your output is high, you begin to think your writing is of good quality only to be demoralized and frustrated by the system. It's unlike any other professional system where if you start at the bottom and if you do good work, you progress up the ladder. In Hollywood, there is no ladder, no merit system. You could be completely out of it one day, and on top of the system the next. There's no common apprenticeship with low-paying wages that graduates to an assistantship with higher wages, which graduates to a professorship with full tenure. The frustrating part is that you really don't know if you'll ever make a living at it. It could be one year, 20 years, or never. You just try to get better at it and hope you'll catch a break.

98. Being Honest with Yourself

A writer knows he's a writer.

—JOHN BARTH

Do you really want to be a screenwriter? I mean *really*. You have to be honest with yourself about what you're meant to do, because only you can tell what you can do with your life. You may be thinking, "I'm a bona fide screenwriter. I bought a book on screenwriting. Why should I waste my time figuring out if it's for me?" Because most beginners are in it for the wrong reasons. They think they can be a writer without really knowing what's involved. They fall in love with the *glamour* of being a writer, the dreams of fame, recognition, and riches, rather than the process of writing. You have to be sure this is it, because the journey is long and life is short. If you're not 100 percent committed and certain that writing is in your blood, you'll be miserable most of the time. Trust me. I know a lot of stubborn "writers" who keep lying to themselves and, as Thoreau would say, "live lives of quiet desperation." To me, there's nothing sadder than a wasted life.

Ron Bass: Do you really love writing? If you can't answer this question honestly, then you're in the wrong business, because the only thing that can sustain a screenwriter through the assault the movie business puts on you, all the unimaginably deflating, rejecting, humiliating experiences, even with all its good intentions, is that you *love* to do it. People who become writers because they want to *be* writers are dead meat. If what you want are the trappings of it, if you like to *think* of yourself as a writer, an artist in your own eyes, because it gives you an inflated feeling of self-worth, or if you think you'll get rich doing it, get fame and praise, go to parties and hang out with beautiful actresses and famous directors all day long, the only bad part of this is that you actually have to write the stuff. Sure, you may live through the writing part and you'll be a writer, but if that's where you're coming from, don't even start. If you don't have that drive, I don't know what else could see you through. Maybe if you thought you had a gift for it and you were incredibly greedy, that greed could drive through the slings and arrows. I've yet to meet a really great writer whom I respect who hates to write and just does it because it is a way to earn a living. Sure, I've known many writers who felt burned out and became directors. They just got tired of writing; their flame went out. But they still had their skill and craft to write and support themselves between directing jobs, because it is the only thing they knew how to do.

Amy Holden Jones: It is common knowledge that people who persevere are more likely to succeed. On the other hand, I know an awful lot of people who persevered when they didn't have the talent. So it's very important to find out whether you have the talent first. If you're a screenwriter, you should have a backup plan because the rate of failure is so high. You have to be willing to do something else if this doesn't work. I think it was Tom Schulman who once said, "Most screenwriters don't fail, they just quit." Unfortunately, half the time they're right to quit. It's a very difficult line. There are a million good reasons to quit. Go start an Internet company, be your own boss, write a novel. This isn't a good way to make a living. You can make a lot more money learning about stocks than writing screenplays, and if you care deeply about your own work, it's emotionally difficult when they massacre your work and take it away from you. I stayed because I was successful at it. Part of life is finding out what you're good at and sticking with it, so figure out first if you're good at writing screenplays, and then if you can handle the frustrations.

Nicholas Kazan: I was a speaker at a conference and I said, "Take your registration form, go back out there and get your money back," and they all laughed. But I told them I was very serious, that if they even thought of following my advice, they'd never make it. You have to believe in yourself and persevere even in the face of massive evidence to the contrary, because sometimes people make leaps in their writing. I know I did, several times, and I couldn't have anticipated these leaps. Your work *can* get better, but it doesn't happen for everybody. There are people who *should* go back home. The trick is knowing which category you fall into. Are you someone with talent who'll make it eventually? Or are you the one who'll work at it for 20 years and never make it?

Scott Rosenberg: To a certain extent, you know if you have it. People are not stupid. Read other scripts and then read your own, and unless you're completely blind, you can tell if your writing meets that high standard needed to get attention in this town. All my jobs, when I had no money, were crappy jobs. The minute I punched the clock at five, I never thought about them again until the next day, because my writing was priority number one. I think that people who take real jobs that consume them beyond that eight-hour day, know at some level that they don't really have it. They are consciously, or unconsciously, hedging their bets; whereas the people who go for broke are so confident and passionate, they always know that if they do their best in this business, they'll eventually make it.

99. Remaining Passionate Despite the Disappointments

A successful man is one who can lay a firm foundation
with the bricks that others throw at him.
—DAVID BRINKLEY

After reading about the downside of being a screenwriter in Hollywood, how even highly successful screenwriters are disrespected and mistreated, how difficult writing a good screenplay actually is, the horrors of dealing with the Hollywood system, and the sacrifices needed to eventually make it, you have to wonder what could possibly motivate our mentors to keep going despite these frustrations? Here's a hint: it starts with a *P* and rhymes with fashion.

Akiva Goldsman: This is what I do for a living. I like it and hate it the same way someone at IBM hates it. If I were at IBM, I'd be having my own set of challenges and rewards and I'd be engaged in them because that's my job. It doesn't mean I don't hate it sometimes and that I don't fantasize about leaving it all behind one day. What it means is that I actually get to do what I want for a living and there's a difference between that and loving every second of it.

Amy Holden Jones: It's the one thing I do well, and at regular intervals movies have been made from my works. If they weren't, I probably would have given up. I know writers who have written a number of interesting scripts that never got made and I understand when they feel like quitting after awhile.

Nicholas Kazan: I try not to answer the phone until I finish work. If I get bad news on another project and it's nine in the morning, it's hard to go back to work. But if you wait until the end of the day, the bad news may make it a lousy day, but at least you got in a few hours of good work.

Eric Roth: There are frustrations along the way, but I'm fairly comfortable. The work is what it is. There's more pressure when you're taking too long (I admit it usually takes me about a year to write one script). The goal is to put together something that you're proud of. You have bigger frustrations when you do good work and the studio screws it up, like giving it to a director that you'd never assume would do this material, so that's a disappointment. You have daily frustrations with any kind of work you do. You may write a scene that just doesn't work, but the upside is that you have stories where it does work, and some wonderful discoveries where you sort of thrill yourself because it's just you and the work at that point. Then, once you turn it in, there's a whole different world that enters into it. What's exciting is working with directors who have the same vision, and that can be fun and stimulating. I also enjoy when we do a table reading of it because there's a sense that something is really there and that it's playing the way you envisioned it. It's very pure, there's no ego involved; we can strike and change lines that don't work. And then, there's the thrill when the movie works and when you're on the set during production. But at some point, you have to let it go because it's not yours anymore.

Michael Schiffer: When I'm working, I try to do the best I can so that there are never any regrets. If I work as hard as I can, and give my best, I never feel that if I worked a little harder, this wouldn't have happened. By the time I turn it in, I have taken it as far as I can take it, and then I just move on. You've got to have a life of your own. The longer I'm at this, the more I feel like the business can't be the only definition of your soul.

Tom Schulman: I hope it's the passion for whatever I'm writing. Despite the terrible things that happen to my various projects in development, the one I'm working on is the baby in the womb with the hope it will someday be a genius. It's what keeps me excited and makes it worth getting up in the morning.

Robin Swicord: There is a sense of mission. In a sense, I feel very lucky that I knew early on I was a storyteller, and it's the one thing I have come here to do. I know that at the most basic level, these frustrations cannot really reach me, because where I really live is not available to them.

100. Not Taking It Too Seriously

I shall live badly if I do not write, and I shall write badly if I do not live.

—FRANÇOISE SAGAN

When breaking into the industry demands such a high level of effort, sacrifice, and obsession, when aspiring screenwriters must give the craft every fiber of their being and think, eat, sleep, and breathe screenwriting 24 hours a day, without a guarantee they'll ever make it, it's difficult to say, "Don't take it too seriously." What I mean is that it shouldn't be *everything* that you're about as a human being. If you're single, with no responsibilities, feel free to be as obsessed as you want to be, while still balancing your life (see Habit 47). But if you have meaningful relationships, a family, children depending on your being there, you have to realize what's important, and act accordingly. Master Habit 47 to balance screenwriting with your life. I can't tell you how many writers have sacrificed everything for a career, only to end up miserable, even when they've "made it." Never sacrifice your loved ones for a screenplay. Successful screenwriters are not as obsessed as you'd think. But they still take their professionalism and the attached responsibilities, such as delivering quality work on time, seriously. As Henry Miller once said, "Develop interest in life as you see it; in people, things, literature, music—the world is so rich, simply throbbing with rich pleasures, beautiful souls, and interesting people. Forget yourself." Simply remember this: There's screenwriting and there's life. Making the distinction will make you a better writer.

Gerald DiPego: You have to be somewhat serious, because writing is an obsession. You're so passionate about it, it's something you have to do, even if you're not getting paid for it. But it's a lot healthier if it's not all that you're about. In fact, you'll probably be better at your writing if it isn't all that you're about. A wider life makes you a fuller person and enables you to see the world outside yourself. If you're so wrapped up in your craft, it becomes too self-involving and you're not really living in the world anymore.

Michael Schiffer: I think young writers tend to be more obsessive. Writing is everything to them, 24 hours a day, and it has to be, in order to get somewhere. But when you have a family, you try to get home and make your family the most important thing in your life. It's such a different universe at home, that you have to shut off all the writing anxieties. It's a discipline that's important to cultivate as a human being. You can't possibly have good relationships if you walk around brooding about stuff all the time.

Ed Solomon: Everything in this town plays into the easy buttons that get pushed and take people off their path: greed, power, glamour, sex, fame. It actually takes more work in this business to stay clear of that. I do the same thing (write) whether I'm paid or not, and I like writing. Ultimately, it all comes down to the work. It's not that I'm really passionate about writing. It's just that I'm far less passionate about driving a bread truck. What is worth taking really seriously? At best, we provide a diversion for people. On rare occasions, we make something that has some value. As an entire media, we definitely have an effect, but nothing we do is worth taking that seriously. Self-importance is the death of creativity. Maybe it's important to express yourself and be heard, but when you start believing you need to make noise because others need to hear you, you're on the road to ruin.

CHAPTER 23
Practice

101. Writing No Matter What . . . Practice, Practice, Practice

Writing energy is like anything else: The more you put in, the more you get out.

—RICHARD REEVES

"Practice makes perfect" has long been the advice given to people who want to improve their performance, whether it's playing sports, learning a musical instrument, or mastering the craft of writing. When people ask you what you're working on, don't tell them about your latest script. Just say, "I'm in training to become a great screenwriter," give them your card, and tell them you'll contact them when you have great material to show. When you finally write that great piece of material, I promise you everything you've just read up to now will materialize. If your script is genuinely good, agents will find you. If a producer is interested, the first thing they'll do is call up their favorite agent and tell them to take a look. This is the one area that no one in the industry has been able to argue against. A great script is the last and final argument.

Jim Kouf: I had the usual beginner's frustrations, like "How come they're not buying this?" I did a lot of writing, figuring it out on my own, because I didn't go to film school. I wrote 11 TV specs before I got someone to take me seriously and then it took six feature scripts before I wrote one that was good enough.

Michael Schiffer: Developing craft is a very slow process. If you were playing the violin, you wouldn't expect to pick it up and then go to Carnegie Hall within six months. And yet people expect their first or second script to sell and become a hit movie. It's a bit delusional. Sure, there may be instances of this happening but I think generally, it's a craft that takes the requisite 5 to 20 years to develop.

Tom Schulman: We all hear the stories of overnight successes. But almost everyone of these successes will tell you that it was an overnight success that took 10 to 20 years. This is by far the rule.

•   •   •

Well, there you have it, 101 habits to model in your training run to become the next great screenwriter. We're just about to wrap it up, so let our mentors congratulate you for being such an attentive apprentice and leave you with some final words of wisdom . . .

EPILOGUE
Fade Out

Do not seek to follow in the footsteps of the wise;
seek what they sought.

—Baslo

Ron Bass: If I have to narrow any advice down to a sound bite, I'd say write every day, only write if you love it, prepare your stories in advance, don't rewrite your own material unless someone is paying you to do it, read other people's stuff, retain the humility that you're not the world's best expert who has all the answers, let it hurt when rejected but don't get hardened against it, keep writing new things, new genres, as different as you can, different characters, different situations. You build your instrument. It's like working with weights. You only get better as you do it. Just keep doing it.

Steven DeSouza: Despite all the frustrations, at the end of the day, nothing really matters except the writing. It must be a lot tougher for a director or a star when a movie falls apart than for a writer, because if a producer is not interested, you can go to the next one, and if a few turn you down, forget the producers and write the damn thing. All you need is a pen and paper. Screw the Pentium IV and the screenwriting software. Go off by yourself and write a killer script that will show that everybody else is wrong, will start a new trend, and make you every struggling writer's new hero.

Gerald DiPego: Always do the very best work you can. Don't rush it. Be as open as you can to feedback. Believe in your work. If it touches you in some deep way, then trust that there are other people out there who will feel the same.

Leslie Dixon: No matter what you do, you have to get an agent. It's like the old real estate maxim "Agent, agent, agent."

Akiva Goldsman: Bruce Beresford taught me something wonderful. He taught me that everyone is really 12 years old. Everyone thinks they're a kid in a grown-up's body, and if you remember this, you stop being scared because, just as I'm scared of being found out, so is the big director across the way and so is the big actor around the corner. Knowing that we are still in our hearts the kids we were, doing our best to wear grown-up clothes, helps us walk a little easier through the world.

Amy Holden Jones: Be absolutely certain you really want to do this. I once asked a writer why she wanted to do it and she said she didn't like to write prose and long descriptions but she loved writing scenes and dialogue. That's a good answer, when screenwriting is the type of writing that you love to do. Get realistic about the nature of the business and study it the way you would any other industry. You'll learn this by getting a job in the business, even if it's an unpaid job.

Nicholas Kazan: If you were a carpenter, I guarantee your 100th desk would be a lot better than your first, just like your 20th screenplay will be a lot better than your first. Just keep going and make sure you really love what you do. I'm perfectly happy about the specs I wrote that haven't sold. I look at them, I worked hard on them, and I'm very proud of them. They're not ruined yet, because they exist only in my head. They still have perfect production values and they're beautifully shot with fantastic performances. Maybe they'll get made one day, maybe not. Who cares? I'm happy about them.

Jim Kouf: I don't think you can learn how to write by listening to anybody tell you how to write. I don't know where the muse comes from or how it's done. You may be able to learn the craft, but how do you teach somebody to be witty? You have to be interested in a lot of stuff and have an almost obsessive compulsive behavior, because you really have to be interested in something to make you want to write about it and spend that much time with it. You have to be able to step back and look at your own work and ask if it's any good. Most of the time, good writing is obvious; it comes alive on the page, but then again, somebody else might hate it, so who the hell knows? But if everybody thinks it's not good, then obviously I've done something wrong. I never believe I'm right above everybody else. That's the kind of script we never send out.

Scott Rosenberg: At the end of the day, I really believe I have the best job in the world. Every day is different. They pay me a fortune of money. I get to work with heroes I've grown up with. In this crazy, wonderful world, I look at the guy who has to go to the office, sit in a cubicle and punch numbers all day, and I wonder what I would have done if it turned out to be me, and I tremble at it. My life is so far away from that. I wake up every morning not knowing what the day will bring and that's really cool.

Eric Roth: Finish what you start. Think of it as a journey.

Michael Schiffer: Aim high. Work harder than you think you should. If it's hard work, you're doing it right. If you're writing about the real world, research it. Be relentless in rewriting. Put it out to people and see what their reactions are. If they give you notes, you may not always agree with them, but always try to figure out what is the underlying problem that made them speak up in the first place. Their articulation of the problem may not give you the answer you need, but their need to fix something probably comes from an underlying problem in the script and you must look beneath the surface to figure out why they were unhappy with this part of the script. If you hand in something utterly brilliant, they will hand it back to you with stars in their eyes and say, "Wow!"

Tom Schulman: Write what you love. Don't write for the market because who knows what the market wants? The best market is yourself.

Ed Solomon: As best you can, try to find the joy and peace in the process, not in the results, because no matter how successful you become, if what you're looking for are results, you'll be very frustrated. Try to have a balanced life. Nothing we do ultimately matters. The success of *Men in Black* was great and I'm sure it entertained millions—but do we really think the world would be any different if *Men in Black* didn't exist? On the rare occasion you do something that really affects someone, that's great, but what's more important are the people you affect in your daily life. That's where you will leave a mark. People who say, "If my movie touches just one person it will be worthwhile," are kidding themselves. If you're interested in touching one person, go out and spend $200 and pay for a school teacher in an African village for a year. If you're going to waste a hundred million dollars and a lot of people's precious time, and be miserable in the process, all you will do is create a lot more misery.

Robin Swicord: This is more to women who are home writing with children and it's a topic worthy of a whole new chapter. It's very important to know that it's perfectly fine to say, "This time is for me and for this other work." It teaches children to be self-reliant. They know you are there but merely aloof. They know they're free to set themselves down on the floor with their own games in front of them and make their own little world. You set a good example by doing this and saying, "This work that I do, which is very important to me, I want to do it now. So you go over there and find your thing to do and we'll do it side by side." This is the best thing to do for yourself, because many women feel guilty about stepping apart from the family and doing this other thing they also came here to do. No one ever said this to me and I just want to say it's a good thing for you and it's good for your kids.

My Final Words

If you haven't mastered Habit 91, and you're in a hurry, here are my top 15, absolutely indispensable habits you can't live without:

1. Have a Driving Reason to Write
2. Educate Yourself
3. Set a High Standard of Excellence
4. Trust Your Instincts and Write What Excites You
5. Plan Your Stories (Outline)
6. Make the Time to Write and Write Regularly
7. Evoke Emotions in the Reader
8. Set Writing Goals
9. Combat Block by Writing Through It
10. Be Open to Outside Criticism and Feedback
11. Realize It's Your Writing That's Important, Not the Relationships
12. Get the Right Agent the Old-Fashioned Way
13. Handle Rejection Like a Pro
14. Remain Passionate Despite the Disappointments
15. Don't Take It Too Seriously

And if these are still a little overwhelming, and you wanted only one piece of advice, one thought as we say "Good-bye," it would be this: The only question in your mind should not be "How do I break into the business," but "How can I write a great script that will excite anyone who reads it?" Remember that no matter how successful screenwriters broke into the business, they first wrote a great script that got the attention of a producer, an agent, their assistants, or their readers.

If you have that one screenplay in a thousand, the one that moves a reader emotionally, I promise you Hollywood will take notice.

Now, remember that the 101 habits are just that, habits, behaviors, skills, and attitudes from a small but representative sample. They are not rules set in stone, just advice and opinions. It is up to you to try them out. If they work for you, fine. If they don't, develop your own and move on. As Habit 100 says, don't take it too seriously. Relax. *Write.* Play. *Write.* Eat. *Write.* Laugh. *Write.* Love. *Write.* Sleep. Repeat daily as necessary.

Good luck!

Index